PEOPLE'S BIBLE COMMENTARY

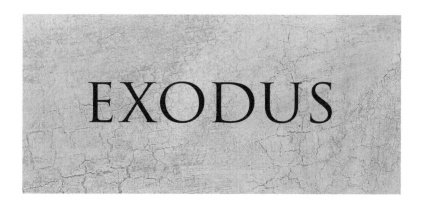

EXODUS

ERNST H. WENDLAND

PBC

CONCORDIA PUBLISHING HOUSE · SAINT LOUIS

Revised edition first printed in 2005.

Copyright © 1992 Concordia Publishing House
3558 S. Jefferson Ave., St. Louis, MO 63118-3968
1-800-325-3040 · www.cph.org

Commentary and pictures are reprinted from EXODUS (The People's Bible Series), copyright © 1984 by Northwestern Publishing House. Used by permission.

Interior illustrations by Glenn Myers.
Map by Dr. John Lawrenz.

Unless otherwise stated, the Scripture quotations in this publication are taken from the HOLY BIBLE, NEW INTERNATIONAL VERSION®. NIV®. Copyright © 1973, 1978, 1984 by International Bible Society. Used by permission of Zondervan Publishing House. All rights reserved.

Manufactured in the United States of America

ISBN 0-7586-0416-5

1 2 3 4 5 6 7 8 9 10   14 13 12 11 10 09 08 07 06 05

CONTENTS

ILLUSTRATIONS

MAP

EDITOR'S PREFACE

The *People's Bible Commentary* is just what the name implies—a Bible and commentary for the people. It includes the complete text of the Holy Scriptures in the popular New International Version. The commentary following the Scripture sections contains personal applications as well as historical background and explanations of the text.

The authors of the *People's Bible Commentary* are men of scholarship and practical insight gained from years of experience in the teaching and preaching ministries. They have tried to avoid the technical jargon which limits so many commentary series to professional Bible scholars.

The most important feature of these books is that they are Christ-centered. Speaking of the Old Testament Scriptures, Jesus himself declared, "These are the Scriptures that testify about me" (John 5:39). Each volume of the *People's Bible Commentary* directs our attention to Jesus Christ. He is the center of the entire Bible. He is our only Savior.

We dedicate these volumes to the glory of God and to the good of his people.

The Publishers

Introduction to Exodus

Exodus is the second book written by Moses as a part of the Pentateuch, the name given to the first five books of the Bible. Genesis ends with the resettling of patriarch Jacob and his family in the land of Egypt and with the death of his son Joseph. It was through Joseph's help during a time of famine that this move had been arranged.

Exodus takes up the story of Jacob's descendants where Genesis leaves off. Jacob's descendants are now called the Israelites. In the opening verses of Exodus, the sons of Jacob are again mentioned. This is followed by the words, "Now Joseph and all his brothers and all that generation died, but the Israelites were fruitful and multiplied greatly and became exceedingly numerous, so that the land was filled with them" (1:6,7). While these verses supply a bridge between the first two books of the Bible, at the same time they cover a span of several hundred years and present us with an entirely new situation in the salvation history of God's people. Exodus presents the important events that follow the Israelites' long stay in Egypt, a sojourn that lasted 430 years in all, as 12:40 tells us.

Title

The title *Exodus* comes from the translation of the Old Testament into the Greek language, a translation known as the Septuagint, which goes back to the year 285 B.C. *Exodus* means "departure" or "going out." Although the book deals with Israel's departure from Egypt so that they could return to the promised land of Canaan, the title *Exodus* does not indicate the book's primary significance in the overall picture of God's salvation history. That will be discussed later in this introduction.

Author

That Moses wrote the entire Pentateuch, including Exodus, needs no detailed proof here. In order that there may be no question regarding our position on this matter, however, it may serve well to review a few points to make this position clear.

Jesus, who frequently used the Old Testament writings in support of his own teachings, referred to the "Law of Moses" as one of the three divisions of the Scriptures that testified of him: "Everything must be fulfilled that is written about me in the Law of Moses, the Prophets and the Psalms" (Luke 24:44). It is clear from Jesus' threefold division of the Old Testament that he used the expression "Law of Moses" in the sense of the entire Pentateuch. At another time in his ministry, Jesus challenged the unbelieving Jews of his day with the words recorded in John 5:46: "If you believed Moses, you would believe me, for he wrote about me." Thus Jesus definitely pointed to Moses as the author of the first five books of the Bible.

Of all the books of the Pentateuch, it is Exodus, of course, that presents the story of Moses' birth and of his activities as God's chosen leader of his people. The contents of the book, moreover, show the author to be a person thoroughly acquainted with Egyptian customs, names, and gods, as well as with that country's climatic and geographical conditions. The description of the Israelites' departure out of Egypt and also of the details of their travels in the desert to Sinai is that of an eyewitness. When we therefore read in the book itself that the Lord directed Moses to write on a scroll so that various events would be remembered (17:14) and that Moses "wrote down everything the LORD had said" (24:4), we are confident that the author of Exodus could be no one but Moses himself.

Content and purpose

During the 430-year sojourn in Egypt, the Israelites developed into a large nation, numbering 600,000 men, not counting women and children. Those who had once been the invited guests of the pharaoh at Joseph's time, however, became a people hated and oppressed. After briefly describing this situation, Exodus introduces us to Moses, the deliverer called by God to lead his people out of bondage and back to the Promised Land (chapters 2,3). The entire rest of the book (chapters 4–40) presents a detailed account of events that took place during a period of less than two years. This two-year period covers the negotiations between Moses and Pharaoh for the Israelites' release from bondage and continues on through the first year of their journey on the way to Canaan.

An event of greatest significance in Israel's salvation history took place shortly after their release from bondage. The Lord of the whole earth adopted Israel as his very own people, through whom he would fulfill the promise of the Savior. He consecrated this people as a covenant nation. He made a solemn agreement with them at Sinai. This constitutes the heart of Exodus. The laws and regulations of God pertaining to this covenantal arrangement between God and Israel make up most of the book's contents.

Outline

This central theme of Israel's consecration as God's covenant nation gives us the basic outline we will follow in our study of Exodus.

Theme: Jehovah's covenant with the people of Israel

I. The deliverance of the covenant people out of Egypt (1:1–18:27)
   A. Birth and early career of Moses (1:1–2:25)
   B. Moses and the burning bush (3:1–4:17)
   C. Moses returns to Egypt (4:18–6:30)
   D. The ten plagues (7:1–11:10)
   E. The Passover and the exodus (12:1–13:22)
   F. Crossing the sea (14:1–16:12)
   G. Manna and quail (16:13-36)
   H. Water from the rock (17:1-7)
   I. The Amalekites defeated at Rephidim (17:8–18:27)

II. The establishment of Jehovah's covenant with Israel (19:1–24:18)
   A. Israel at Mount Sinai (19:1-25)
   B. The Ten Commandments (20:1-21)
   C. Laws regarding worship, people, and property (20:22–23:13)
   D. The three annual festivals (23:14-19)
   E. Ratification of the covenant (23:20–24:18)

III. The entry into the place of the covenant, the tabernacle (25:1–40:38)
   A. Construction of the ark (25:1-22)
   B. The pattern of the tabernacle (25:23–31:18)
   C. The golden calf (32:1–33:23)
   D. The second set of stone tablets (34:1-28)

    E. The radiant face of Moses (34:29-35)

    F. Construction of the tabernacle (35:1–40:38)

According to this outline, the covenant of Jehovah, the Savior-God, with his chosen people Israel receives the emphasis it deserves.

The first 18 chapters of Exodus—which present the birth and call of Moses, the negotiations between Moses and Pharaoh over Israel's release from bondage, the plagues, the institution of the feast of the Passover, the exodus itself, the passage of Israel through the Red Sea and the wilderness to Mount Sinai—are preparatory to the establishment of the Sinai covenant.

The next six chapters (19–24) give us the establishment of the Sinai covenant itself: the immediate preparations for its declaration, its regulations as expressed in the Ten Commandments and the fundamental ordinances pertaining to Israel's life as covenant people, and its formal ratification.

Beginning with chapter 25, we have God's directions concerning the erection and arrangement of the tabernacle, the central place of the covenant as the dwelling place of Jehovah in Israel. Beginning work on the building of the tabernacle is interrupted by the incident of Israel's worship of the golden calf. But following Moses' intercession, the covenant is renewed, the tabernacle is built, and the book closes with its solemn dedication as "the glory of the LORD filled the tabernacle" (40:34).

Historical setting

For many years Bible students and historians have debated the question as to where the events recorded in Exodus fit into world history. Who is the "new king" referred to in the first chapter of Exodus "who did not know about

Joseph" (verse 8)? Which pharaoh oppressed the Israelites? With whom did Moses plead to let God's people go? These questions are all related to the actual date of Israel's departure out of Egypt, concerning which there has been considerable difference of opinion.

Our own position on the date of the exodus is influenced primarily by Scripture itself. In 1 Kings 6:1 we are told that Solomon began to build the temple of the Lord in the fourth year of his reign over Israel and that this occurred "in the four hundred and eightieth year after the Israelites had come out of Egypt." Through archeological discoveries, particularly a list of Assyrian eponyms (officials), historians are pretty well agreed that the fourth year of Solomon's reign was on or about 966 B.C. Adding 480 years to this gives us the year 1446 B.C. as the date of Israel's exodus. While some scholars prefer to follow the archeological findings of Nelson Glueck and Kathleen Kenyon, which seem to support a later date, there also are archeologists, such as John Garstang, who favor the earlier one as suggested by the reference in 1 Kings. We prefer, of course, to follow the date that fits best with the chronology of Scripture.

Following the above line of thought, the "new king, who did not know about Joseph," would come out of the dynasty that expelled the Hyksos, a Semitic tribe that ruled Egypt in the 16th century B.C. Historically, this Egyptian dynasty that drove out the Hyksos would fall into the period of the New Kingdom, which ruled approximately between the years 1580 to 1085 B.C.

According to this reckoning, the pharaoh of the oppression would be Thutmose III, who ruled from about 1500 to 1450 B.C., and the pharaoh of the exodus would be Amenhotep II, who ruled from about 1450 to 1425 B.C. As is to be expected, Egyptian records themselves do not mention an event such as the exodus, because it would reflect adversely upon Egypt's power and glory.

We mention these names and dates as matters of historical interest, not of absolute certainty. While archeological findings can certainly supply interesting information about scriptural truth, they cannot determine this truth for us. Where Scripture does provide specific historical information, as in the case of 1 Kings 6:1, we accept this as true.

Above all, these matters should not detract from the purpose for which our Savior-God gave this inspired record to Moses, namely, to impress upon us the covenant that he made with his people Israel.

PART ONE

The Deliverance of the Covenant People out of Egypt
(1:1–18:27)

From Genesis to Exodus

1 These are the names of the sons of Israel who went to Egypt with Jacob, each with his family: ²Reuben, Simeon, Levi and Judah; ³Issachar, Zebulun and Benjamin; ⁴Dan and Naphtali; Gad and Asher. ⁵The descendants of Jacob numbered seventy in all; Joseph was already in Egypt.

⁶Now Joseph and all his brothers and all that generation died, ⁷but the Israelites were fruitful and multiplied greatly and became exceedingly numerous, so that the land was filled with them.

The opening verses of Exodus provide an excellent link between Genesis and Exodus. The final chapters of Genesis tell about the move of Jacob's family to Egypt at the time of the great famine. Here a reference to this resettlement is repeated. The sons of Jacob are listed according to their mothers, first those of Leah and Rachel, then of the handmaids Zilpah and Bilhah. Joseph, of course, was already in Egypt. The total number of 70 descendants of Jacob involved here agrees with the figure previously given in Genesis 46:27.

Briefly, then, the scene is set for what is to follow. We hear that the generation just mentioned died. The generations that followed experienced an unusual increase. The land of Goshen, where they had settled, was filled with Israelites. God's promise to Abraham in Genesis 22:17 came true: "I will surely bless you and make your descendants as numerous as the stars in the sky and as the sand on the seashore." We know that it took several centuries for this remarkable growth to take place, centuries spent in a strange land and in isolated circumstances. We know very little about this period, since very little is reported. We can see in this isolated development, however, God's plan to prepare for himself a nation set apart from all other nations, a nation that was to become his covenant people. The Egyptian people despised shepherds, and the Israelites were primarily a people of shepherds. Consequently, the Israelites for centuries carried on a separate existence, which was just as God had planned during these formative years of their development as a nation.

We pause to consider what this must have meant to this people of God. This time period in Israel's history involves several centuries. Our own country, the United States of America, celebrated two hundred years of its existence not that many years ago. Often the faithful Israelites must have said during these many years, "What is happening to that promise God made to our fathers, Abraham, Isaac, and Jacob? We are strangers in a foreign land. This is not the Land of Promise. Our whole situation does not agree at all with what God said he had planned for us!"

As far as we can determine, the Israelites still observed circumcision, the sign of God's covenant with Abraham. They brought sacrifices to the Lord. They observed the Sabbath Day as a day of worship and praise. But God was strangely silent. We have no indication that he spoke to them during all this time as he had with the patriarchs. Yet we know that even here God was daily fulfilling a promise made to their fathers to make of them a great nation. Their isolation in Egypt served God's plan well.

Christians today are strangers and foreigners in this world of sin. Often in times of loneliness and anguish, they ask with the psalmist, "How long, O LORD?" (Psalm 13:1). Heaven seems so far away, and God's reassuring voice is nothing but a word of promise that does not seem to be reaching fulfillment.

How important to remember that God will never forsake his promise and that his plans are being fulfilled according to his perfect plans for our salvation! Yes, how necessary that this be kept in mind especially when earthly problems increase and the evil forces of this world threaten to destroy us!

Israel's time of testing through anguish and persecution became more bitter for them, as our next verses show.

The Israelites oppressed

⁸**Then a new king, who did not know about Joseph, came to power in Egypt. ⁹"Look," he said to his people, "the Israelites have become much too numerous for us. ¹⁰Come, we must deal shrewdly with them or they will become even more numerous and, if war breaks out, will join our enemies, fight against us and leave the country."**

¹¹**So they put slave masters over them to oppress them with forced labor, and they built Pithom and Rameses as store cities for Pharaoh. ¹²But the more they were oppressed, the more they multiplied and spread; so the Egyptians came to dread the Israelites ¹³and worked them ruthlessly. ¹⁴They made their lives bitter with hard labor in brick and mortar and with all kinds of work in the fields; in all their hard labor the Egyptians used them ruthlessly.**

As mentioned in the introduction, the "new king, who did not know about Joseph" and who "came to power in Egypt" was very likely the founder of a new dynasty. The history of Egypt reports the establishment of a New Kingdom at about the year 1580 B.C., when the troublesome Hyksos invaders were driven out of the country and when Egypt entered one of the most prosperous times in its development. The little we do know about the Hyksos leads us to believe that they were not as hostile toward the Hebrews as the Egyptians, since they also were foreigners in this land. This situation changed abruptly, however, with the rise of the Egyptian new dynasty, which was not bound any longer by feelings of gratitude for what Joseph had done for Egypt a long time ago.

The "new king" considered the people of Israel a threat to his country and his rule and instituted the harsh measures described in the above verses to keep them under control. Although he feared the Israelites, at the same time he did not wish to see them leave his country. They were too valuable to him as a source of slave labor in building up store cities, such as Pithom and Rameses. Pharaoh's plan to hinder Israel's growth by these harsh methods failed miserably. From Israel's viewpoint, we can well imagine that this oppression only served to increase their desire to return to their homeland. This desire could have waned if this stay in Egypt had proved satisfying. God, we know, wanted his people back in Canaan. Again we can clearly see God's hand in this turn of events, even though for a time the Israelites had to face trials that were extremely difficult to bear.

That the fear of the Lord sustained the Israelites during this severe time of testing becomes apparent in the verses that follow.

The oppression intensified

¹⁵**The king of Egypt said to the Hebrew midwives, whose names were Shiphrah and Puah, ¹⁶"When you help the Hebrew**

women in childbirth and observe them on the delivery stool, if it is a boy, kill him; but if it is a girl, let her live." [17]The midwives, however, feared God and did not do what the king of Egypt had told them to do; they let the boys live. [18]Then the king of Egypt summoned the midwives and asked them, "Why have you done this? Why have you let the boys live?"

[19]The midwives answered Pharaoh, "Hebrew women are not like Egyptian women; they are vigorous and give birth before the midwives arrive."

[20]So God was kind to the midwives and the people increased and became even more numerous. [21]And because the midwives feared God, he gave them families of their own.

[22]Then Pharaoh gave this order to all his people: "Every boy that is born you must throw into the Nile, but let every girl live."

Shiphrah and Puah were no doubt the two women in charge of midwifery for the Hebrews. The "delivery stool" was two stones, or stools, used by women in those times to kneel or sit upon during the delivery of babies.

The question is sometimes raised as to whether or not these midwives were justified in deceiving the king with their excuse that Hebrew women delivered their babies so quickly that the children were born before the midwives could arrive to assist with the birth. Apparently, the midwives simply refused to act. They obeyed God rather than men. They could not with good conscience carry out the king's murderous command. And God blessed them for fearing him rather than the king. We see that a feeling of awesome respect for the almighty God was surely present in Israel, even after these many years in a strange land and after suffering severe hardships.

"The midwives, however, feared God. . . ." We too need to remember that in times of severe trial and temptation, the fear of the Lord can sustain us. This is not a slavish fear of punishment. It is rather a consciousness on our part that God is still there, no matter how severe the affliction is that threatens. This awesome respect for his presence will bring with it a childlike trust that his power will prevail, no matter how severe the threat of danger may be.

This fear of the Lord in believers, of course, can incite unbelievers to greater acts of hatred and violence. Pharaoh was determined to show his power over these Israelites, who continued to increase in numbers and became a threat to his kingdom. This time he issued an open decree: "Every boy that is born you must throw into the Nile."

But even this ruthless attempt to exterminate Israel not only failed; God actually used it to preserve his people, as we see in the next chapter.

The birth of Moses

2 Now a man of the house of Levi married a Levite woman, ²and she became pregnant and gave birth to a son. When she saw that he was a fine child, she hid him for three months. ³But when she could hide him no longer, she got a papyrus basket for him and coated it with tar and pitch. Then she placed the child in it and put it among the reeds along the bank of the Nile. ⁴His sister stood at a distance to see what would happen to him.

⁵Then Pharaoh's daughter went down to the Nile to bathe, and her attendants were walking along the river bank. She saw the basket among the reeds and sent her slave girl to get it. ⁶She opened it and saw the baby. He was crying, and she felt sorry for him. "This is one of the Hebrew babies," she said.

⁷Then his sister asked Pharaoh's daughter, "Shall I go and get one of the Hebrew women to nurse the baby for you?"

⁸"Yes, go," she answered. And the girl went and got the baby's mother. ⁹Pharaoh's daughter said to her, "Take this baby and nurse him for me, and I will pay you." So the woman took the baby and nursed him. ¹⁰When the child grew older, she took him to Pharaoh's daughter and he became her son. She named him Moses, saying, "I drew him out of the water."

Moses now introduces himself. In these verses he tells how his life was protected from the murderous edict of

Pharaoh. The details of this story are known to every Sunday school child. But it is important to remember that Moses is here recording his own story, a story involving the God-fearing efforts of his own family. Theirs was truly a heroic faith. The writer of Hebrews declares, "By faith Moses' parents hid him for three months after he was born, because they saw he was no ordinary child, and they were not afraid of the king's edict" (11:23).

It took courage for the parents of Moses to have sons in those perilous times. Miriam, the older sister of Moses, was not endangered by Pharaoh's decree. Somehow the parents had managed to preserve Aaron, Moses' older brother. Moses' mother, whose name is not given in these verses, sensed something about her next son to indicate that he was "no ordinary child." Our text says that he was "a fine child," beautiful and healthy. For three months it was possible to keep the baby in hiding. When the child's voice could be heard outside the house, however, another way to protect him became necessary.

The method chosen—placing the baby in a little ark made out of interwoven papyrus stems coated with tar and pitch, and placing it into a protected place in the Nile River—was actually placing him into God's care. Was this place chosen because the parents knew that Pharaoh's daughter came here to bathe? Was this all done in the hope that the baby would become the foster child of an Egyptian princess? Moses does not tell us. What is important is that the outcome of this incident was ideal for the training of one chosen to become Israel's great leader.

Arrangements were made so that the child's own mother would be his nurse. In those days this meant a period of about three years. The education that the child would one day receive, as Stephen later pointed out in Acts 7:22, was "in all the wisdom of the Egyptians." The best in Egypt in those days meant the best in the world, since this was a time when the greatest achievements in all the various sciences were to be found in Egypt. This was just the kind of training needed for the work to which God would call Moses. We now can see how God made use of the wisdom of Egypt, Israel's persecutors, to carry out his mighty act of deliverance.

We also see from this text that the name "Moses" was given to him by Pharaoh's daughter. Although Bible students have tried to interpret the meaning of this name in many different ways, Moses gives us his own interpretation: "[drawn] out of the water." Truly, it was also through Moses that Israel was drawn out of its slavery in Egypt!

As a sidelight to this story, it is interesting to note the important place of children in the Israelite family. They were truly regarded as a heritage from the Lord. These parents put their own lives in danger in order to have children and protect them as God's highest earthly blessing. What a contrast to our society today, when people actually murder unborn gifts of God, very often simply because children are no longer wanted!

Moses flees to Midian

¹¹One day, after Moses had grown up, he went out to where his own people were and watched them at their hard labor. He saw an Egyptian beating a Hebrew, one of his own people. ¹²Glancing this way and that and seeing no one, he killed the Egyptian and hid him in the sand. ¹³The next day he went out and saw two Hebrews fighting. He asked the one in the wrong, "Why are you hitting your fellow Hebrew?"

¹⁴The man said, "Who made you ruler and judge over us? Are you thinking of killing me as you killed the Egyptian?" Then Moses was afraid and thought, "What I did must have become known."

¹⁵When Pharaoh heard of this, he tried to kill Moses, but Moses fled from Pharaoh and went to live in Midian, where he sat down by a well.

According to Acts 7:23, Moses was 40 years old when he fled to Midian. Moses tells us nothing about the period when he was educated at Pharaoh's court in all the wisdom of the Egyptians. During all this time, however, Moses did not lose sight of the fact that he was an Israelite. His sympathies were with his own people, who were being cruelly oppressed as slaves.

Moses soon showed that he was on the side of his people, as displayed by his actions. In his zeal to take sides, he killed an Egyptian. It was an impulsive act, a sin that cannot be condoned. Moses' actions, "glancing this way and that" and hiding the Egyptian in the sand, show that Moses himself knew that what he did was a crime. Yet the fact that he chose to take sides with his own people was an act of faith, as the writer of Hebrews states: "By faith Moses, when he had grown up, refused to be known as the son of Pharaoh's daughter. He chose to be mistreated along with the people of God rather than to enjoy the pleasures of sin for a short time. He regarded disgrace for the sake of Christ as of greater value than the treasures of Egypt" (11:24-26).

In this act of violence against an Egyptian, "Moses thought that his own people would realize that God was using him to rescue them," as Stephen declared while on trial before the Jews (Acts 7:25). Already at that time, Moses saw himself as a deliverer of his people. He soon found out that his own people were not ready for this. When attempting to settle a dispute between two of his own people, he received only a negative reaction. They also let Moses know that his murderous act had become well known in the land. This brought him to the realization that he was in deep trouble. Killing the Egyptian was an act of open rebellion. To save his life, Moses fled to a remote area on the peninsula of Sinai, where a branch of the Midianite people were living as shepherds.

Already at this early time in life, we see Moses as a man of great courage and dedication. He was not afraid to risk his own life to help the cause of his people. He turned his back upon all the earthly pleasures that he could have enjoyed as an adopted member of Pharaoh's family. He was convinced that God wanted to use his services in some way to deliver his people out of their desperate situation. His act of murder, however, showed poor judgment. He reminds us of Peter when Jesus was arrested in the Garden of Gethsemane. Peter grabbed his sword and cut off the ear of Malchus in his misplaced zeal to save Christ.

We too can become impatient in our zeal to serve the Lord. We may have the best of intentions. What we do may require great courage. But we are never justified in trying to help the cause of the Lord by a wrongful act, no matter how "helpful" that act may seem to us at the time. The end does not justify the means.

Moses had to learn patience before the Lord's chosen time for Israel's deliverance. The next chapter in Moses' life was spent far away from Egypt, where the act of deliverance would take place. That chapter of his life lasted another 40 years!

Moses in the land of Midian

¹⁶**Now a priest of Midian had seven daughters, and they came to draw water and fill the troughs to water their father's flock. ¹⁷Some shepherds came along and drove them away, but Moses got up and came to their rescue and watered their flock.**

¹⁸**When the girls returned to Reuel their father, he asked them, "Why have you returned so early today?"**

¹⁹**They answered, "An Egyptian rescued us from the shepherds. He even drew water for us and watered the flock."**

²⁰**"And where is he?" he asked his daughters. "Why did you leave him? Invite him to have something to eat."**

²¹**Moses agreed to stay with the man, who gave his daughter Zipporah to Moses in marriage. ²²Zipporah gave birth to a son, and Moses named him Gershom, saying, "I have become an alien in a foreign land."**

The Midianites, among whom Moses sought refuge in the Sinai Peninsula, were descended from Abraham through Keturah. Abraham married her after Sarah died, as we read in Genesis chapter 25. Although the Midianite people lived mostly east of Canaan, the people referred to here in our text were a branch that had settled farther to the south and west in this remote area. The Midianites were a nomadic people, moving about from place to place. We hear more of them especially during the time of the judges, when they invaded the land of Canaan and greatly troubled God's people.

Reuel (also called "Jethro" in the very next chapter), the man whom Moses served as shepherd during his stay in this land, was a priest. The name Reuel means "friend of God." His other name, "Jethro," probably designated his rank or position in his tribe. How much of the true God was known by Reuel at this time is difficult to say. It appears later on that through Moses, he became a convert to the worship of the God of Israel.

Here Moses married Zipporah, one of Reuel's seven daughters. The name that Moses and Zipporah gave to their son, "Gershom," shows that Moses still felt himself to be a stranger among these people even though he lived with them for 40 years. The name *Gershom* means "stranger,

18

alien." Later on, Moses and Zipporah were blessed with a son whom they named "Eliezer," which means "God is a helper." The name of the second son indicates that Moses' confidence in the Lord was strengthened.

We can well imagine that these years were difficult for Moses. Just imagine this great future leader serving all these years as a humble shepherd! Moses learned patience. He also learned much about the kind of land through which he was to lead God's people later on. God was training, testing, and strengthening Moses for the years ahead, even though at the time Moses must have found this difficult to appreciate. When God was ready, he called his chosen leader.

People who serve God in a special way often find it difficult to appreciate God's purposes for them, especially if they carry on this service in some remote area where their labors are often little appreciated and perhaps go unrecognized. But God always knows what he is doing. When he sees fit, through his church he will call his servants to places of higher responsibilities. In the meanwhile, God's servants learn patience in faithful service, wherever this may be.

God's concern for his people

²³**During that long period, the king of Egypt died. The Israelites groaned in their slavery and cried out, and their cry for help because of their slavery went up to God. ²⁴God heard their groaning and he remembered his covenant with Abraham, with Isaac and with Jacob. ²⁵So God looked on the Israelites and was concerned about them.**

These verses now serve as a bridge to what follows in the next chapter. The scene is prepared for the Savior-God to make his presence known to his people in remarkable ways.

The death of the king of Egypt meant that there was finally nothing to prevent Moses' return. When the text says that God "remembered" his covenant with Abraham, Isaac, and Jacob, we know that God never forgot these promises. God is always the same, and he always knows all things. This is the holy writer's way of saying that God has now decided to take direct action in behalf of his people. God's loving concern now moves him to take this appropriate action at the right time.

Moses and the burning bush

3 **Now Moses was tending the flock of Jethro his father-in-law, the priest of Midian, and he led the flock to the far side of the desert and came to Horeb, the mountain of God. ²There the angel of the LORD appeared to him in flames of fire from within a bush. Moses saw that though the bush was on fire it did not burn up. ³So Moses thought, "I will go over and see this strange sight—why the bush does not burn up."**

⁴When the LORD saw that he had gone over to look, God called to him from within the bush, "Moses, Moses!"

And Moses said, "Here I am."

⁵"Do not come any closer," God said. "Take off your sandals, for the place where you are standing is holy ground." ⁶Then he said, "I am the God of your father, the God of Abraham, the God of Isaac and the God of Jacob." At this, Moses hid his face, because he was afraid to look at God.

⁷The LORD said, "I have indeed seen the misery of my people in Egypt. I have heard them crying out because of their slave drivers, and I am concerned about their suffering. ⁸So I have come down to rescue them from the hand of the Egyptians and to bring them up out of that land into a good and spacious land, a land flowing with milk and honey—the home of the Canaanites, Hittites, Amorites, Perizzites, Hivites and Jebusites. ⁹And now the cry of the Israelites has reached me, and I have seen the way the Egyptians are oppressing them. ¹⁰So now, go. I am sending you to Pharaoh to bring my people the Israelites out of Egypt."

¹¹But Moses said to God, "Who am I, that I should go to Pharaoh and bring the Israelites out of Egypt?"

¹²**And God said, "I will be with you. And this will be the sign to you that it is I who have sent you: When you have brought the people out of Egypt, you will worship God on this mountain."**

¹³**Moses said to God, "Suppose I go to the Israelites and say to them, 'The God of your fathers has sent me to you,' and they ask me, 'What is his name?' Then what shall I tell them?"**

In these verses Moses relates how God appeared to him while he was tending the flock of his father-in-law and called him to bring the Israelites out of Egypt. The place was Horeb, a mountain range that Moses calls "the mountain of God." It was here on Mount Sinai, one of Horeb's mountain peaks, that God later gave the Israelites the law.

We are told that "the angel of the LORD" appeared to Moses. This expression, "angel of the LORD," is often used in the Old Testament for the second person of the triune God before he came to this earth in human form at Bethlehem. To Hagar, he appeared as a man (Genesis 16:7); to Abraham, as one of three visitors (18:1,2) or as a voice from heaven (22:11); to Joshua, as the commander of God's army (Joshua 5:13-15); to Balaam, as an angel with a drawn sword (Numbers 22:31). In our text "angel of the LORD," "God," and "Lord" are used interchangeably, so there can be no question that "angel of the LORD" means God himself in a special manifestation of his presence.

In this situation God appeared to Moses in a bush that burned with fire and yet was not consumed. Surely, this was a miracle of God! As Moses came near this unusual sight, God called him by name. He told Moses to take off his sandals, because he was standing on holy ground. In those days, when people entered a holy place such as a church, they would take off their sandals. It was a sign of a deep respect for that place.

God first of all made himself known to Moses as "the God of Abraham, the God of Isaac and the God of Jacob."

Moses could not bear to look up. Think of it—the God who had spoken to the forefathers of Israel, who for hundreds of years had been silent, was now speaking to Moses out of this burning bush!

God now assured Moses that he would rescue the people of Israel from their slavery in Egypt. He would bring them to the land that had been promised to Abraham, a rich land "flowing with milk and honey." He called Moses as the one to go to Pharaoh to bring the Israelites out of Egypt.

As we hear these words of this text, we too should "take off our sandals." We are about to approach a manifestation of God that is one of the most revealing passages in all of Scripture. With holy awe we stand before God's presence, a God who makes himself known to us in his Holy Word, a God who promises to do great and wondrous things for us. We are not surprised that Moses reacts as we hear of him in the following verses.

Moses, overwhelmed by this miraculous appearance of God, says, "Who am I, that I should go to Pharaoh and bring the Israelites out of Egypt?" This is a different Moses. Many years before this, he had wanted to take on this job of deliverer all by himself when he killed an Egyptian and tried to settle an argument between two of his people. Now he doubts his own ability to do this work. Forty years as a shepherd had taught him humility!

God reassures Moses. He says, "I will be with you." He even gives Moses a sign as a pledge. "On this same mountain," God promises, "you will worship me!" It was at this very same place that Israel was to receive God's law as his very own covenant people.

Moses now asks God what he should say to the Israelites in case they would ask him for the name of the God of their fathers. This question too, we can understand. After all, Moses had been away for 40 years. How could he remove all accusations that he was perhaps nothing but an impostor? How could he identify the true God in a way that would be unmistakably clear?

In his reply, which we read in the verses that follow, God declares his name to Moses in a most wonderful way, a way in which he distinguishes himself as the God above all other gods, a God in whom one could have absolute confidence. This revelation of God's name is without doubt one of the most meaningful in all Scripture.

God reveals his name

¹⁴**God said to Moses, "I AM WHO I AM. This is what you are to say to the Israelites: 'I AM has sent me to you.'"**

¹⁵**God also said to Moses, "Say to the Israelites, 'The LORD, the God of your fathers—the God of Abraham, the God of Isaac and the God of Jacob—has sent me to you.' This is my name forever, the name by which I am to be remembered from generation to generation.**

"I AM WHO I AM." This is God's very own revelation of his name and of himself. The words seem so simple. Yet there is a world of truth in these few words about the God who speaks of himself this way.

"I AM," God declares. He is an "I," a personal being. He is not merely an indefinite force or magical power somewhere out in nature, as many people believe. As a person he compares himself to people who think, who feel, who speak, who decide, who act.

"I AM WHO I AM." These words also breathe the spirit of absolute independence. God moves with unlimited freedom. As Paul writes in Romans, "Who has known the mind of the Lord? Or who has been his counselor? Who has ever given to

God, that God should repay him? For from him and through him and to him are all things. To him be the glory forever! Amen" (11:34-36).

"I AM,'" God says. God is timeless, constant, unchangeable. Scripture refers to this "I AM" frequently. In the book of Revelation, God says, "I am the Alpha and the Omega, . . . who is, and who was, and who is to come, the Almighty" (1:8). In John 8:58 Jesus says of himself, "Before Abraham was born, I am!" The writer of Hebrews declares Jesus to be "the same yesterday and today and forever" (13:8). Through the prophet Malachi, God declares, "I the LORD do not change" (3:6).

For Moses and for the Israelites, these qualities that God here revealed were to reassure God's people that the promises of grace and mercy given to their fathers were still in effect. God had not forgotten them. Now he was about to demonstrate to them that every one of these gracious promises would be fulfilled.

Those who are familiar with the Hebrew will see something else of significance in God's "I AM." The letters of the Hebrew stem for the word "I AM" are the same letters used in the Hebrew word that we translate as "LORD." This word occurs already in Genesis 2:4. God used this name when he revealed himself to Abraham. This was the God of the covenant, the God of free and faithful grace. The Hebrew word for this name, "LORD," is pronounced *Yahweh.* Because the Jews later on in their history feared to utter this holy name, they substituted the title "LORD" for the name Yahweh whenever reading it aloud. The "I AM WHO I AM" was thus God's way of telling Moses and the Israelites that he was the same covenant-God who in grace and mercy had called them to be his people, the God who would surely now keep all these promises made to them.

In verse 14 and 15 of this text, God closely connects his "I AM" with the name "the LORD," the God of their fathers,

24

and declares, "This is my name forever, the name by which I am to be remembered from generation to generation."

With this assurance, Moses is told in the following verses to go to the elders of Israel.

The Lord's instructions to Moses

¹⁶"**Go, assemble the elders of Israel and say to them, 'The LORD, the God of your fathers—the God of Abraham, Isaac and Jacob—appeared to me and said: I have watched over you and have seen what has been done to you in Egypt. ¹⁷And I have promised to bring you up out of your misery in Egypt into the land of the Canaanites, Hittites, Amorites, Perizzites, Hivites and Jebusites—a land flowing with milk and honey.'**

¹⁸"**The elders of Israel will listen to you. Then you and the elders are to go to the king of Egypt and say to him, 'The LORD, the God of the Hebrews, has met with us. Let us take a three-day journey into the desert to offer sacrifices to the LORD our God.' ¹⁹But I know that the king of Egypt will not let you go unless a mighty hand compels him. ²⁰So I will stretch out my hand and strike the Egyptians with all the wonders that I will perform among them. After that, he will let you go.**

²¹"**And I will make the Egyptians favorably disposed toward this people, so that when you leave you will not go empty-handed. ²²Every woman is to ask her neighbor and any woman living in her house for articles of silver and gold and for clothing, which you will put on your sons and daughters. And so you will plunder the Egyptians."**

Several questions arise as we consider these verses more closely.

First of all, was the request to Pharaoh to let Israel take a "three-day journey into the desert" to offer sacrifices to the Lord a way of deceiving him? Why not tell Pharaoh that a permanent freedom was Israel's purpose? This question is not difficult to answer. Coming with a lesser request, as Moses was instructed to do here, was simply to be a first step.

And it showed good diplomacy. At the same time, it would indicate what Pharaoh's feelings were in giving any kind of consideration toward God's people.

God knew in advance, as he informed Moses, that Pharaoh would refuse even this modest request. Then why go at all with a request? God here told Moses in advance that in the events which would follow, God would have to reveal his mighty hand with miracles in order to compel Pharaoh to let Israel go. The blame for this would rest upon Pharaoh's obstinacy, a trait that he would show from the very beginning.

Through this demonstration of God's power, as God also foretells, the Egyptians would see to it that the Israelites would not leave Egypt empty-handed. But wasn't the request of the Israelites for precious gifts unworthy of God's people? How could the Lord recommend such a thing? As we think of the many years of hard labor in Egypt, however, this request was not at all unreasonable. (Incidentally, the translation in the King James Version that these treasures were to be "borrowed" from the Egyptians is inaccurate. The Hebrew word clearly means "ask.") According to God's plan, the Israelites would leave Egypt as a conquering nation, bringing with them the spoils of a victory that God had graciously bestowed upon them.

Signs for Moses

4 Moses answered, "What if they do not believe me or listen to me and say, 'The LORD did not appear to you'?"

²Then the LORD said to him, "What is that in your hand?"

"A staff," he replied.

³The LORD said, "Throw it on the ground."

Moses threw it on the ground and it became a snake, and he ran from it. ⁴Then the LORD said to him, "Reach out your hand and take it by the tail." So Moses reached out and took hold of the snake and it turned back into a staff in his hand. ⁵"This," said the LORD, "is so that they may believe that the LORD, the God of their fathers—the God of Abraham, the God of Isaac and the God of Jacob—has appeared to you."

⁶Then the LORD said, "Put your hand inside your cloak." So Moses put his hand into his cloak, and when he took it out, it was leprous, like snow.

⁷"Now put it back into your cloak," he said. So Moses put his hand back into his cloak, and when he took it out, it was restored, like the rest of his flesh. ⁸Then the LORD said, "If they do not believe you or pay attention to the first miraculous sign, they may believe the second. ⁹But if they do not believe these two signs or listen to you, take some water from the Nile and pour it on the dry ground. The water you take from the river will become blood on the ground."

Previously, Moses had expressed humility when faced with the Lord's commission. But now after the Lord had given specific directions as to how he was to go to the people and to Pharaoh to carry out his task, doubts began to fill his mind. "What if they do not believe me . . . and say, 'the LORD did not appear to you'?" he asks the Lord.

What if . . . ? How often don't all sorts of questions like this fill our hearts and minds when we're confronted with a specific task? Moses was no different from any of us when it comes to being faced with the responsibility of carrying out certain duties that we know the Lord wants us to do. Our first reaction, perhaps, is one of humility. The closer we come to the time when action is required, however, we often begin to doubt that anyone will listen to us. Surely we can all think of times when we knew it was our duty to bear witness to our faith before some unbeliever, and how these "what ifs" entered our minds!

The Lord answered Moses by giving him the power to perform these miracles. This is the first time that we have a record of God bestowing to some person the power to perform miracles like this. Abraham and Sarah were blessed with Isaac at an age when the birth of a child was a miracle. Joseph received miraculous power from God to interpret dreams. The power to perform miracles of this unusual nature, however, happened here for the first time in biblical history.

The miracles themselves—Moses' staff becoming a snake, his hand becoming leprous, water from the Nile turning into blood—have been interpreted as having all sorts of fanciful meanings. The staff of Moses, we are told, represents his calling as a shepherd. By throwing it down, he shows himself ready to face dangers; the leprous hand, they say, represents Israel's condition of bondage in Egypt; the Nile River had become a god in Egypt, and turning it to blood demonstrated Moses' power to destroy Pharaoh's gods.

While we find these explanations interesting, we prefer to stay with a simple, straightforward interpretation of these signs. They were a testimony both to Israel and to Egypt that God's presence and his power accompanied his chosen messenger. How could anyone see these signs and doubt that Moses was God's very own representative! And how could Moses, for that matter, still be filled with doubts concerning his mission!

Yet Moses is still not satisfied that he should be the one to carry out this great task.

Excuses, excuses

¹⁰**Moses said to the LORD, "O Lord, I have never been eloquent, neither in the past nor since you have spoken to your servant. I am slow of speech and tongue."**

¹¹**The LORD said to him, "Who gave man his mouth? Who makes him deaf or mute? Who gives him sight or makes him blind? Is it not I, the LORD?** ¹²**Now go; I will help you speak and will teach you what to say."**

¹³**But Moses said, "O Lord, please send someone else to do it."**

¹⁴**Then the L**ORD**'s anger burned against Moses and he said, "What about your brother, Aaron the Levite? I know he can speak well. He is already on his way to meet you, and his heart will be glad when he sees you. ¹⁵You shall speak to him and put words in his mouth; I will help both of you speak and will teach you what to do. ¹⁶He will speak to the people for you, and it will be as if he were your mouth and as if you were God to him. ¹⁷But take this staff in your hand so you can perform miraculous signs with it."**

As Moses comes closer to the reality of facing the Israelites and Pharaoh, he seems to try harder to find excuses. He uses his lack of eloquence, his slowness of speech, as a reason for not being well equipped for his assignment. Again, this excuse amounts to doubting God's ability to give him the powers of speech adequate for the task, as the Lord immediately points out to Moses when he says, "Who gave man his mouth? . . . Now go; I will help you speak."

Finally Moses pleads with the Lord to send someone else. He thereby expresses the real reason behind these excuses. He simply does not want to go.

We are not surprised that "the LORD's anger burned against Moses." Just how God expressed this anger we are not told. Yet even an angry God, a God who will not be turned aside by poor excuses, shows his compassion to Moses by calling attention to Moses' brother, Aaron, who can accompany him on his difficult mission and speak for him. The Lord also commands Moses finally to take his staff in hand and do the work assigned to him, assuring him that he can rely on the Lord's help to do miracles.

This account of Moses concerning himself should serve as an encouragement to anyone who receives a call into the public ministry through the church or who is chosen to some special assignment in the Lord's work. In Numbers

12:3 Moses writes of himself as "a very humble man, more humble than anyone else on the face of the earth." Humility is a high virtue in the Lord's service. But feelings of humility should not lead us to think up all sorts of excuses when the Lord calls us to do some special task for him. Which person is by nature worthy to do the Lord's work? Who is adequate to serve as the Lord's own representative? Yet we can trust that the Lord who supplies the message and calls us to do his work will also give us the necessary strength to carry out his commands. It is in this spirit that we say, "Here am I. Send me!" (Isaiah 6:8).

Moses returns to Egypt

¹⁸Then Moses went back to Jethro his father-in-law and said to him, "Let me go back to my own people in Egypt to see if any of them are still alive."

Jethro said, "Go, and I wish you well."

¹⁹Now the Lord had said to Moses in Midian, "Go back to Egypt, for all the men who wanted to kill you are dead." ²⁰So Moses took his wife and sons, put them on a donkey and started back to Egypt. And he took the staff of God in his hand.

²¹The Lord said to Moses, "When you return to Egypt, see that you perform before Pharaoh all the wonders I have given you the power to do. But I will harden his heart so that he will not let the people go. ²²Then say to Pharaoh, 'This is what the Lord says: Israel is my firstborn son, ²³and I told you, "Let my son go, so he may worship me." But you refused to let him go; so I will kill your firstborn son.'"

²⁴At a lodging place on the way, the Lord met Moses and was about to kill him. ²⁵But Zipporah took a flint knife, cut off her son's foreskin and touched Moses' feet with it. "Surely you are a bridegroom of blood to me," she said. ²⁶So the Lord let him alone. (At that time she said "bridegroom of blood," referring to circumcision.)

²⁷The Lord said to Aaron, "Go into the desert to meet Moses." So he met Moses at the mountain of God and kissed

him. ²⁸Then Moses told Aaron everything the LORD had sent him to say, and also about all the miraculous signs he had commanded him to perform.

²⁹Moses and Aaron brought together all the elders of the Israelites, ³⁰and Aaron told them everything the LORD had said to Moses. He also performed the signs before the people, ³¹and they believed. And when they heard that the LORD was concerned about them and had seen their misery, they bowed down and worshiped.

Having received the consent of his father-in-law, Jethro, to return to Egypt, we read that "Moses took his wife and sons, put them on a donkey and started back to Egypt. And he took the staff of God in his hand." What an incongruous picture! A husband and wife traveling with their two sons on a desert road to Egypt, with a donkey as beast of burden and a shepherd's staff as a weapon. Were these poor travelers on a mission to lead an entire nation out of Egypt against the wishes of the most powerful ruler on earth? Yes, they were. The "staff of God" was in Moses' hand!

Again the Lord forewarned Moses about the way that Pharaoh would not agree to let the Israelites depart. "I will harden his heart so that he will not let the people go," God declared. God thereby foretold what would happen in the future in Pharaoh's case. As we follow the events in the chapters that lie ahead, we will notice that it was Pharaoh himself who was responsible for having a heart that was hard so that he would not listen to the Lord's command delivered through Moses to let the people of Israel go. We also know from Scripture that the Lord does not take pleasure in the death of the wicked (Ezekiel 33:11), that he wants all men to be saved and to come to a knowledge of the truth (1 Timothy 2:3,4). And so it was only after Pharaoh repeatedly rejected God's call to repentance, displaying a defiant spirit and an obdurate heart, that God finally stepped in and completed the process. God here forewarns Moses as to what would happen.

Even so today, the Lord is not wanting anyone to perish, but everyone to come to repentance. God earnestly desires the salvation of all people. When people are lost, it is their own fault entirely. Yes, when they persistently and obdurately refuse to heed God's gracious call to repentance, hardening their hearts against the work of God's Holy Spirit, then God steps in and declares the process complete. He pronounces his judgment upon them. Already in this life their eternal doom is sealed. Such people no longer hear God's gracious call to repentance.

"Israel," God also declared to Moses at this time, "is my firstborn son." They were God's chosen people. Because Pharaoh in his hardness of heart would refuse to let God's chosen firstborn people go, he would suffer the death of his own firstborn son at the hand of God. Thus God here in this brief way foretells the grim events that would happen in the days ahead, as well as the victorious outcome for Israel in their deliverance.

On the way to Egypt, an incident occurred in which the Lord threatened Moses with death. Just how God sought to kill Moses we are not told. Perhaps it was some sudden and severe sickness. It was only when Zipporah, Moses' wife, circumcised Moses' son that his life was spared.

Did Moses neglect to circumcise his son because of Zipporah's dislike for circumcision? Is that why Zipporah now called Moses a "bridegroom of blood," indicating that it was only through this bloody act that she could bring her husband back to life? These are possible explanations for an incident that is told us in but a few words. This incident does make very clear, however, that God expected a man who was to serve as a leader of God's people to be faithful to the covenant of grace in his own family. Failure to obey the command to circumcise brought with it the threat to "be cut off" from God's people (Genesis 17:14).

In the closing verses of this chapter, we see how Moses and Aaron met according to God's promise, how they went to the elders of the Israelites, and how they met with a favorable response. The people "believed" and "bowed down and worshiped." The promises of the fathers still were alive in Israel.

Bricks without straw

5 Afterward Moses and Aaron went to Pharaoh and said, "This is what the LORD, the God of Israel, says: 'Let my people go, so that they may hold a festival to me in the desert.'"

²Pharaoh said, "Who is the LORD, that I should obey him and let Israel go? I do not know the LORD and I will not let Israel go."

³Then they said, "The God of the Hebrews has met with us. Now let us take a three-day journey into the desert to offer sacrifices to the LORD our God, or he may strike us with plagues or with the sword."

⁴But the king of Egypt said, "Moses and Aaron, why are you taking the people away from their labor? Get back to your work!" ⁵Then Pharaoh said, "Look, the people of the land are now numerous, and you are stopping them from working."

⁶That same day Pharaoh gave this order to the slave drivers and foremen in charge of the people: ⁷"You are no longer to supply the people with straw for making bricks; let them go and gather their own straw. ⁸But require them to make the same number of bricks as before; don't reduce the quota. They are lazy; that is why they are crying out, 'Let us go and sacrifice to our God.' ⁹Make the work harder for the men so that they keep working and pay no attention to lies."

¹⁰Then the slave drivers and the foremen went out and said to the people, "This is what Pharaoh says: 'I will not give you any more straw. ¹¹Go and get your own straw wherever you can find it, but your work will not be reduced at all.'" ¹²So the people scattered all over Egypt to gather stubble to use for straw. ¹³The

slave drivers kept pressing them, saying, "Complete the work required of you for each day, just as when you had straw." [14]The Israelite foremen appointed by Pharaoh's slave drivers were beaten and were asked, "Why didn't you meet your quota of bricks yesterday or today, as before?"

[15]Then the Israelite foremen went and appealed to Pharaoh: "Why have you treated your servants this way? [16]Your servants are given no straw, yet we are told, 'Make bricks!' Your servants are being beaten, but the fault is with your own people."

[17]Pharaoh said, "Lazy, that's what you are—lazy! That is why you keep saying, 'Let us go and sacrifice to the Lord.' [18]Now get to work. You will not be given any straw, yet you must produce your full quota of bricks."

[19]The Israelite foremen realized they were in trouble when they were told, "You are not to reduce the number of bricks required of you for each day." [20]When they left Pharaoh, they found Moses and Aaron waiting to meet them, [21]and they said, "May the Lord look upon you and judge you! You have made us a stench to Pharaoh and his officials and have put a sword in their hand to kill us."

[22]Moses returned to the Lord and said, "O Lord, why have you brought trouble upon this people? Is this why you sent me? [23]Ever since I went to Pharaoh to speak in your name, he has brought trouble upon this people, and you have not rescued your people at all."

Pharaoh's reply to the request of Moses and Aaron was a flat, decisive no. We note that the two leaders of Israel presented their request to let Israel hold a festival in the desert as a command of the Lord: "This is what the Lord, the God of Israel, says. . . ." "Who is the Lord, that I should obey him . . . ?" was Pharaoh's harsh reply. As far as he was concerned, this "Lord" was some kind of foreign god. Pharaoh considered himself to be the only true intermediary between the high-gods and the people of the world. To him the great superpowers were those of nature, like the sun and the moon, and he was the great high priest who could approach these high-gods in the beautiful temples along the Nile built in their honor. Thus his reply is more an expression of contempt than a question.

Moses and Aaron patiently explained that "the God of the Hebrews" expected his people to perform this service of sacrifices in the desert. Failing to comply with their Lord's request would make their God angry. Surely, they thought, even one who did not believe in their Lord could respect their desire to take part in this act of worship.

Pharaoh's answer was to add to Israel's labors. It was a vindictive act. When making bricks out of clay and stubble, the Israelites would no longer be supplied with straw. (Straw was mixed with clay in order to increase the strength of the bricks.) They would have to get their own straw and still meet the same quota of bricks. Those Israelite foremen whose workers failed to complete the daily task were to be beaten without mercy.

The Israelites blamed Moses and Aaron for this added oppression. "You have made us a stench to Pharaoh and his officials," they said. In other words, their name was now spoiled. Pharaoh and his officials would destroy them. It is strange how the Israelites could even call upon the Savior-God to judge Moses and Aaron for this. These very people who showed that they had lost all confidence in God still called upon this same God to punish their leaders! Moses begins to experience the perversity of Israel!

And even Moses himself shows signs of becoming discouraged. "O Lord," he prays, "why have you brought trouble upon this people? Is this why you sent me?"

Does this prayer of Moses sound familiar? We hear this questioning of God's ways throughout the book of Job, as Job and his friends wrestled with the problem of God's dealing with people in times of trouble and disappointment. Frequently, the psalms also asked "Why, O LORD, . . . ?" and "How long, O Lord?" (Read Psalms 10 and 13.)

It happens today that Christians who conscientiously do God's will and follow his commands suffer nothing but contempt and persecution at the hands of unbelievers. When even their own friends and relatives criticize them for continuing in their faithful witness to Christ, the burden sometimes seems almost more than they can bear. "Why, O Lord? How long, O Lord?" they pray. God is there. He hears this prayer. In his way and in his time, he promises to bring relief and show his saving power. In the meantime, he assures them that in all things, even in those ways that are past finding out at the moment, he is working "for the good of those who love him, who have been called according to his purpose," as Romans 8:28 tells us.

In our next chapter we see how quickly the Lord comes to Moses and reassures him in this time of uncertainty.

God promises deliverance

6 Then the LORD said to Moses, "Now you will see what I will do to Pharaoh: Because of my mighty hand he will let them go; because of my mighty hand he will drive them out of his country."

²God also said to Moses, "I am the LORD. ³I appeared to Abraham, to Isaac and to Jacob as God Almighty, but by my name the LORD I did not make myself known to them. ⁴I also established my covenant with them to give them the land of Canaan, where they lived as aliens. ⁵Moreover, I have heard the groaning of the Israelites, whom the Egyptians are enslaving, and I have remembered my covenant.

⁶"Therefore, say to the Israelites: 'I am the LORD, and I will bring you out from under the yoke of the Egyptians. I will free you from being slaves to them, and I will redeem you with an outstretched arm and with mighty acts of judgment. ⁷I will take you as my own people, and I will be your God. Then you will

know that I am the L ORD your God, who brought you out from under the yoke of the Egyptians. ⁸And I will bring you to the land I swore with uplifted hand to give to Abraham, to Isaac and to Jacob. I will give it to you as a possession. I am the L ORD.'"

⁹Moses reported this to the Israelites, but they did not listen to him because of their discouragement and cruel bondage.

¹⁰Then the L ORD said to Moses, ¹¹"Go, tell Pharaoh king of Egypt to let the Israelites go out of his country."

¹²But Moses said to the L ORD, "If the Israelites will not listen to me, why would Pharaoh listen to me, since I speak with faltering lips?"

"Now you will see . . ." God reassured Moses in his time of doubt and uncertainty. "Because of my mighty hand" Pharaoh would be compelled to let Israel go; that was God's sure promise. "I am the L ORD. I appeared to Abraham, to Isaac and to Jacob as God Almighty," God declared. Again the Lord pointed to the covenant which he, the "L ORD," the covenant-God, had made with the Israelites' forefathers. By calling himself "L ORD," he reminded Moses of that solemn contract which he in his mercy had made with the fathers of Israel. As the covenant-God, he had placed himself under obligation to rescue his people. He also showed himself to these patriarchs as "God Almighty," the God who had demonstrated his power in the miraculous birth of Isaac, and who by his might had preserved and multiplied this family so that it grew into a mighty nation.

Having said all this, God added the words of reassurance "but by my name the L ORD I did not make myself known to them." The forefathers of Israel were, in fact, acquainted with the name L ORD (Yahweh—the God of the covenant). Abraham built an altar to this name, as Genesis chapters 12 and 13 attest, and called upon this name. This was the very name God used to reveal himself to Moses while tending sheep on Mount Horeb, the name that Moses was told to use when making himself known to the

Israelites as God's true representative. Surely, the Israelites were already quite familiar with the name LORD.

The full implications of this name, however, were still to be revealed. What this name would mean as to how God would carry out his promise of redemption for his people, the Israelites would soon experience. God would now show his "mighty hand" as the God of the covenant, the Lord of grace and mercy, the God who now would show his "remembrance" of his covenant by taking direct action into their affairs. What the forefathers did not know about this LORD, the Israelites would see revealed before their very eyes! In the very next verses (6-8), the Lord explains this further. God would deliver Israel from bondage in Egypt. God would adopt this nation as his very own people. God would bring this nation into the Land of Promise. "I am the LORD," he declared. What tremendous assurances the Lord here brings to Moses and to his people Israel!

Some Bible scholars say that these words of the Lord ("but by my name the LORD I did not make myself known to them") show that Abraham, Isaac, and Jacob knew only the name "God Almighty." The patriarchs, in other words, had a more primitive form of religion. As their religion developed, these critics of the Bible say, they learned later on to know God by the name "LORD" also. These same critics, of course, do not accept the Bible as God's verbally inspired Word; neither do they accept Moses as the author of the Pentateuch. Their faulty interpretation of this passage is another example of how they take certain words of Scripture completely out of context in an effort to fit their own theories. At the same time, they try to empty Scripture of that great saving purpose for which God gave us his Word. We interpret Scripture with Scripture, and as we do so, we see how beautifully the passages of the Bible fit together to bring us God's entire plan of salvation.

In spite of God's reassurance, the Israelites again, blinded by their own feelings of self-pity, failed to listen. Their despondency had its effect on Moses. If even God's people would not listen to him, how could he expect Pharaoh to listen? "I speak with faltering lips," Moses complained. The Hebrew word he used here really means "uncircumcised lips," indicating the same complaint he used previously: "I am slow of speech" (4:10).

God's reply to this objection of Moses is given us in the next chapter. In the meantime, Moses introduces his own family record in the remaining verses of chapter 6 that follow here.

The family record of Moses and Aaron

¹³Now the LORD spoke to Moses and Aaron about the Israelites and Pharaoh king of Egypt, and he commanded them to bring the Israelites out of Egypt.

¹⁴These were the heads of their families:

The sons of Reuben the firstborn son of Israel were Hanoch and Pallu, Hezron and Carmi. These were the clans of Reuben.

¹⁵The sons of Simeon were Jemuel, Jamin, Ohad, Jakin, Zohar and Shaul the son of a Canaanite woman. These were the clans of Simeon.

¹⁶These were the names of the sons of Levi according to their records: Gershon, Kohath and Merari. Levi lived 137 years.

¹⁷The sons of Gershon, by clans, were Libni and Shimei.

¹⁸The sons of Kohath were Amram, Izhar, Hebron and Uzziel. Kohath lived 133 years.

¹⁹The sons of Merari were Mahli and Mushi.

These were the clans of Levi according to their records.

²⁰Amram married his father's sister Jochebed, who bore him Aaron and Moses. Amram lived 137 years.

²¹The sons of Izhar were Korah, Nepheg and Zicri.

²²The sons of Uzziel were Mishael, Elzaphan and Sithri.

²³Aaron married Elisheba, daughter of Amminadab and sister of Nahshon, and she bore him Nadab and Abihu, Eleazar and Ithamar.

²⁴The sons of Korah were Assir, Elkanah and Abiasaph. These were the Korahite clans.

²⁵Eleazar son of Aaron married one of the daughters of Putiel, and she bore him Phinehas.

These were the heads of the Levite families, clan by clan.

²⁶It was this same Aaron and Moses to whom the LORD said, "Bring the Israelites out of Egypt by their divisions." ²⁷They were the ones who spoke to Pharaoh king of Egypt about bringing the Israelites out of Egypt. It was the same Moses and Aaron.

²⁸Now when the LORD spoke to Moses in Egypt, ²⁹he said to him, "I am the LORD. Tell Pharaoh king of Egypt everything I tell you."

³⁰But Moses said to the LORD, "Since I speak with faltering lips, why would Pharaoh listen to me?"

Why this unusual interruption in the account of Israel's deliverance from Egypt? Why this list of names? Before we are tempted to dismiss this as "just another list of names," a list which we can pass over quickly because "it really doesn't add much to the story," let us look more closely at the list itself.

First of all, the families of Reuben and Simeon, the first two sons of Jacob, are introduced. Then we come to Levi, the third son in line, whose family is listed in more detail. This clearly reminds us again where Levi, the forefather of Moses and Aaron, fits into the genealogy of Jacob.

Coming to Levi, we see that not only is Levi's age recorded, but also the three sons of Levi are listed: Gershon, Kohath, and Merari. These are important names to remember. The three branches of Levi's family are referred to frequently according to these three names in the Bible records that follow, since each branch had a special duty to perform in carrying out the functions of Israel's priesthood.

Of the three sons of Levi, Kohath is next singled out. His age is given also, as was that of Levi. Moses and Aaron, we see, descended from the family branch of Kohath.

Of the sons of Kohath, the name Amram is emphasized by giving his age. Amram, who "married his father's sister Jochebed," was the forefather of Moses and Aaron. The word "sister" here, incidentally, can be understood in a more general sense as "relative." Many scholars, by the way, conclude from verse 20 that Amram and Jochebed were indeed the names of Moses and Aaron's parents. If that is the case, then the Amram listed as the son of Kohath must be an earlier Amram in the family genealogy, since there were many more generations between Levi and Moses than just three. What we have here, as in other places of Scripture, is a summary listing of names.

Note also that Aaron is listed before Moses, indicating that he was the older of the two.

Following the names of Moses and Aaron, we have many other important names: Korah, Nadab, Abihu, Eleazar, Ithamar, Phinehas. These names play important roles in Israel's later history, particularly in the development of Israel's priesthood.

We come back to the questions raised before: Why this list of names? Why interrupt the story to bring us a family record? Remember, Moses had been called by God to be Israel's deliverer. His brother, Aaron, had been chosen to be his coworker. Both are to play prominent roles in the account that follows. The difficult situation that lies ahead of these two chosen leaders has been clearly presented. The big confrontation between them and Pharaoh is about to take place, a confrontation that begins with the performing of miracles, the plagues, and leads to the eventual deliverance. What better place could there be for a genealogy of Moses and Aaron than at precisely this point? To those critics who again argue here that the Bible is a book of loosely connected documents put together by some later editor, we say, "Study God's Word with an open mind. Look at it positively. See for yourself how beautifully every detail fits together as a history of God's saving acts in behalf of all mankind." And by "all mankind," we include ourselves!

At the close of this chapter, we come back to "this same Aaron and Moses," whose leadership roles have been substantiated by this genealogy of their family and who are now about to engage in this tremendous struggle with the most powerful ruler in the world at that time. Moses will have Aaron to help his own "faltering lips," because Aaron will serve as spokesman. God assures Moses of this, as we see in the next chapter.

The plagues

7 Then the Lord said to Moses, "See, I have made you like God to Pharaoh, and your brother Aaron will be your prophet. ²You are to say everything I command you, and your brother Aaron is to tell Pharaoh to let the Israelites go out of his country. ³But I will harden Pharaoh's heart, and though I multiply my miraculous signs and wonders in Egypt, ⁴he will not listen to you. Then I will lay my hand on Egypt and with mighty acts of judgment I will bring out my divisions, my people the Israelites. ⁵And the Egyptians will know that I am the Lord when I stretch out my hand against Egypt and bring the Israelites out of it."

These words of our text are God's general announcement to Moses about the plagues that are to follow. God tells Moses that he would make Moses "like God to Pharaoh, and your brother Aaron will be your prophet." Moses would receive authority and miraculous power from God. These signs and wonders in Egypt, God would "multiply," pointing to the many plagues just ahead. Their end result would be that God would "bring the Israelites out of [Egypt]."

God also sets forth the purpose of these plagues. Previously, he had already said that because of his mighty acts, Israel would come to know that they were God's own people, and he would be revealed as their God. Now God adds, "And the Egyptians will know that I am the LORD." To Israel, God's mighty acts meant deliverance. To Egypt these same mighty acts brought severe judgment. To Pharaoh, because of his own persistent hardening of heart in the face of God's repeated warnings, they eventually led to this—that God himself would harden Pharaoh's heart, just as God had already indicated.

Before considering each plague individually as they are recorded for us in the coming chapters, a survey of the first nine plagues provides some interesting observations. They are recorded as follows:

1. Blood (7:14-25)	4. Flies (8:20-32)	7. Hail (9:13-35)
2. Frogs (8:1-15)	5. Animal Disease	8. Locusts (10:1-20)
3. Gnats (8:16-19)	(9:1-7)	9. Darkness
	6. Boils (9:8-12)	(10:21-27)

By placing these miracles into three groups of three each (3 x 3), as above, we can see some interesting patterns emerge:

- In each series, the first and second plagues are announced to Pharaoh in advance. The third is given without previous warning.
- The grouping of 3 x 3 leads to a climax in the number 10, the number that is the symbol for completeness.

- Within the plagues as a whole, there is a progression, an increase in severity. These last three are especially severe and destructive.

- The Egyptian magicians vie with Moses in duplicating the very first two plagues. At the third they try but no longer succeed in their magic arts. They must confess, "This is the finger of God" (8:19).

- Beginning with the second series of plagues (4, 5, and 6), a distinction is made between the Israelites and the Egyptians. The land of Goshen, where the Israelites live, is spared.

- The first nine plagues deal with phenomena that have to do with the world of nature. For this reason, some scholars try to explain the plagues as natural happenings, occurrences that possibly took place "as natural disasters and in the course of time were exaggerated to make up the account as recorded in Exodus." We believe, however, that each plague was a miracle of God, in which God used the natural means of that country to manifest his supernatural power. Since the Egyptians worshiped these powers of nature, in what more effective way could God display his power over all things, even those things the Egyptians looked upon as deities!

Moses and the magicians

⁶**Moses and Aaron did just as the LORD commanded them. ⁷Moses was eighty years old and Aaron eighty-three when they spoke to Pharaoh.**

⁸The Lᴏʀᴅ said to Moses and Aaron, ⁹"When Pharaoh says to you, 'Perform a miracle,' then say to Aaron, 'Take your staff and throw it down before Pharaoh,' and it will become a snake."

¹⁰So Moses and Aaron went to Pharaoh and did just as the Lᴏʀᴅ commanded. Aaron threw his staff down in front of Pharaoh and his officials, and it became a snake. ¹¹Pharaoh then summoned wise men and sorcerers, and the Egyptian magicians also did the same things by their secret arts: ¹²Each one threw down his staff and it became a snake. But Aaron's staff swallowed up their staffs. ¹³Yet Pharaoh's heart became hard and he would not listen to them, just as the Lᴏʀᴅ had said.

When Moses and Aaron displayed to Pharaoh the sign of throwing down the staff so that it became a snake, we are told that "the Egyptian magicians also did the same things by their secret arts."

Werner Franzmann, in his *Bible History Commentary* on the Old Testament, has a fitting comment on this point:

> Here the question arises: Did the magicians actually perform supernatural feats? The text leaves no doubt as to the reality of their "miracles." True, we can explain their turning rods or staffs into serpents as a magician's trick, since even today travelers can see Oriental jugglers perform the feat of making serpents look stiff as a rod and then on command "restore them to life." But we cannot explain in the same way the feats they performed in connection with the first two plagues (water turned to blood, bringing up frogs). However, their feats were not genuine miracles and signs in the sense that God was performing supernatural acts through them and was thereby signifying ("signs") his approval of their words and actions, as he did in the case

of Moses and Aaron. Note that "the magicians also did the same things by their secret arts." These secret arts always stand in the service of Satan. Through the power that God permits the devil to use, the open enemies of God and false teachers can perform acts that seem like genuine miracles. But they are always "counterfeit signs" and "counterfeit wonders," as St. Paul calls the "miracles" advanced by the Antichrist (the Papacy) in support of his blasphemous claims (2 Thessalonians 2:8,9). Note also that this power of Satan is strictly limited. In 8:18,19 we hear that when the magicians were unable to turn dust into lice, they admitted, "This is the finger of God." (page 227)

Even here we note that Aaron's staff swallowed up the staffs of the magicians. Yet instead of recognizing the superior power of the God of Moses and Aaron, "Pharaoh's heart became hard." His obstinate refusal to heed God's warnings persisted.

The plague of blood

¹⁴Then the LORD said to Moses, "Pharaoh's heart is unyielding; he refuses to let the people go. ¹⁵Go to Pharaoh in the morning as he goes out to the water. Wait on the bank of the Nile to meet him, and take in your hand the staff that was changed into a snake. ¹⁶Then say to him, 'The LORD, the God of the Hebrews, has sent me to say to you: Let my people go, so that they may worship me in the desert. But until now you have not listened. ¹⁷This is what the LORD says: By this you will know that I am the LORD: With the staff that is in my hand I will strike the water of the Nile, and it will be changed into blood. ¹⁸The fish in the Nile will die, and the river will stink; the Egyptians will not be able to drink its water.'"

¹⁹The LORD said to Moses, "Tell Aaron, 'Take your staff and stretch out your hand over the waters of Egypt—over the streams

and canals, over the ponds and all the reservoirs'—and they will turn to blood. Blood will be everywhere in Egypt, even in the wooden buckets and stone jars."

²⁰Moses and Aaron did just as the LORD had commanded. He raised his staff in the presence of Pharaoh and his officials and struck the water of the Nile, and all the water was changed into blood. ²¹The fish in the Nile died, and the river smelled so bad that the Egyptians could not drink its water. Blood was everywhere in Egypt. ²²But the Egyptian magicians did the same things by their secret arts, and Pharaoh's heart became hard; he would not listen to Moses and Aaron, just as the LORD had said. ²³Instead, he turned and went into his palace, and did not take even this to heart. ²⁴And all the Egyptians dug along the Nile to get drinking water, because they could not drink the water of the river.

Moses was instructed by God to confront Pharaoh at the bank of the Nile, as the king would take his customary walk there. Undoubtedly, this was an act of worship on Pharaoh's part, since the Nile was regarded by the Egyptians as a god.

Was this turning of the Nile into "blood" to be interpreted as merely changing its color, perhaps intensifying a natural phenomenon that happened there at certain times of the year? This is how many Bible scholars wish to "explain" this miracle. That the water actually experienced a chemical change by means of a supernatural force is evident from the fact that the fish died, the river stank, and the water was undrinkable. It did not merely change its color, as occurs naturally every year when the Nile is at flood stage, carrying as it does many particles of fine red earth. It so happens that at this stage, the water is more suitable for drinking than at lower stages.

When the magicians successfully employed their secret arts to accomplish the same act of turning water into blood, Pharaoh's heart again became hard, and he refused to heed Moses and Aaron's request. These magicians, as we have pointed out, were instruments of Satan. Especially in times of great crisis, Satan summons all his considerable powers to oppose the works of the Lord. For the present, God permitted Satan to show this power through his agents. Even here, however, what the magicians accomplished in no way equaled the power of God's miracle. Later on, God also called a halt to their limited show of satanic power.

The plague of frogs

8 ²⁵Seven days passed after the LORD struck the Nile. ¹Then the LORD said to Moses, "Go to Pharaoh and say to him, 'This is what the LORD says: Let my people go, so that they may worship me. ²If you refuse to let them go, I will plague your whole country with frogs. ³The Nile will teem with frogs. They will come up into your palace and your bedroom and onto your bed, into the houses of your officials and on your people, and into your ovens and kneading troughs. ⁴The frogs will go up on you and your people and all your officials.'"

⁵Then the LORD said to Moses, "Tell Aaron, 'Stretch out your hand with your staff over the streams and canals and ponds, and make frogs come up on the land of Egypt.'" ⁶So Aaron stretched out his hand over the waters of Egypt, and the frogs came up and covered the land. ⁷But the magicians did the same things by their secret arts; they also made frogs come up on the land of Egypt.

⁸Pharaoh summoned Moses and Aaron and said, "Pray to the LORD to take the frogs away from me and my people, and I will let your people go to offer sacrifices to the LORD."

⁹Moses said to Pharaoh, "I leave to you the honor of setting the time for me to pray for you and your officials and your people that you and your houses may be rid of the frogs, except for those that remain in the Nile."

¹⁰"Tomorrow," Pharaoh said.

Moses replied, "It will be as you say, so that you may know there is no one like the LORD our God. ¹¹The frogs will leave you and your houses, your officials and your people; they will remain only in the Nile."

¹²After Moses and Aaron left Pharaoh, Moses cried out to the LORD about the frogs he had brought on Pharaoh. ¹³And the LORD did what Moses asked. The frogs died in the houses, in the court-

yards and in the fields. **¹⁴They were piled into heaps, and the land reeked of them. ¹⁵But when Pharaoh saw that there was relief, he hardened his heart and would not listen to Moses and Aaron, just as the LORD had said.**

The plague of frogs occurred seven days after the plague of blood, we are told. This raises the question as to the duration of the entire series of plagues. Nowhere else is the time that intervened between the plagues mentioned. We know that the seventh plague (hail) happened in February, the time when "the barley had headed and the flax was in bloom" (9:31). The tenth plague took place in April, the month called Abib in the Israelite calendar. Thus there was an interval of perhaps two months between plague seven and plague ten. This indicates, at least, an approximate time interval between the various plagues. Bible scholars reckon the entire period of the plagues as somewhere around nine months.

While swarms of frogs were a common source of trouble in Egypt, this again was a miracle wrought by God as Aaron stretched out his staff over the waters of the land. Frogs were everywhere—even in Pharaoh's palace, in food supplies, and upon the people themselves.

In a limited way, the magicians were able to imitate this miracle also, but they were unable to take away the menace caused by the frogs as these animals invaded every possible place. Pharaoh, therefore, turned to Moses and Aaron for help this time, promising to let Israel perform their sacrifices to the Lord if the plague was removed. Moses even let Pharaoh choose the day when this was to take place. But when Pharaoh saw that the plague was removed, he refused to let Israel go.

This treacherous action of Pharaoh set the pattern for his reaction to the remaining plagues. Moses made it clear by word and deed that these plagues were acts of the

almighty God. In his heart Pharaoh never really acknowl-
edged this. Seeking relief, he would plead for mercy. Yet
as soon as relief came, "he hardened his heart" and persisted in his obduracy until God himself sealed his doom.

It happens frequently that people today act in defiance
of God just as Pharaoh did. In a time of crisis, they cry to
the Lord for help and are willing to promise anything if only
the threat of trouble is taken away. As soon as the crisis has
passed, however, they quickly forget whatever promises
they may have made to mend their sinful ways. The warning in this text against persistent indifference in regard to
God's warnings is clear. Through a process of repeated
hardening of their hearts, such people can no longer hear
God's call to repentance.

God's word of warning is always in place: "Today, if you
hear his voice, do not harden your hearts" (Hebrews 3:15).

The plague of gnats

¹⁶**Then the LORD said to Moses, "Tell Aaron, 'Stretch out your
staff and strike the dust of the ground,' and throughout the land of
Egypt the dust will become gnats." ¹⁷They did this, and when Aaron
stretched out his hand with the staff and struck the dust of the
ground, gnats came upon men and animals. All the dust throughout
the land of Egypt became gnats. ¹⁸But when the magicians tried to
produce gnats by their secret arts, they could not. And the gnats
were on men and animals.**

¹⁹**The magicians said to Pharaoh, "This is the finger of God."
But Pharaoh's heart was hard and he would not listen, just as the
LORD had said.**

The King James Version of the Bible as well as Luther's
German translation use the word "lice" to describe this
plague. Our NIV translation uses "gnats." The latter word
better designates the tiny, almost-invisible insects known
in Egypt which cause considerable discomfort. In this case,

by a miracle of God, as Aaron struck the dust of the ground with his staff, they rose in such swarms that they were unbearable.

Bible scholars call attention to the fact that again God used an element of nature to which the Egyptians attached divine powers. The first two plagues were connected with the waters of the Nile, supposedly inhabited by the Egyptian god Osiris. This one came out of the dust of the earth, venerated by the Egyptians as the dwelling place of the goddess Isis.

This time the magicians failed to produce anything resembling this miracle. Even they were compelled to say, "This is the finger of God." God had placed a limit upon Satan's power. God does the same for his believers today. "God is faithful;" Paul writes in 1 Corinthians 10:13, "he will not let you be tempted beyond what you can bear. But when you are tempted, he will also provide a way out so that you can stand up under it." Luther also assures us concerning the devil's power in his Reformation hymn: "One little word can fell him" (*Christian Worship: A Lutheran Hymnal* 200:3).

Pharaoh, however, remained stubborn even when he saw his own magicians defeated by a power higher than theirs.

The plague of flies

²⁰**Then the LORD said to Moses, "Get up early in the morning and confront Pharaoh as he goes to the water and say to him, 'This is what the LORD says: Let my people go, so that they may worship me. ²¹If you do not let my people go, I will send swarms of flies on you and your officials, on your people and into your houses. The houses of the Egyptians will be full of flies, and even the ground where they are.**

²²**"'But on that day I will deal differently with the land of Goshen, where my people live; no swarms of flies will be there, so that you will know that I, the LORD, am in this land. ²³I will make a**

distinction between my people and your people. This miraculous sign will occur tomorrow.'"

²⁴And the LORD did this. Dense swarms of flies poured into Pharaoh's palace and into the houses of his officials, and throughout Egypt the land was ruined by the flies.

²⁵Then Pharaoh summoned Moses and Aaron and said, "Go, sacrifice to your God here in the land."

²⁶But Moses said, "That would not be right. The sacrifices we offer the LORD our God would be detestable to the Egyptians. And if we offer sacrifices that are detestable in their eyes, will they not stone us? ²⁷We must take a three-day journey into the desert to offer sacrifices to the LORD our God, as he commands us."

²⁸Pharaoh said, "I will let you go to offer sacrifices to the LORD your God in the desert, but you must not go very far. Now pray for me."

²⁹Moses answered, "As soon as I leave you, I will pray to the LORD, and tomorrow the flies will leave Pharaoh and his officials and his people. Only be sure that Pharaoh does not act deceitfully again by not letting the people go to offer sacrifices to the LORD."

³⁰Then Moses left Pharaoh and prayed to the LORD, ³¹and the LORD did what Moses asked: The flies left Pharaoh and his officials and his people; not a fly remained. ³²But this time also Pharaoh hardened his heart and would not let the people go.

With the beginning of the fourth plague, we note several differences. This time there is no staff of Aaron smiting the water or the dust. God simply announces through Moses that at such and such a time, this plague will happen!

The other difference is that a distinction is made between the area where the Egyptians live and the land of Goshen, where the Israelites live. The plague affects the Egyptians only!

In these ways even greater pressure is put upon Pharaoh to acknowledge the presence of the Lord in all these happenings. As dense swarms of disease-bringing flies infest the houses of rich and poor alike among the Egyptians, bringing desolation everywhere except in the land of Goshen, it seems that Pharaoh weakens. He grants permission to the

The plagues

Israelites to offer sacrifices. But he wants to set the terms. This is to be done in Egypt!

Moses points out that such a sacrifice would be an offense to the Egyptians. To them, sacrificial animals such as cows were sacred. To follow Pharaoh's orders would only bring greater confusion. Pharaoh then grants permission to leave the land to offer these sacrifices, but again he hardens his heart as soon as the plague of flies is removed and does not let the Israelites go.

Pharaoh does this is spite of Moses' warning that he should "not act deceitfully again." The hardening process is increasing. God continues to act leniently. God alone knows how long this process is to continue in order to accomplish his purposes. We know also that "God cannot be mocked. A man reaps what he sows. The one who sows to please his sinful nature, from that nature will reap destruction" (Galatians 6:7,8).

The plague on livestock

9 Then the LORD said to Moses, "Go to Pharaoh and say to him, 'This is what the LORD, the God of the Hebrews, says: "Let my people go, so that they may worship me." ²If you refuse to let them go and continue to hold them back, ³the hand of the LORD will bring a terrible plague on your livestock in the field—on your horses and donkeys and camels and on your cattle and sheep and goats. ⁴But the LORD will make a distinction between the livestock of Israel and that of Egypt, so that no animals belonging to the Israelites will die.'"**

⁵The LORD set a time and said, "Tomorrow the LORD will do this in the land." ⁶And the next day the LORD did it: All the livestock of the Egyptians died, but not one animal belonging to the Israelites died. ⁷Pharaoh sent men to investigate and found that not even one of the animals of the Israelites had died. Yet his heart was unyielding and he would not let the people go.

Again Pharaoh is given advance warning of a severe disease that would come upon all livestock in the field. This disease would infect horses, donkeys, camels, cattle, sheep, and goats. Usually such animal diseases afflict one or another kind. This plague would strike many and various kinds. Pharaoh is also told that "no animal belonging to the Israelites will die." Again Pharaoh refuses to listen.

The statement is made that "all the livestock of the Egyptians died." This is to be understood in light of another passage that occurs later in this same chapter which again refers to the livestock of the Egyptians. The word "all" in this first case simply stresses the vast number that died. This exaggerated way of speaking is used by us also. We say, for example, "Everybody knows it," meaning, of course, a great many people.

The plague of boils

⁸Then the LORD said to Moses and Aaron, "Take handfuls of soot from a furnace and have Moses toss it into the air in the presence of Pharaoh. ⁹It will become fine dust over the whole land of Egypt, and festering boils will break out on men and animals throughout the land."

¹⁰So they took soot from a furnace and stood before Pharaoh. Moses tossed it into the air, and festering boils broke out on men and animals. ¹¹The magicians could not stand before Moses because of the boils that were on them and on all the Egyptians. ¹²But the LORD hardened Pharaoh's heart and he would not listen to Moses and Aaron, just as the LORD had said to Moses.

This time ashes scattered in the air by Moses in the presence of Pharaoh produced festering boils on people and animals throughout the land. This plague happened without advance warning.

We note that even the magicians were afflicted with these boils. We also note that this was the first disaster to strike the bodies of people directly. We note finally that this time "the LORD hardened Pharaoh's heart." The prophetic words of 4:21 were now fulfilled. Because Pharaoh had repeatedly refused to heed the many warnings he had received from the Lord, the Lord pronounced his own judgment upon this hardened sinner. Pharaoh's eternal doom was now sealed.

The plague of hail

[13]Then the LORD said to Moses, "Get up early in the morning, confront Pharaoh and say to him, 'This is what the LORD, the God of the Hebrews, says: Let my people go, so that they may worship me, [14]or this time I will send the full force of my plagues against you and against your officials and your people, so you may know that there is no one like me in all the earth. [15]For by now I could have stretched out my hand and struck you and your people with a plague that would have wiped you off the earth. [16]But I have raised you up for this very purpose, that I might show you my power and that my name might be proclaimed in all the earth. [17]You still set yourself against my people and will not let them go. [18]Therefore, at this time tomorrow I will send the worst hailstorm that has ever fallen on Egypt, from the day it was founded till now. [19]Give an order now to bring your livestock and everything you have in the field to a place of shelter, because the hail will fall on every man and animal that has not been brought in and is still out in the field, and they will die.'"

[20]Those officials of Pharaoh who feared the word of the LORD hurried to bring their slaves and their livestock inside. [21]But those who ignored the word of the LORD left their slaves and livestock in the field.

[22]Then the LORD said to Moses, "Stretch out your hand toward the sky so that hail will fall all over Egypt—on men and animals and on everything growing in the fields of Egypt." [23]When Moses stretched out his staff toward the sky, the LORD sent thunder and hail, and lightning flashed down to the ground. So the LORD rained hail on the land of Egypt; [24]hail fell and lightning flashed back and forth. It was the worst storm in all the land of Egypt since it had become a nation. [25]Throughout Egypt hail struck everything in the

fields—both men and animals; it beat down everything growing in the fields and stripped every tree. ²⁶The only place it did not hail was the land of Goshen, where the Israelites were.

²⁷Then Pharaoh summoned Moses and Aaron. "This time I have sinned," he said to them. "The LORD is in the right, and I and my people are in the wrong. ²⁸Pray to the LORD, for we have had enough thunder and hail. I will let you go; you don't have to stay any longer."

²⁹Moses replied, "When I have gone out of the city, I will spread out my hands in prayer to the LORD. The thunder will stop and there will be no more hail, so you may know that the earth is the LORD's. ³⁰But I know that you and your officials still do not fear the LORD God."

³¹(The flax and barley were destroyed, since the barley had headed and the flax was in bloom. ³²The wheat and spelt, however, were not destroyed, because they ripen later.)

³³Then Moses left Pharaoh and went out of the city. He spread out his hands toward the LORD; the thunder and hail stopped, and the rain no longer poured down on the land. ³⁴When Pharaoh saw that the rain and hail and thunder had stopped, he sinned again: He and his officials hardened their hearts. ³⁵So Pharaoh's heart was hard and he would not let the Israelites go, just as the LORD had said through Moses.

This plague introduces the final group of three referred to previously, the three plagues in which the Lord would strike with full fury, so that Pharaoh should know that there was no one like the God of Israel in all the earth. Our text declares, "It was the worst storm in all the land of Egypt since it had become a nation." Again the land of Goshen, however, was spared.

Terrible storms, of course, do occur. But this storm came as a special act of God. What added to its miraculous significance was that it came directly upon a preannounced signal of Moses. As Moses stretched out his staff to the sky, the Lord sent this violent storm. This storm, we see, struck enough terror into the heart of Pharaoh that he summoned Moses and Aaron and declared, "This time I have sinned."

While at first this has the sound of repentance, we note at once that it had a condition attached to it: "this time." What about all the other times, Pharaoh?

As Pharaoh continues his so-called words of remorse, we can sense a tone of arrogance about them: "The LORD is in the right, and I and my people are in the wrong. Pray to the Lord, for we have had enough thunder and hail. I will let you go; you don't have to stay any longer." The words proceed quickly out of Pharaoh's mouth. He wants them to state just enough so that Moses gets out of his presence as fast as possible and puts a stop to the troublesome storm.

Moses senses this lack of true fear of the Lord God in Pharaoh's words. He says as much. Nevertheless, he puts a stop to the storm, and just as expected, Pharaoh "sinned again." In other words, he continued in his sin. His repentance had been a sham, a momentary fright that caused him to speak words of remorse just to get Moses to put an end to the plague. If anything at all, Pharaoh's hardening was worse than ever, if such a thing were still possible!

The plague of locusts

10 Then the LORD said to Moses, "Go to Pharaoh, for I have hardened his heart and the hearts of his officials so that I may perform these miraculous signs of mine among them ²that you may tell your children and grandchildren how I dealt harshly with the Egyptians and how I performed my signs among them, and that you may know that I am the LORD."

³So Moses and Aaron went to Pharaoh and said to him, "This is what the LORD, the God of the Hebrews, says: 'How long will you refuse to humble yourself before me? Let my people go, so that they may worship me. ⁴If you refuse to let them go, I will bring locusts into your country tomorrow. ⁵They will cover the face of the ground so that it cannot be seen. They will devour what little

you have left after the hail, including every tree that is growing in your fields. ⁶They will fill your houses and those of all your officials and all the Egyptians—something neither your fathers nor your forefathers have ever seen from the day they settled in this land till now.'" Then Moses turned and left Pharaoh.

⁷Pharaoh's officials said to him, "How long will this man be a snare to us? Let the people go, so that they may worship the LORD their God. Do you not yet realize that Egypt is ruined?"

⁸Then Moses and Aaron were brought back to Pharaoh. "Go, worship the LORD your God," he said. "But just who will be going?"

⁹Moses answered, "We will go with our young and old, with our sons and daughters, and with our flocks and herds, because we are to celebrate a festival to the LORD."

¹⁰Pharaoh said, "The LORD be with you—if I let you go, along with your women and children! Clearly you are bent on evil. ¹¹No! Have only the men go; and worship the LORD, since that's what you have been asking for." Then Moses and Aaron were driven out of Pharaoh's presence.

¹²And the LORD said to Moses, "Stretch out your hand over Egypt so that locusts will swarm over the land and devour everything growing in the fields, everything left by the hail."

¹³So Moses stretched out his staff over Egypt, and the LORD made an east wind blow across the land all that day and all that night. By morning the wind had brought the locusts; ¹⁴they invaded all Egypt and settled down in every area of the country in great numbers. Never before had there been such a plague of locusts, nor will there ever be again. ¹⁵They covered all the ground until it was black. They devoured all that was left after the hail—everything growing in the fields and the fruit on the trees. Nothing green remained on tree or plant in all the land of Egypt.

¹⁶Pharaoh quickly summoned Moses and Aaron and said, "I have sinned against the LORD your God and against you. ¹⁷Now forgive my sin once more and pray to the LORD your God to take this deadly plague away from me."

¹⁸Moses then left Pharaoh and prayed to the LORD. ¹⁹And the LORD changed the wind to a very strong west wind, which caught up the locusts and carried them into the Red Sea. Not a locust was left anywhere in Egypt. ²⁰But the LORD hardened Pharaoh's heart, and he would not let the Israelites go.

At first reading, this plague seems to begin with the usual pattern experienced previously. Yet we can see things becoming more intense, drawing to a climax.

First of all, God tells Moses that he himself has hardened the heart of Pharaoh and his officials. Yet God still has his purpose in sending another plague in spite of Pharaoh's obduracy. This is to serve Israel in generations to come, God says to Moses, as a sign of his power. They are to tell these events to their children. From Psalms 78 and 105, we know the manner in which this was done. "He spoke, and the locusts came, grasshoppers without number; they ate up every green thing in their land, ate up the produce of their soil" (105:34,35).

Pharaoh's doom, in other words, is already sealed. The events to follow would enforce the purpose of these plagues as demonstrations of God's almighty power, both to Israel as well as to Pharaoh. All the earth should know that he is the Lord over all! "Give thanks to the LORD, call on his name; make known among the nations what he has done," Israel later sang in Psalm 105:1.

We see, moreover, that Pharaoh's officials are becoming impatient. They have had enough. "How long will this man be a snare to us?" they ask their king. This is the first time that we hear about unrest among the Egyptian officials because of the troublesome plagues.

Finally, upon hearing that his own counselors are urging him to let the Israelites go, Pharaoh begins to show definite signs of losing his grip. First he asks Moses and Aaron to return. . . . Then he grants permission to leave the country. . . . Immediately after this he asks who will be going. Moses stands his ground and says the expedition will include all people, not only the men. . . . Then we read Pharaoh's strange statement: "The LORD be with you—

if I let you go, along with your women and children! Clearly you are bent on evil. No! Have only the men go; and worship the LORD, since that's what you have been asking for."

These words of Pharaoh have been variously interpreted—as irony, as contempt, as ill will, as indecision, as mere hypocrisy and caprice. We see a bit of all these things in his strange words. But above all, we see in them the words of a hardened sinner who feels himself threatened, who is gradually entering into a state of shock because he doesn't know what to do anymore, who lashes out angrily with whatever power he still thinks he can muster. They are the words of a thoroughly evil man reaching the end of his strength. They are the words of a man under the judgment of God.

Locusts were not an unusual pest in Egypt. But the coming of the locusts as described in this miracle was again most unusual. As one Bible scholar says, the fact that the wind blew for a day and a night before bringing the locusts shows that they must have come from a great distance. This surely was proof to the Egyptians that the power of Jehovah reached far beyond the borders of Egypt. Usually the swarms of locusts come into Egypt from the south. These locusts came from the east, and their destruction was without parallel.

"I have sinned," Pharaoh says as he summons Moses and pleads with him to take the plague away. We don't suppose that even Moses was fooled very much by this outward admission of sin. We know that the Lord surely wasn't! God's purposes were being served. His power was being demonstrated for all to behold. And the end was drawing near.

The plague of darkness

[21]Then the LORD said to Moses, "Stretch out your hand toward the sky so that darkness will spread over Egypt—darkness that can be felt." [22]So Moses stretched out his hand toward the sky, and total darkness covered all Egypt for three days. [23]No one could see anyone else or leave his place for three days. Yet all the Israelites had light in the places where they lived.

[24]Then Pharaoh summoned Moses and said, "Go, worship the LORD. Even your women and children may go with you, only leave your flocks and herds behind."

[25]But Moses said, "You must allow us to have sacrifices and burnt offerings to present to the LORD our God. [26]Our livestock too must go with us; not a hoof is to be left behind. We have to use some of them in worshiping the LORD our God, and until we get there we will not know what we are to use to worship the LORD."

[27]But the LORD hardened Pharaoh's heart, and he was not willing to let them go. [28]Pharaoh said to Moses, "Get out of my sight! Make sure you do not appear before me again! The day you see my face you will die."

[29]"Just as you say," Moses replied. "I will never appear before you again."

"Darkness that can be felt" is how our text describes this plague. What an ominous darkness this must have been! The Egyptians, who worshiped the sun, even building the city Heliopolis as a place dedicated to this sun-god, now found themselves completely cut off from all light for three days.

Some would explain this miracle by the great sand-storms that come to this region periodically, with particles of sand blown by the wind so intensely that the sky is covered as with a thick veil. While this could have been the way in which God caused this plague to happen, we cannot be sure. Its miraculous nature was still evident in the fact that "all the Israelites had light in the places where they lived."

Pharaoh again states a condition when he offers permission to the Israelites to leave: "Leave your flocks and herds behind." Moses, of course, refuses on the grounds that these are necessary for the sake of the sacrifices that are to be performed.

"Get out of my sight!" Pharaoh shouts in a rage. "Make sure you do not appear before me again! The day you see my face you will die." Pharaoh pronounces his own doom.

"Just as you say," Moses replies. Moses knew that the end was coming. That is why he could say to Pharaoh so definitely, "I will never appear before you again." Moses was so sure about this because God had already given Moses information concerning the last plague. He knew that this plague would claim the life of every firstborn son in Egypt and would secure the release of the Israelites.

The words with which the Lord had previously made these things known to Moses are given to us in the next chapter.

The plague on the firstborn

11 Now the LORD had said to Moses, "I will bring one more plague on Pharaoh and on Egypt. After that, he will let you go from here, and when he does, he will drive you out completely. ²Tell the people that men and women alike are to ask their neighbors for articles of silver and gold." ³(The LORD made the Egyptians favorably disposed toward the people, and Moses himself was highly regarded in Egypt by Pharaoh's officials and by the people.)

⁴So Moses said, "This is what the LORD says: 'About midnight I will go throughout Egypt. ⁵Every firstborn son in Egypt will die, from the firstborn son of Pharaoh, who sits on the throne, to the firstborn son of the slave girl, who is at her hand mill, and all the firstborn of the cattle as well. ⁶There will be loud wailing throughout Egypt—worse than there has ever been or ever will be again. ⁷But among the Israelites not a dog will bark at any man or animal.' Then you will know that the LORD makes a distinction between Egypt and Israel. ⁸All these officials of yours will come to me, bowing down before me and saying, 'Go, you and all the people who follow you!' After that I will leave." Then Moses, hot with anger, left Pharaoh.

⁹**The LORD had said to Moses, "Pharaoh will refuse to listen to you—so that my wonders may be multiplied in Egypt." ¹⁰Moses and Aaron performed all these wonders before Pharaoh, but the LORD hardened Pharaoh's heart, and he would not let the Israelites go out of his country.**

In the previous chapter, Moses had said to Pharaoh after the plague of darkness, "I will never appear before you again." What is reported here in chapter 11, where Moses announces to Pharaoh the next and final plague, actually took place some time *before* the words of Moses recorded in 10:29. Chapter 11, in other words, is what we would call a flashback. This manner of historical writing was familiar in those days, just as we make use of it today. Moses was sure that he would never appear before Pharaoh again. He was so sure because of something that had happened previously. Now we are told what that was. (Unless we understand the sequence of events in this way, the words in chapter 11 would seem to contradict what Moses had just flatly declared in chapter 10.)

Very correctly, the New International Version therefore translates at the beginning of chapter 11, "Now the Lord *had* said to Moses . . ." One more plague after the plague of darkness would descend upon Egypt. This one would result in Israel's exodus from Egypt. Before that departure Moses was reminded to have the Israelites request articles of silver and gold from the Egyptians. God himself promised again to see to it that the Egyptians would be willing to comply with this request.

Moses' last words to Pharaoh concerning the final plague—and let us remember that these words were spoken prior to his words in 10:29—tell us the awesome impact of the Lord's final judgment upon Pharaoh as well as all Egypt. Every firstborn male offspring of people and cattle belonging to the Egyptians would die. What a terrible threat to bring! And what a woeful effect it would have! In Egypt, wailing and crying. In Israel, not even a dog would bark!

Does this threatened action of God seem too harsh? Let us remember the many stern warnings God had given Pharaoh and the Egyptians through these plagues over an extended period of time. Even though the Lord had increased their intensity, Pharaoh simply became more set than ever in his obduracy. God is gracious and merciful, slow to anger. But there does come a time when he must act in his perfect justice and carry out his threats of divine retribution. If that were not true, then his threats would be meaningless.

This same truth applies to all humanity. People often ask, How can a loving God condemn people to everlasting punishment? They don't seem to believe that such a thing could be at all possible. A God who is in earnest about his gracious promise to save, however, is equally serious about his threat to punish all disobedience. God's own conclusion to the Ten Commandments, as we have learned in Luther's Small Catechism, makes this abundantly clear. "Whoever believes and is baptized will be saved, but whoever does not believe will be condemned," we read in Mark 16:16. The story of the plagues is a demonstration that God means what he says. It is also a stern warning.

In this case, the death of the firstborn son of man and beast in Egypt was to be the punishment for the Egyptians' cruel decision to hold God's people in slavery all these many years. "Israel is my firstborn son," God had declared to Moses when Moses was on his way back to Egypt from the land of Midian (4:22). Already then God had summarized the future series of events for Moses. Because Pharaoh would refuse to let Israel, God's "firstborn son," go, Moses would announce to Pharaoh, "I will kill your firstborn son"

(4:23). The concluding verses of chapter 11 once more summarize the situation for us, bringing this phase of Israel's history to a close.

With the next chapter, which records how Israel was finally delivered from bondage in Egypt, we enter a new phase in Israel's history.

The Passover

12 **The LORD said to Moses and Aaron in Egypt, ²"This month is to be for you the first month, the first month of your year. ³Tell the whole community of Israel that on the tenth day of this month each man is to take a lamb for his family, one for each household. ⁴If any household is too small for a whole lamb, they must share one with their nearest neighbor, having taken into account the number of people there are. You are to determine the amount of lamb needed in accordance with what each person will eat. ⁵The animals you choose must be year-old males without defect, and you may take them from the sheep or the goats. ⁶Take care of them until the fourteenth day of the month, when all the people of the community of Israel must slaughter them at twilight. ⁷Then they are to take some of the blood and put it on the sides and tops of the doorframes of the houses where they eat the lambs. ⁸That same night they are to eat the meat roasted over the fire, along with bitter herbs, and bread made without yeast. ⁹Do not eat the meat raw or cooked in water, but roast it over the fire—head, legs and inner parts. ¹⁰Do not leave any of it till morning; if some is left till morning, you must burn it. ¹¹This is how you are to eat it: with your cloak tucked into your belt, your sandals on your feet and your staff in your hand. Eat it in haste; it is the LORD's Passover.**

¹²"On that same night I will pass through Egypt and strike down every firstborn—both men and animals—and I will bring judgment on all the gods of Egypt. I am the LORD. ¹³The blood will be a sign for you on the houses where you are; and when I see the blood, I will pass over you. No destructive plague will touch you when I strike Egypt.

All of the Holy Scripture is God's Word and is useful for our study. There are certain chapters of the Bible, however, that are particularly outstanding. Genesis chapter 3, which brings us the story of the fall into sin and the first promise of a Savior, is one of these. Leviticus chapter 16, which presents the regulations for Israel's great Day of Atonement, is another. The chapter that we are now about to look at more closely, Exodus chapter 12, is especially noteworthy because it presents to us one of the most important Old Testament types of the Savior Jesus Christ. A type is a sign or an event that represents something still to come. We look to the Scriptures to identify these types. Chapter 12 brings us God's institution of the Passover festival. The Passover lamb, on which this feast was centered, is a type, or picture, of Christ, "the Lamb of God, who takes away the sin of the world" (John 1:29).

God instituted this Passover festival in order to carry on his work of setting apart the people of Israel as his very own people. God declared through his prophet Hosea, "When Israel was a child, I loved him, and out of Egypt I called my son" (Hosea 11:1). God was now about to separate his people from the land of Egypt by delivering them from slavery in that land. He was adopting them as his children. Israel was God's firstborn son.

The Passover festival was to be celebrated by the Israelites every year and was to remind them of their special place as God's chosen people. The time for this celebration, as the Lord said to Moses and Aaron at the very beginning of this chapter, was to be "the first month of your year." The Hebrew name for this month was "Abib," or "ear-month," because the grain was then in the ear (see 13:4). It is our month of April.

As we look at the directions God gave for preparing the Passover meal, we see step-for-step how the entire ritual points to Christ, our Passover Lamb:

- The *Passover lamb* was to be a year-old male, chosen from the sheep or the goats. — John the Baptist, when calling attention to the promised Messiah whose way he was to prepare, pointed to Jesus and said, "Look, the *Lamb of God,* who takes away the sin of the world!" (John 1:29). When writing to the Corinthians, Paul declared, "Christ, our *Passover lamb,* has been sacrificed" (1 Corinthians 5:7).

- God directed that this Passover lamb was to be *"without defect."* — Peter wrote to the scattered Christians of Asia Minor that they were redeemed "with the precious blood of Christ, a lamb *without blemish or defect"* (1 Peter 1:19).

- The Passover lamb was to be slaughtered as a *sacrifice.* — Paul reminded his fellow believers that "Christ loved us and gave himself up for us as a fragrant offering and *sacrifice* to God" (Ephesians 5:2). The writer of the book of Hebrews repeatedly refers to Christ as an "offering" and a "sacrifice."

- The Israelites were to "take some of the *blood* and put it on the sides and tops of the doorframes of the houses." On the night of the Passover feast, when he would pass through Egypt and strike down every firstborn, God had promised the Israelites, "When I see the blood, I will pass over you. No destructive plague will touch you when I strike Egypt." Israel, in other words, was saved from destruction by the blood of the Passover lamb. — This points, of course, to the central teaching of

Scripture, that we are redeemed from the power of sin, death, and Satan "with the precious *blood of Christ,* a lamb without blemish or defect."

- Later on in this same chapter, the Lord directed Moses and Aaron concerning the Passover lamb, "Do not *break* any of *the bones*" (verse 46). — After Jesus' death on the cross, the soldiers did not break his bones as they did to those who were crucified with him. John writes, "These things happened so that the scripture would be fulfilled: *'Not one of his bones will be broken'* " (19:36).

In all these ways we see how the Passover lamb clearly pointed to Christ, the Lamb of God, our only Redeemer, who gave his life as a sacrifice for the sins of the world. The Lord gave Moses and Aaron other instructions about how the people were to roast the Passover lamb, how they were to eat it with bitter herbs and bread made without yeast, and how they were to be prepared to leave the land very quickly—with cloak tucked into their belts, sandals on their feet, and staff in hand. All of the lamb was to be eaten. Anything that was left over was to be burned.

The time of deliverance had finally come! As God in that night of the Passover feast would strike down the firstborn of Egypt, so he would also deliver Israel, his firstborn son.

A day to be remembered

¹⁴"This is a day you are to commemorate; for the generations to come you shall celebrate it as a festival to the LORD—a lasting ordinance. ¹⁵For seven days you are to eat bread made without yeast. On the first day remove the yeast from your houses, for whoever eats anything with yeast in it from the first day through the seventh must be cut off from Israel. ¹⁶On the first day hold a sacred assembly, and another one on the seventh day. Do no work at all on

these days, except to prepare food for everyone to eat—that is all you may do.
¹⁷Celebrate the Feast of Unleavened Bread, because it was on this very day that I brought your divisions out of Egypt. Celebrate this day as a lasting ordinance for the generations to come. ¹⁸In the first month you are to eat bread made without yeast, from the evening of the fourteenth day until the evening of the twenty-first day. ¹⁹For seven days no yeast is to be found in your houses. And whoever eats anything with yeast in it must be cut off from the community of Israel, whether he is an alien or native-born. ²⁰Eat nothing made with yeast. Wherever you live, you must eat unleavened bread."

These verses explain how the people of Israel were to remember this Passover occasion in the future. For seven days before the Passover meal itself, the Israelites were not to work and were to eat bread without yeast. This was called the Feast of Unleavened Bread. Those who disobeyed this regulation were to be "cut off from the community of Israel." Yeast, which starts the process of fermentation in dough, is a natural symbol of moral corruption. Since it was therefore considered ceremonially unclean, it was not to be found in the house during the Passover celebration. By putting away the old yeast, the Israelites were to remind themselves of the new life they experienced as God's people when they left Egypt behind.

The apostle Paul refers to this Feast of the Unleavened Bread when he tells his congregation at Corinth, "Get rid of the old yeast that you may be a new batch without yeast— as you really are. For Christ, our Passover lamb, has been sacrificed. Therefore let us keep the Festival, not with the old yeast, the yeast of malice and wickedness, but with bread without yeast, the bread of sincerity and truth" (1 Corinthians 5:7,8). Paul used this Old Testament picture to encourage Christians to remember with joyful celebration the great victory that Christ, their New Testament Passover

Lamb, accomplished by his sacrifice on the cross. As the Israelites got rid of the old yeast at the time of their Passover feast, so Christians should put off their old sinful ways and strive to live in new ways pleasing to God.

The epistle lesson that is customarily read in our churches on Easter Sunday includes these words of Paul from 1 Corinthians. They can serve as a fitting encouragement to Christians to remember Christ's victory over the powers of sin, death, and hell by resolving to dedicate their Christian lives to the glory of his name. This is a fitting way to celebrate Easter.

Instructions given and obeyed

²¹Then Moses summoned all the elders of Israel and said to them, "Go at once and select the animals for your families and slaughter the Passover lamb. ²²Take a bunch of hyssop, dip it into the blood in the basin and put some of the blood on the top and on both sides of the doorframe. Not one of you shall go out the door of his house until morning. ²³When the LORD goes through the land to strike down the Egyptians, he will see the blood on the top and sides of the doorframe and will pass over that doorway, and he will not permit the destroyer to enter your houses and strike you down.

²⁴"Obey these instructions as a lasting ordinance for you and your descendants. ²⁵When you enter the land that the LORD will give you as he promised, observe this ceremony. ²⁶And when your children ask you, 'What does this ceremony mean to you?' ²⁷then tell them, 'It is the Passover sacrifice to the LORD, who passed over the houses of the Israelites in Egypt and spared our homes when he struck down the Egyptians.'" Then the people bowed down and worshiped. ²⁸The Israelites did just what the LORD commanded Moses and Aaron.

The instructions that God gave to Moses and Aaron concerning the Passover lamb were now passed on to the people through their elders. Hyssop is a leafy plant, which they were to use to dip into the basin containing the blood of the lamb and sprinkle it on the doorposts and lintel of every home. Later hyssop was used as a picture for cleansing from sin, as we read in Psalm 51:7.

At the same time, Moses impressed upon the people how they were to celebrate this Passover ceremony every year to remember how God delivered them from slavery in Egypt and how through the promised Savior, God would deliver them from the bondage of sin.

The people were thus fully prepared for God's mighty act of deliverance. In thankful worship they agreed and acted according to God's instructions. The great liberation from their many years of slavery was now about to take place!

The exodus

²⁹At midnight the LORD struck down all the firstborn in Egypt, from the firstborn of Pharaoh, who sat on the throne, to the firstborn of the prisoner, who was in the dungeon, and the firstborn of all the livestock as well. ³⁰Pharaoh and all his officials and all the Egyptians got up during the night, and there was loud wailing in Egypt, for there was not a house without someone dead.

³¹During the night Pharaoh summoned Moses and Aaron and said, "Up! Leave my people, you and the Israelites! Go, worship the LORD as you have requested. ³²Take your flocks and herds, as you have said, and go. And also bless me."

³³The Egyptians urged the people to hurry and leave the country. "For otherwise," they said, "we will all die!" ³⁴So the people took their dough before the yeast was added, and carried it on their shoulders in kneading troughs wrapped in clothing. ³⁵The Israelites did as Moses instructed and asked the Egyptians for articles of silver and gold and for clothing. ³⁶The LORD had made the Egyptians favorably disposed toward the people, and they gave them what they asked for; so they plundered the Egyptians.

³⁷The Israelites journeyed from Rameses to Succoth. There were about six hundred thousand men on foot, besides women and children. ³⁸Many other people went up with them, as well as large droves of livestock, both flocks and herds. ³⁹With the dough they had brought from Egypt, they baked cakes of unleavened bread.

The dough was without yeast because they had been driven out of Egypt and did not have time to prepare food for themselves.
⁴⁰**Now the length of time the Israelite people lived in Egypt was 430 years.** ⁴¹**At the end of the 430 years, to the very day, all the Lᴏʀᴅ's divisions left Egypt.** ⁴²**Because the Lᴏʀᴅ kept vigil that night to bring them out of Egypt, on this night all the Israelites are to keep vigil to honor the Lᴏʀᴅ for the generations to come.**

"At midnight," our text begins. The hour of God's reckoning has come! This time the plague has no connection with a phenomenon from nature, such as gnats or frogs or hail. This time the Lord himself strikes down "all the first-born in Egypt." The effect is devastating: "There was not a house without someone dead."

The following events progress quickly. Pharaoh urges the Israelites to leave. They carry along their dough without yeast; there is no time for such things as adding yeast to the dough or starting new batches. The Israelites ask for articles of silver and gold and clothing, as wages long overdue—which the Egyptians are only too happy to give them so that they go at once. As victors laden with plunder, the Israelites depart from the land that has held them captive for so many years. The Lord has given them freedom from slavery!

The place from which the Israelites set out is Rameses, a store city that they themselves have built with sweat and blood and tears. There are surely no tears connected with leaving such a place! Their journey is toward Succoth, to the southeast. What a multitude: 600,000 men—including women and children, about two million people in total! Imagine the sight of this mass of people marching along with all their livestock!

"Many other people went up with them," we are told. This was a mixed multitude of non-Israelites, some of them perhaps servants, some no doubt Egyptians who thought there would be some advantage in going along. Every

73

large crowd has its hangers-on. Later on these people caused trouble on the way, as Numbers chapter 11 tells us.

The length of time the Israelites lived in Egypt is given here as 430 years. We do not question this figure. It fits into the historical situation of that time. God spoke prophetically to Abram about Israel's enslavement for "four hundred years" (Genesis 15:13); he was using a round number. The apostle Paul used the same figure as here in Exodus, 430 years, to show that God's covenant with Abraham came many years before the giving of the law on Mount Sinai. Paul knew this figure to be correct. He made use of an understatement, to show that the one covenant (the promise of a Savior) preceded the other (the law) by at least that period of time.

Israel's day of deliverance was truly a day to be remembered. Israel was to keep a night watch on that same night in the years to follow to honor the Lord who "kept vigil that night to bring them out of Egypt."

Passover restrictions

⁴³The LORD said to Moses and Aaron, "These are the regulations for the Passover:

"No foreigner is to eat of it. ⁴⁴Any slave you have bought may eat of it after you have circumcised him, ⁴⁵but a temporary resident and hired worker may not eat of it.

⁴⁶"It must be eaten inside one house; take none of the meat outside the house. Do not break any of the bones. ⁴⁷The whole community of Israel must celebrate it.

⁴⁸"An alien living among you who wants to celebrate the LORD's Passover must have all the males in his household circumcised; then he may take part like one born in the land. No uncircumcised male may eat of it. ⁴⁹The same law applies to the native-born and to the alien living among you."

⁵⁰All the Israelites did just what the LORD had commanded Moses and Aaron. ⁵¹And on that very day the LORD brought the Israelites out of Egypt by their divisions.

Since the regulations concerning the Passover are found in this chapter, Moses no doubt added these regulations and put them here in the book of Exodus to safeguard the Passover's proper use. No foreigners were to partake of this celebration. No uncircumcised male was to be allowed to eat of it. If a foreigner wished to honor the true God of Israel and to keep the Passover, he was first to be received into the Israelite community by submitting to all its rules and regulations. For males this meant circumcision. Through partaking of the Passover meal, God's people confessed their fellowship with their God and with one another. "The whole community of Israel must celebrate it," God said.

We can see a comparison here between the Old Testament rites prescribed for God's people and the New Testament sacraments instituted by Christ. Both circumcision and Baptism were to establish a covenant with God and receive the person into the fellowship of his family. Both Passover and the Lord's Supper were instituted to strengthen this fellowship. They are not the same, of course. In their respective dispensations, however, there are strong similarities.

The Passover, we see, was not for everybody. Neither is the Lord's Supper today. Our Lutheran church practices close communion. By this we mean that the Lord's Supper is for those who are one in their fellowship of faith. "We, who are many," Paul says, "are one body" (1 Corinthians 10:17). Those who are not one with us in faith are restricted from celebrating this sacrament with us.

Consecration of the firstborn

13 **The LORD said to Moses, ²"Consecrate to me every firstborn male. The first offspring of every womb among the Israelites belongs to me, whether man or animal."**

³Then Moses said to the people, "Commemorate this day, the day you came out of Egypt, out of the land of slavery, because the

LORD brought you out of it with a mighty hand. Eat nothing containing yeast. ⁴Today, in the month of Abib, you are leaving. ⁵When the LORD brings you into the land of the Canaanites, Hittites, Amorites, Hivites and Jebusites—the land he swore to your forefathers to give you, a land flowing with milk and honey—you are to observe this ceremony in this month: ⁶For seven days eat bread made without yeast and on the seventh day hold a festival to the LORD. ⁷Eat unleavened bread during those seven days; nothing with yeast in it is to be seen among you, nor shall any yeast be seen anywhere within your borders. ⁸On that day tell your son, 'I do this because of what the LORD did for me when I came out of Egypt.' ⁹This observance will be for you like a sign on your hand and a reminder on your forehead that the law of the LORD is to be on your lips. For the LORD brought you out of Egypt with his mighty hand. ¹⁰You must keep this ordinance at the appointed time year after year.

¹¹"After the LORD brings you into the land of the Canaanites and gives it to you, as he promised on oath to you and your forefathers, ¹²you are to give over to the LORD the first offspring of every womb. All the firstborn males of your livestock belong to the LORD. ¹³Redeem with a lamb every firstborn donkey, but if you do not redeem it, break its neck. Redeem every firstborn among your sons.

¹⁴"In days to come, when your son asks you, 'What does this mean?' say to him, 'With a mighty hand the LORD brought us out of Egypt, out of the land of slavery. ¹⁵When Pharaoh stubbornly refused to let us go, the LORD killed every firstborn in Egypt, both man and animal. This is why I sacrifice to the LORD the first male offspring of every womb and redeem each of my firstborn sons.' ¹⁶And it will be like a sign on your hand and a symbol on your forehead that the LORD brought us out of Egypt with his mighty hand."

"Consecrate to me every firstborn male . . . whether man or animal." These words were probably commanded by the Lord at Succoth, shortly after the exodus. The consecration of the firstborn to the Lord was closely connected with the Passover. Since the firstborn of the Israelites had been spared, the Lord commanded that these be set apart for special service to him as a reminder of his grace to the people. The Lord had also declared that the nation of Israel was his "firstborn son" (4:22). By dedicating their own firstborn to the Lord, the Israelites constantly remembered their gracious deliverance by the Lord's hand.

This act of consecrating the firstborn was to be carried out after the Lord would bring his people into the land of Canaan. More detailed regulations as to how this was to be done are found in this book as well as in Numbers and Deuteronomy. Here in our text we are briefly told that the firstborn males of people were to be given over to the Lord. The firstborn of clean (acceptable for food and sacrifice) domestic animals were to "belong to the LORD," that is, to be sacrificed to him; the firstborn of unclean domestic animals, which were unacceptable for sacrifice, such as donkeys, were to be "redeem[ed] with a lamb" or were to be killed by breaking their necks.

Later on in the book of Numbers, we are told how God set aside the tribe of Levi for special service in his house. This was a constant reminder to Israel that all that she was and all that she possessed were continually to be presented to the Lord, who had redeemed her. Although we are not bound by all these Old Testament regulations, the apostle Paul tells us as New Testament believers, "Do you not know that your body is a temple of the Holy Spirit, who is in you, whom you have received from God? You are not your own; you were bought at a price. Therefore honor God with your body" (1 Corinthians 6:19,20).

Even in the years ahead when the Israelites would be living in the land of Canaan, God wanted his people never to forget their gracious deliverance out of Egypt. That was the great purpose of this consecration of the firstborn. "It will be like a sign on your hand and a symbol on your forehead that the LORD brought us out of Egypt with his mighty hand," Moses impressed upon the people.

Some Jewish sects later on interpreted these words of Moses literally. Out of the skin of ceremonially clean animals, they made small pouches, called phylacteries. They strapped these pouches to men's foreheads or to their left arms. Inside these pouches were strips of parchment on which were written passages from the law. This literal interpretation, of course, was not according to God's command. God intended these words to be a constant reminder to his people in all their thoughts (forehead) and deeds (arm) of his ever-present grace and mercy toward them. "Whether you eat or drink or whatever you do," Paul also tells us in New Testament times, "do it all for the glory of God" (1 Corinthians 10:31).

God leads his people

¹⁷**When Pharaoh let the people go, God did not lead them on the road through the Philistine country, though that was shorter. For God said, "If they face war, they might change their minds and return to Egypt."** ¹⁸**So God led the people around by the desert road toward the Red Sea. The Israelites went up out of Egypt armed for battle.**

¹⁹**Moses took the bones of Joseph with him because Joseph had made the sons of Israel swear an oath. He had said, "God will surely come to your aid, and then you must carry my bones up with you from this place."**

²⁰**After leaving Succoth they camped at Etham on the edge of the desert.** ²¹**By day the Lᴏʀᴅ went ahead of them in a pillar of cloud to guide them on their way and by night in a pillar of fire to give them light, so that they could travel by day or night.** ²²**Neither the pillar of cloud by day nor the pillar of fire by night left its place in front of the people.**

The most direct route from Egypt to Canaan would have been by way of a road that led to the northeast through the country of the warlike Philistines. God knew that his people were not prepared for war so soon after leaving Egypt, so he led them to the southeast on a road that led toward the Red Sea. The Israelites were not equipped with weapons. The expression translated in the NIV as "armed for battle" according to the Hebrew text simply means that they went "in orderly procedure."

"Moses took the bones of Joseph with him," we are told. In Genesis 50:25 we read, "Joseph made the sons of Israel swear an oath and said, 'God will surely come to your aid, and then you must carry my bones up from this place.'" Joseph trusted firmly in God's promise to Abraham that the land of Canaan was the place where his descendants would become a great nation, and where through one of his off-spring all nations on earth would be blessed. Moses now remembered that request of Joseph made hundreds of years ago, and so also showed his trust in God's promises.

Etham, the place where Israel camped next, was on Egypt's eastern border, right next to desert territory. Here we are told that "the LORD went ahead of them in a pillar of cloud to guide them on the way and by night in a pillar of fire to give them light." The Lord showed his presence among his people by means of this cloud. He used it to lead them. He used it in the very next chapter to protect them from the enemy. He used it above all, as we shall note carefully later on, to manifest his glory to his people. This visible sign of the Lord's presence, we are told, did not depart from Israel throughout their journey through the wilderness.

In our journey as Christians through this life, God assures us of his abiding presence. "Never will I leave you; never will I forsake you," he declares (Hebrews 13:5). We recall those beautiful words of Isaiah:

> This is what the LORD says—
>> he who created you, O Jacob,
>> he who formed you, O Israel:

"Fear not, for I have redeemed you;
　　I have summoned you by name; you are mine.
When you pass through the waters,
　　I will be with you;
and when you pass through the rivers,
　　they will not sweep over you.
When you walk through the fire,
　　you will not be burned;
　　the flames will not set you ablaze.
For I am the LORD, your God,
　　the Holy One of Israel, your Savior;
I give Egypt for your ransom,
　　Cush and Seba in your stead." (43:1-3)

We remember also the words of the risen Christ as he gave his great commission to his followers to make disciples of all nations and then added these words of assurance: "Surely I am with you always, to the very end of the age" (Matthew 28:20).

What is our pillar of cloud by day and our pillar of fire by night? We can turn to our God confidently and say with the psalmist, "Your word is a lamp to my feet and a light for my path" (Psalm 119:105).

"Take my hand and lead me," the Christian prays in days of joy—and in days of sadness. Israel too had to learn that in spite of God's gracious presence and guidance, many bitter experiences were to follow before they would reach the promised land of Canaan.

Israel encamps by the sea

14 Then the LORD said to Moses, ²"Tell the Israelites to turn back and encamp near Pi Hahiroth, between Migdol and the sea. They are to encamp by the sea, directly opposite Baal Zephon. ³Pharaoh will think, 'The Israelites are wandering around the land in confusion, hemmed in by the desert.' ⁴And I will harden Pharaoh's heart, and he will pursue them. But I will gain glory for myself through Pharaoh and all his army, and the Egyptians will know that I am the LORD." So the Israelites did this.

At Etham, where Israel had camped after leaving Succoth, the Lord told Moses to turn back and encamp at a place called Pi Hahiroth, near the sea. God's purpose in giving this command was to lead the Egyptians into thinking that the Israelites were confused.

The Hebrew word for the body of water near which Israel camped is translated "Sea of Reeds." This sea was an extension of the Red Sea, which was situated to the south. Critics of the Bible who try to explain away the force of the miracle that took place here claim that this "sea" was nothing but a low, marshy area which could easily have been dry at a period of ebb tide. Their explanation does not make sense to those who are acquainted with the natural conditions of that area. Neither does it agree with the text of the Bible itself, which describes this sea in such a way that only by a miracle of God could it be crossed successfully.

The Lord announced to Moses his plan of leading Israel in this unusual direction. It would give the Lord an opportunity to demonstrate again his glory to Pharaoh and the Egyptians.

The Egyptians pursue

⁵When the king of Egypt was told that the people had fled, Pharaoh and his officials changed their minds about them and said, "What have we done? We have let the Israelites go and have lost their services!" ⁶So he had his chariot made ready and took his army with him. ⁷He took six hundred of the best chariots, along with all the other chariots of Egypt, with officers over all of them. ⁸The LORD hardened the heart of Pharaoh king of Egypt, so that he pursued the Israelites, who were marching out boldly. ⁹The Egyptians—all Pharaoh's horses and chariots, horsemen and troops—pursued the

Israelites and overtook them as they camped by the sea near Pi Hahiroth, opposite Baal Zephon.

The news was brought to Pharaoh that the people "had fled." This was no journey of several days into the desert to offer sacrifices. This was a permanent exodus! Gone was the Egyptians' precious slave labor!

With an army led by six hundred of his best chariots, Pharaoh pursued the Israelites and caught up with them near their camp at Pi Hahiroth. To the Egyptians, the Israelites seemed confused, wandering about aimlessly and in the wrong direction. "This should be an easy victory," they must have thought.

¹⁰As Pharaoh approached, the Israelites looked up, and there were the Egyptians, marching after them. They were terrified and cried out to the Lord. ¹¹They said to Moses, "Was it because there were no graves in Egypt that you brought us to the desert to die? What have you done to us by bringing us out of Egypt? ¹²Didn't we say to you in Egypt, 'Leave us alone; let us serve the Egyptians'? It would have been better for us to serve the Egyptians than to die in the desert!"
¹³Moses answered the people, "Do not be afraid. Stand firm and you will see the deliverance the Lord will bring you today. The Egyptians you see today you will never see again. ¹⁴The Lord will fight for you; you need only to be still."

We can understand that the Israelites were terrified when they saw this well-armed host of Pharaoh approaching swiftly. Ahead of them was the sea. With all their women and children and livestock, how could they hope to fight against this organized army? That they should cry to the Lord for help was to be expected.

But we see that their cry to the Lord had little trust in it. This was apparent in their cowardly complaint to Moses: Were there no graves in Egypt? "It would have been better to serve the Egyptians than to die in the desert."

The words spoken by Moses in reply are well worth remembering: "Do not be afraid. Stand firm. . . . The LORD will fight for you; . . . you need only to be still."

Under the circumstances, these words of Moses must have seemed like pious wishful thinking to the Israelites. What was wrong with Moses? Couldn't he see the enemy? Didn't he appreciate the danger of the situation?

How like our fearful nature in moments of distress! We see the enemy. We see the dangerous situation before us. In our weakness we fail to lift up our eyes to the Lord, who promises to help us and to deliver us from every evil of body and soul. God's assurances in Scripture—as we can find in places like Psalm 121 or Romans 8:18-39—are not pious platitudes. They are real promises of deliverance. When Jesus says to us, "Everything is possible for him who believes" (Mark 9:23), may we respond, "I do believe; help me overcome my unbelief!" (verse 24).

In this situation, the Lord quickly comes to Moses' aid, as we see in the next verses.

Israel moves forward

[15]Then the LORD said to Moses, "Why are you crying out to me? Tell the Israelites to move on. [16]Raise your staff and stretch out your hand over the sea to divide the water so that the Israelites can go through the sea on dry ground. [17]I will harden the hearts of the Egyptians so that they will go in after them. And I will gain glory through Pharaoh and all his army, through his chariots and his horsemen. [18]The Egyptians will know that I am the LORD when I gain glory through Pharaoh, his chariots and his horsemen."

[19]Then the angel of God, who had been traveling in front of Israel's army, withdrew and went behind them. The pillar of cloud also moved from in front and stood behind them, [20]coming between the armies of Egypt and Israel. Throughout the night the cloud brought darkness to the one side and light to the other side; so neither went near the other all night long.

²¹**Then Moses stretched out his hand over the sea, and all that night the LORD drove the sea back with a strong east wind and turned it into dry land. The waters were divided, ²²and the Israelites went through the sea on dry ground, with a wall of water on their right and on their left.**

"Tell the Israelites to move on!" With these stirring words to Moses, the Lord gives the command to his people to move forward. He also tells Moses how this is to be accomplished. As Moses raises his staff over the water of the sea, it will separate so that the Israelites can cross this area on dry land. Even as Pharaoh chases after them with his army, the Lord will deal with him so that a glorious victory will be won.

After this, events happen quickly. God uses the pillar of cloud to separate the Israelites from the Egyptians, so that the enemy is enveloped in darkness and God's people have light. As Moses stretches out his staff over the sea, a mighty wind divides the water so that the Israelites can pass through the sea on dry land with walls of water piled up on either side.

Bible story books try to illustrate this event, but pictures cannot do justice to the greatness of this miracle. Imagine two million people with all their livestock and baggage passing through a large sea in the time interval of one night! The space of dry land on which they walked must have been at least one-half mile wide, if not more. The wind must have been unusually powerful to turn a sea bottom into dry land, and the walls of water on either side must have been immense indeed!

There are skeptics who go to great lengths to "explain" this event as a natural happening, showing how at the right time at ebb tide with the aid of a heavy wind, this occurrence would not be unusual. We prefer to let Scripture itself offer the correct explanations. The psalmist declares of the God of his salvation, "It was you who split open the sea by your power" (Psalm 74:13). And in Psalm 77 we read:

> Your path led through the sea,
>   your way through the mighty waters,
>   though your footprints were not seen.
> You led your people like a flock
>   by the hand of Moses and Aaron.
>
> (verses 19,20)

What a beautiful expression: "Though your footprints were not seen." We do not have to *see* all of God's footprints to *believe* in his miraculous power. Peter also reminds us in his epistle as he points believers to Jesus Christ, "Though you have not seen him, you love him; and even though you do not see him now, you believe in him and are filled with an inexpressible and glorious joy, for you are receiving the goal of your faith, the salvation of your souls" (1 Peter 1:8,9).

"Tell the Israelites to move on." Yes, tell the church of Jesus Christ to move on! Sometimes we see only the dangers ahead. The forces of godlessness increase. The frontiers of an unbelieving world close in. Whatever financial gains we make are more than used up by inflationary costs. We can scarcely maintain the church activities that we have begun. How can we hope to advance in our mission work? And besides, who will listen to us anymore in this corrupt, evil world! How did we ever get involved in all our expansion work? Let's dig a hole for ourselves and crawl in!

Tell the people of God to move on! What will happen to their enemy is vividly pictured in the following verses.

The enemy destroyed

²³The Egyptians pursued them, and all Pharaoh's horses and chariots and horsemen followed them into the sea. ²⁴During the last watch of the night the LORD looked down from the pillar of fire and cloud at the Egyptian army and threw it into confusion. ²⁵He made the wheels of their chariots come off so that they had difficulty driving. And the Egyptians said, "Let's get away from the Israelites! The LORD is fighting for them against Egypt."

²⁶Then the LORD said to Moses, "Stretch out your hand over the sea so that the waters may flow back over the Egyptians and their chariots and horsemen." ²⁷Moses stretched out his hand over the sea, and at daybreak the sea went back to its place. The Egyptians were fleeing toward it, and the LORD swept them into the sea. ²⁸The water flowed back and covered the chariots and horsemen—the entire army of Pharaoh that had followed the Israelites into the sea. Not one of them survived.

²⁹But the Israelites went through the sea on dry ground, with a wall of water on their right and on their left. ³⁰That day the LORD saved Israel from the hands of the Egyptians, and Israel saw the Egyptians lying dead on the shore. ³¹And when the Israelites saw the great power the LORD displayed against the Egyptians, the people feared the LORD and put their trust in him and in Moses his servant.

When the Israelites had arrived at the eastern side of the sea, the pillar of cloud rose and the Egyptians saw the Israelites ahead. The way through the sea was still open, and so the Egyptians went in after the Israelites in hot pursuit. God then demonstrated his power in various ways. He threw the Egyptian army "into confusion." The psalmist adds a word of comment concerning this confusion:

> The waters saw you, O God,
>> the waters saw you and writhed;
>> the very depths were convulsed.
> The clouds poured down water,
>> the skies resounded with thunder;
>> your arrows flashed back and forth.
>
> (Psalm 77:16,17)

A violent storm came down upon the Egyptian army. God "made the wheels of their chariots come off so that they had difficulty driving." Some ancient Bible manuscripts read, "God jammed the wheels of their chariots." We can picture them, stuck in the exposed sandy bottom of the sea. Then as Moses stretched forth his hand over the sea, the water that had piled up on either side flowed back and covered Pharaoh's entire army so that "not one of them survived."

This awesome destruction of Pharaoh's host produced a wholesome fear of the Lord in the Israelites, so that they "put their trust in him and in Moses." God was both deliverer as well as judge. This the Israelites were to experience more and more in the days ahead.

In the following chapter, Moses expresses the glory of this victory in a song of praise to the Lord.

The song of Moses

The Cambridge Bible calls this song in chapter 15 "one of the finest products of Hebrew poetry" but rejects the idea that Moses could have written it. Bible critics are of the opinion that poetry of this quality must have been written at a much later time in history, when Israel was more developed.

We, on the other hand, agree with scholars who state that its Mosaic authorship is placed beyond all doubt by both content and form. Moses had just taken part in a glorious miracle in which God's people had been delivered and the enemies of the Lord had been destroyed. What could have been more fitting than that Moses should write this song and lead his people in their praise to the Lord!

We will follow the song's division into three stanzas in this presentation:

Stanza one

15 Then Moses and the Israelites sang this song to the LORD:
"I will sing to the LORD,
for he is highly exalted.
The horse and its rider
he has hurled into the sea.
² The LORD is my strength and my song;
he has become my salvation.
He is my God, and I will praise him,
my father's God, and I will exalt him.
³ The LORD is a warrior;
the LORD is his name.
⁴ Pharaoh's chariots and his army
he has hurled into the sea.
The best of Pharaoh's officers
are drowned in the Red Sea.
⁵ The deep waters have covered them;
they sank to the depths like a stone.

Hebrew poetry is similar to poems with which we are acquainted in its unusual use of descriptive words, comparisons, and figures of speech. In this first stanza, for example, we see the many different words used by Moses to describe and praise the Lord: "my strength," "my song," "my salvation," "my God," "my father's God," "a warrior." By way of contrast, the enemy is described as being without strength at all: "they sank to the depths like a stone." By means of this choice of words, the poet conveys the main idea of this first stanza, namely, the greatness of the Lord who has shown his power in destroying Israel's enemy.

Hebrew poetry is different from much of our present-day poetry in that it does not use words that rhyme at the end of the sentences. It has a different method of connecting its thought patterns. After stating a thought in a certain way, the same thought is repeated in different words. This balancing of ideas in separate sentences is called *parallelism*. The second statement is often like an echo of the first. Note how this is done, for example, in verse 2 of our stanza:

> The LORD is my strength and my song;
> > he has become my salvation.

The same effect is produced in verse 4:

> Pharaoh's chariots and his army
> > he has hurled into the sea.
> The best of Pharaoh's officers
> > are drowned in the Red Sea.

In stanza 2 of this song, we see how Moses again in a beautifully poetic way praises the Lord for his great victory over the enemy:

Stanza two

> ⁶ "Your right hand, O LORD,
> > was majestic in power.
> Your right hand, O LORD,
> > shattered the enemy.
> ⁷ In the greatness of your majesty
> > you threw down those who opposed you.
> You unleashed your burning anger;
> > it consumed them like stubble.
> ⁸ By the blast of your nostrils
> > the waters piled up.
> The surging waters stood firm like a wall;
> > the deep waters congealed in the heart of the sea.
>
> ⁹ "The enemy boasted,
> > 'I will pursue, I will overtake them.
> I will divide the spoils;
> > I will gorge myself on them.
> I will draw my sword
> > and my hand will destroy them.'
> ¹⁰ But you blew with your breath,
> > and the sea covered them.

> **They sank like lead
> in the mighty waters.**

The right hand of the Lord is frequently used in Hebrew poetry as a symbol of God's power, as in Psalms 18:35 and 98:1. Here the Lord's right hand is described as "majestic in power" as it "shattered the enemy."

In the case of Egypt, Moses declares, God unleashed his anger at the very moment that the enemy was boasting and savoring how he would enjoy his victory. Yet "they sank like lead in the mighty waters."

In the third stanza of this song, Moses looks ahead to the time when the Lord will use this same power to bring his people to their promised inheritance:

Stanza three

> ¹¹ **"Who among the gods is like you, O Lord?**
> **Who is like you—**
> > **majestic in holiness,**
> > **awesome in glory,**
> > **working wonders?**
> ¹² **You stretched out your right hand**
> > **and the earth swallowed them.**
>
> ¹³ **"In your unfailing love you will lead**
> > **the people you have redeemed.**
> **In your strength you will guide them**
> > **to your holy dwelling.**
> ¹⁴ **The nations will hear and tremble;**
> > **anguish will grip the people of Philistia.**
> ¹⁵ **The chiefs of Edom will be terrified,**
> > **the leaders of Moab will be seized with trembling,**
> **the people of Canaan will melt away;**
> ¹⁶ > **terror and dread will fall upon them.**
> **By the power of your arm**
> > **they will be as still as a stone—**
> **until your people pass by, O Lord,**
> > **until the people you bought pass by.**

[17] You will bring them in and plant them
on the mountain of your inheritance —
the place, O LORD, you made for your dwelling,
the sanctuary, O Lord, your hands established.
[18] The LORD will reign
for ever and ever."

How beautifully these words praise the Lord's power, his glory and majesty, and especially his unfailing love! As we read its closing words, "The LORD will reign for ever and ever," we are reminded of the song of heavenly praise to God recorded for us in Revelation 11:15:

The kingdom of the world has become the
kingdom of our Lord and of his Christ,
and he will reign for ever and ever.

We also think of the redeemed in heaven, of whom John writes, "They will see his face, and his name will be on their foreheads. There will be no more night. They will not need the light of a lamp or the light of the sun, for the Lord God will give them light. And they will reign for ever and ever" (Revelation 22:4,5). Truly, the Lord's victory in behalf of his people Israel is a picture of his glorious victory won for his redeemed people of all ages, including our own, and of the heavenly home they will inherit as a result of it.

Miriam's refrain

[19]When Pharaoh's horses, chariots and horsemen went into the sea, the LORD brought the waters of the sea back over them, but the Israelites walked through the sea on dry ground. [20]Then Miriam the prophetess, Aaron's sister, took a tambourine in her hand, and all the women followed her, with tambourines and dancing. [21]Miriam sang to them:

"Sing to the LORD,
for he is highly exalted.

> The horse and its rider
> he has hurled into the sea."

Miriam, the sister of Moses and Aaron, also had prophetic gifts. We are told that she led a chorus of women, who played tambourines and danced at this joyous occasion of praise to the Lord. Very likely Miriam's song with the women was a refrain, sung as a response after the singing of each stanza of the song of Moses.

The waters of Marah and Elim

²²Then Moses led Israel from the Red Sea and they went into the Desert of Shur. For three days they traveled in the desert without finding water. ²³When they came to Marah, they could not drink its water because it was bitter. (That is why the place is called Marah.) ²⁴So the people grumbled against Moses, saying, "What are we to drink?"

²⁵Then Moses cried out to the LORD, and the LORD showed him a piece of wood. He threw it into the water, and the water became sweet.

There the LORD made a decree and a law for them, and there he tested them. ²⁶He said, "If you listen carefully to the voice of the LORD your God and do what is right in his eyes, if you pay attention to his commands and keep all his decrees, I will not bring on you any of the diseases I brought on the Egyptians, for I am the LORD, who heals you."

²⁷Then they came to Elim, where there were twelve springs and seventy palm trees, and they camped there near the water.

The wilderness of Shur, into which the Israelites traveled after their deliverance at the Red Sea, was a desolate area. There were places where animals could graze, but there were also bare limestone hills and rocky valleys through which they had to travel. For such a large number of people in a dry area, of course, water was a problem. Their supply gave out. At a place called Marah, the Israelites came to a small spring where the water was

Miriam's song of joy

so bitter that they could not drink it. The name Marah means "bitter." In their usual way the people grumbled, and the Lord again miraculously took care of them, as our text describes.

This was Israel's first real test of desert travel. God warned them here by this example of bitter water that their way ahead would have similar trials. These would be a test of their faith. If they would patiently look to the Lord for help, he would save and protect them. God gave them that promise.

A familiar hymn comes to mind:

> Savior, I follow on, guided by thee,
> Seeing not yet the hand that leadeth me.
> Hushed be my heart and still; fear I no further ill.
> Only to meet thy will my will shall be.
>
> Often to Marah's brink have I been brought;
> Shrinking the cup to drink, help I have sought,
> And with the prayer's ascent
>   Jesus the branch hath rent,
> Quickly relief hath sent, sweet'ning the draught.
>
> (CW 473:1,3)

At Elim, not many miles away, the Israelites found a lovely oasis. It is said that this place is still today one of the principal stopping places for people traveling along this way. Just ahead was another desert, where again something most unusual happened.

The glory of the Lord

16 **The whole Israelite community set out from Elim and came to the Desert of Sin, which is between Elim and Sinai, on the fifteenth day of the second month after they had come out of Egypt. ²In the desert the whole community grumbled against Moses and Aaron. ³The Israelites said to them, "If only we had died by the LORD's hand in Egypt! There we sat around pots of meat and ate all**

the food we wanted, but you have brought us out into this desert to starve this entire assembly to death."

⁴Then the LORD said to Moses, "I will rain down bread from heaven for you. The people are to go out each day and gather enough for that day. In this way I will test them and see whether they will follow my instructions. ⁵On the sixth day they are to prepare what they bring in, and that is to be twice as much as they gather on the other days."

⁶So Moses and Aaron said to all the Israelites, "In the evening you will know that it was the LORD who brought you out of Egypt, ⁷and in the morning you will see the glory of the LORD, because he has heard your grumbling against him. Who are we, that you should grumble against us?" ⁸Moses also said, "You will know that it was the LORD when he gives you meat to eat in the evening and all the bread you want in the morning, because he has heard your grumbling against him. Who are we? You are not grumbling against us, but against the LORD."

⁹Then Moses told Aaron, "Say to the entire Israelite community, 'Come before the LORD, for he has heard your grumbling.'"

¹⁰While Aaron was speaking to the whole Israelite community, they looked toward the desert, and there was the glory of the LORD appearing in the cloud.

¹¹The LORD said to Moses, ¹²"I have heard the grumbling of the Israelites. Tell them, 'At twilight you will eat meat, and in the morning you will be filled with bread. Then you will know that I am the LORD your God.'"

From the oasis at Elim, the Israelites came into the Desert of Sin. Travelers describe this area as an arid wasteland. After nearly a month of travel, it is not surprising that whatever food supplies had been brought along from Egypt were used up. Again the people complained.

In his mercy the Lord promised to send help to these grumbling people. He also gave them the special assurance of his presence. The people saw "the glory of the LORD" appearing in the cloud by which he led them. A radiant light appeared in this cloud as they "looked toward the desert."

This is the first time that the expression "glory of God" occurs in the book of Exodus. Moses had previously seen an appearance of the Lord's glory in the burning bush on Mount Horeb. The Israelites had seen this glory of the Lord in the pillars of cloud and of fire that led them on their way. But this is the first time the expression itself is used. Here the words "glory of the LORD" are used in connection with this bright cloud. As we continue our study of this book, we will see this expression used frequently. It was a visible sign of the Lord's burning determination to carry out his gospel promise. Usually the appearance involved a cloud of flame and smoke. Wherever it occurs, the Lord of grace and mercy makes his presence known to his people in a special way. We should watch for these words as they occur in Scripture and see how they emphasize the Lord's gracious abiding presence and help.

This time the Lord wanted the people to know that he had heard their grumbling and that he would demonstrate his power to them and satisfy their need of food in the desert. "You will know that I am the LORD your God," he said to Moses.

The verses that follow report how God not only showed his glory in a cloud but also demonstrated his concern for his people's need for food in a wonderful way.

Manna and quail

¹³That evening quail came and covered the camp, and in the morning there was a layer of dew around the camp. ¹⁴When the dew was gone, thin flakes like frost on the ground appeared on the desert floor. ¹⁵When the Israelites saw it, they said to each other, "What is it?" For they did not know what it was.

Moses said to them, "It is the bread the LORD has given you to eat. ¹⁶This is what the LORD has commanded: 'Each one is to gather as much as he needs. Take an omer for each person you have in your tent.'"

¹⁷The Israelites did as they were told; some gathered much, some little. ¹⁸And when they measured it by the omer, he who gathered much did not have too much, and he who gathered little did not have too little. Each one gathered as much as he needed.

¹⁹Then Moses said to them, "No one is to keep any of it until morning."

²⁰However, some of them paid no attention to Moses; they kept part of it until morning, but it was full of maggots and began to smell. So Moses was angry with them.

²¹Each morning everyone gathered as much as he needed, and when the sun grew hot, it melted away. ²²On the sixth day, they gathered twice as much—two omers for each person—and the leaders of the community came and reported this to Moses. ²³He said to them, "This is what the LORD commanded: 'Tomorrow is to be a day of rest, a holy Sabbath to the LORD. So bake what you want to bake and boil what you want to boil. Save whatever is left and keep it until morning.'"

²⁴So they saved it until morning, as Moses commanded, and it did not stink or get maggots in it. ²⁵"Eat it today," Moses said, "because today is a Sabbath to the LORD. You will not find any of it on the ground today. ²⁶Six days you are to gather it, but on the seventh day, the Sabbath, there will not be any."

²⁷Nevertheless, some of the people went out on the seventh day to gather it, but they found none. ²⁸Then the LORD said to Moses, "How long will you refuse to keep my commands and my instructions? ²⁹Bear in mind that the LORD has given you the Sabbath; that is why on the sixth day he gives you bread for two days. Everyone is to stay where he is on the seventh day; no one is to go out." ³⁰So the people rested on the seventh day.

People who say that the miracles recorded in the Bible are nothing but exaggerated stories have their own explanations for what is reported in the above verses.

Quail are migratory birds, they say, which fly in vast numbers at certain times of the year. When they rest on the ground, it is easy for people to capture them by hand. In this case, however, the quail came at a time designated by the Lord. They came to the very place where he wanted them to come. They came in sufficient numbers to satisfy two million people. Surely, this did not happen without God's direction!

In the region where Israel was traveling, these same doubters of miracles explain, a certain tree called the tamarisk drops small pellets of a honeylike substance to the ground, which the Arabs gather and use for food. This, they claim, was no doubt the "manna" that the Israelites found on the desert floor. The manna reported in Scripture, however, was not only found here in the desert where there were tamarisk trees. The Israelites received it for 40 years, wherever they went. Unlike the produce of the tamarisk tree, manna could be baked or boiled, in addition to being eaten raw. And it came to the Israelites in the exact amount as the situation required. "Each one gathered as much as he needed." This amounted to an omer, or about two quarts, for each person per day. When a two-day supply was required—as on the day before the Sabbath—this is precisely what the Lord supplied.

Since the Israelites had never seen this kind of food before, they asked, "What is it?" The name "manna," a Hebrew word, is derived from the two words that make up this question. All these facts certainly point to an extraordinary miracle by which God supplied daily bread to his people.

When supplying manna at this time, it is interesting to see how the Lord took into consideration the command that he would give later to keep the Sabbath, or seventh day of the week, as a day of rest. On the sixth day the people were commanded to gather enough manna for two days. On the seventh day no manna would be supplied since that was to be a day of rest. The command to "remember the Sabbath day by keeping it holy," recorded in 20:8, was given on Mount Sinai some time after this. No work was to be done on that day, according to the Lord's command on Sinai. But it is possible that the people at this time already had the custom of observing the seventh day of the week as a day of rest. God, we know, followed this arrangement when he created the world in six days and rested on the seventh day. On Sinai he incorporated this principle as a custom that Israel was to observe throughout the Old Testament period.

A memorial for the future

³¹**The people of Israel called the bread manna. It was white like coriander seed and tasted like wafers made with honey. ³²Moses said, "This is what the LORD has commanded: 'Take an omer of manna and keep it for the generations to come, so they can see the bread I gave you to eat in the desert when I brought you out of Egypt.'"**

³³**So Moses said to Aaron, "Take a jar and put an omer of manna in it. Then place it before the LORD to be kept for the generations to come."**

³⁴**As the LORD commanded Moses, Aaron put the manna in front of the Testimony, that it might be kept. ³⁵The Israelites ate manna forty years, until they came to a land that was settled; they ate manna until they reached the border of Canaan.**

³⁶**(An omer is one tenth of an ephah.)**

These verses give a final instruction about manna. An omer (two quarts) of manna was to be kept in a jar and put "in front of the Testimony." The "Testimony," according to 25:16, was the name given to the law written on tablets of stone that the Lord gave Moses on Mount Sinai. In the New Testament, Hebrews 9:4 tells us, "This ark [of the covenant] contained the gold jar of manna, Aaron's staff that had budded, and the stone tablets of the covenant." We will hear more about this ark of the covenant, which was placed in the Most Holy Place of the tabernacle, as we consider the later chapters in this book. The manna, kept later in the ark of the covenant with the Testimony, was to remind the Israelites of the way the Lord had provided for his people as they traveled through the desert on their way to the promised land of Canaan. During all 40 years of this journey, the daily gift of manna never stopped.

On our journey to our eternal inheritance in heaven, we too should remember the preserving care of our heavenly Father, who daily provides us with all that we need to keep our body and life. To this end, our Lord Jesus teaches us to pray, "Give us each day our daily bread" (Luke 11:3).

One more item pertaining to manna should be mentioned. Jesus called attention to manna when speaking to the Jews about the purpose of his coming into this world. "I am the bread of life. Your forefathers ate the manna in the desert, yet they died. But here is the bread that comes down from heaven, which a man may eat and not die. I am the living bread that came down from heaven. If anyone eats of this bread, he will live forever. This bread is my flesh, which I will give for the life of the world" (John 6:48-51). As manna sustained Israel's earthly life, Jesus sustains our spiritual life. The life that he, the Bread of Life, offers is eternal. "God so loved the world," he said to Nicodemus, "that he gave his one and only Son, that whoever believes in him shall not perish but have eternal life" (John 3:16).

"Lord, give us this bread," we pray. We ask God to strengthen our faith in Jesus as our only Savior, who has ascended to our heavenly Father's house to prepare a place for us there and who is the way to that eternal inheritance in heaven.

Water from the rock

17 **The whole Israelite community set out from the Desert of Sin, traveling from place to place as the Lord commanded.**

They camped at Rephidim, but there was no water for the people to drink. ²So they quarreled with Moses and said, "Give us water to drink."

Moses replied, "Why do you quarrel with me? Why do you put the LORD to the test?"

³But the people were thirsty for water there, and they grumbled against Moses. They said, "Why did you bring us up out of Egypt to make us and our children and livestock die of thirst?"

⁴Then Moses cried out to the LORD, "What am I to do with these people? They are almost ready to stone me."

⁵The LORD answered Moses, "Walk on ahead of the people. Take with you some of the elders of Israel and take in your hand the staff with which you struck the Nile, and go. ⁶I will stand there before you by the rock at Horeb. Strike the rock, and water will come out of it for the people to drink." So Moses did this in the sight of the elders of Israel. ⁷And he called the place Massah and Meribah because the Israelites quarreled and because they tested the LORD saying, "Is the LORD among us or not?"

Rephidim, the next camping place of the Israelites reported in Exodus after the Desert of Sin, was not far from Mount Sinai. The rock that Moses struck there to get water was "at Horeb." Horeb, as we have mentioned before, was the mountain range where Moses had tended sheep for his father-in-law, Jethro. Mount Sinai was one of the peaks in this Horeb mountain range. After the experience of receiving manna and quail in the Desert of Sin, the Israelites camped at two other places before reaching Rephidim. These two places, Dophkah and Alush, were mentioned by Moses later when he gave a list of all the places where Israel camped, as we read in Numbers 33:12,13.

Nothing of special note seems to have happened at Dophkah and Alush, but we call attention to this in order to appreciate better the situation at Rephidim. Israel had been on the move again for several days. The hills were getting higher, the valleys were narrower and full of huge rocks, and springs of water were nowhere to be found.

This time the Israelites not only complained. They "quarreled" with Moses. They even threatened to stone him. How thankless of those who under his leadership had been so wondrously fed with manna and quail! But the Lord patiently deals with the Israelites as a father with little children in distress. He directs Moses to strike a certain rock in the presence of his elders. As Moses obeys, water comes out of the rock for the people to drink.

Who would have blamed Moses at this point if he had felt like taking his staff and going back to tend sheep for his father-in-law, who lived nearby! After putting forth his every effort to serve the people, they were ready to turn against him as soon as the first trouble arises. "What am I to do with these people?" he asks the Lord in his dismay. Yet he accepts the Lord's direction to strike a rock, trusting that the Lord will bring water out of that rock. No wonder that he called the place "Massah," which means "testing," and "Meribah," which means "quarreling." Through their quarreling the Israelites were testing the Lord, demanding proof that he was still among them. In his mercy the Lord again gave evidence of his love to these undeserving people.

The apostle Paul uses this incident as a metaphor for God's mercy through Christ, the Rock of our salvation.

> I do not want you to be ignorant of the fact, brothers, that our forefathers were all under the cloud and that they all passed through the sea. They were all baptized into Moses in the cloud and in the sea. They all ate the same spiritual food and drank the same spiritual drink; for they drank from the spiritual rock that accompanied them, and that rock was Christ. (1 Corinthians 10:1-4)

The Savior-God showered his grace on his people Israel by means of this rock in the desert, just as God has blessed us in Christ beyond all that we sinful creatures deserve. "Nevertheless," Paul continues, "God was not pleased with most of them; their bodies were scattered over the desert. These things happened to them as examples and were written down as warnings for us, on whom the fulfillment of the ages has come. So, if you think you are standing firm, be careful that you don't fall! No temptation has seized you except what is common to man. And God is faithful; he will not let you be tempted beyond what you can bear. But when you are tempted, he will also provide a way out so that you can stand up under it" (verses 5,11-13).

What a fitting application of this Old Testament event! Paul says it all! We all need to turn again and again to that Savior who declared in John chapter 4, "Whoever drinks the water I give him will never thirst. Indeed, the water I give him will become in him a spring of water welling up to eternal life" (verse 14). Yet how often are we not tempted to complain about God's ways of dealing with us, forgetting that eternal purpose he has planned for us in Christ.

"Sir," we need to say to our Lord, as the Samaritan woman did, "give me this water so that I won't get thirsty" (verse 15).

The Amalekites defeated

⁸The Amalekites came and attacked the Israelites at Rephidim. ⁹Moses said to Joshua, "Choose some of our men and go out to fight the Amalekites. Tomorrow I will stand on top of the hill with the staff of God in my hands."

¹⁰So Joshua fought the Amalekites as Moses had ordered, and Moses, Aaron and Hur went to the top of the hill. ¹¹As long as Moses held up his hands, the Israelites were winning, but whenever he lowered his hands, the Amalekites were winning. ¹²When Moses'

103

hands grew tired, they took a stone and put it under him and he sat on it. Aaron and Hur held his hands up—one on one side, one on the other—so that his hands remained steady till sunset. ¹³So Joshua overcame the Amalekite army with the sword.

¹⁴Then the LORD said to Moses, "Write this on a scroll as something to be remembered and make sure that Joshua hears it, because I will completely blot out the memory of Amalek from under heaven."

¹⁵Moses built an altar and called it The LORD is my Banner. ¹⁶He said, "For hands were lifted up to the throne of the LORD. The LORD will be at war against the Amalekites from generation to generation."

The Amalekites were descendants of Amalek, a grandson of Esau, as Genesis 36:12 tells us. In this story we see that they were the first nation to attack God's people after they left Egypt. Moses later on describes the cowardly nature of their attack. When the Israelites "were weary and worn out," the Amalekites "cut off all who were lagging behind; they had no fear of God" (Deuteronomy 25:18). For this reason the Lord directed Moses to record this incident on a scroll, to make sure that some day the people of God would "completely blot out the memory of Amalek from under heaven."

On this occasion Moses directed Joshua to lead the fight against the Amalekites. This is the first time we hear about Joshua, the man later chosen by God to succeed Moses as Israel's leader. While Joshua fought against the enemy, Moses stood on a hill holding the staff of God in his hands. As long as Moses held up his hands with this staff, the Israelites were winning. When Moses became tired, Aaron and Hur held up his hands until the Amalekites were defeated.

The staff of the Lord was Israel's banner of victory, the Lord's own assurance that he was fighting for his people. In order to thank the Lord for this victory, Moses built an altar here and named it "The LORD is my Banner."

Moses' act of holding up his hands during the battle has been interpreted as being symbolic of prayer, since people in those days would hold up their hands when they prayed to God. One of our familiar mission hymns expressed this thought as follows:

> If you cannot be a watchman,
>> standing high on Zion's wall,
> Pointing out the path to heaven,
>> off'ring life and peace to all,
> With your prayers and with your off'rings
>> you can do what God demands;
> You can be like faithful Aaron,
>> holding up the prophet's hands. (CW 573:3)

As Christians, we should also be reminded as we struggle against our spiritual enemies to take "the sword of the Spirit, which is the word of God" (Ephesians 6:17). That Word of God, which is centered in our Savior Jesus Christ, assures us that "we are more than conquerors through him who loved us" (Romans 8:37). Yes, as we go forward in our mission work, Isaiah assures us that "the Root of Jesse [Christ] will stand as a banner for the peoples" (11:10).

> He will raise a banner for the nations
>> and gather the exiles of Israel. (verse 12)

"The LORD is my Banner." Onward, Christian soldiers! Sin cannot conquer us. Satan cannot rule us. Even the heathen nations cannot stop the advance of the gospel. Our Savior-God is fighting for us!

Jethro visits Moses

18 Now Jethro, the priest of Midian and father-in-law of Moses, heard of everything God had done for Moses and for his people Israel, and how the LORD had brought Israel out of Egypt.

²After Moses had sent away his wife Zipporah, his father-in-law Jethro received her ³and her two sons. One son was named Gershom, for Moses said, "I have become an alien in a foreign land"; ⁴and the other was named Eliezer, for he said, "My father's God was my helper; he saved me from the sword of Pharaoh."

⁵Jethro, Moses' father-in-law, together with Moses' sons and wife, came to him in the desert, where he was camped near the mountain of God. ⁶Jethro had sent word to him, "I, your father-in-law Jethro, am coming to you with your wife and her two sons."

⁷So Moses went out to meet his father-in-law and bowed down and kissed him. They greeted each other and then went into the tent. ⁸Moses told his father-in-law about everything the LORD had done to Pharaoh and the Egyptians for Israel's sake and about all the hardships they had met along the way and how the LORD had saved them.

⁹Jethro was delighted to hear about all the good things the LORD had done for Israel in rescuing them from the hand of the Egyptians. ¹⁰He said, "Praise be to the LORD, who rescued you from the hand of the Egyptians and of Pharaoh, and who rescued the people from the hand of the Egyptians. ¹¹Now I know that the LORD is greater than all other gods, for he did this to those who had treated Israel arrogantly." ¹²Then Jethro, Moses' father-in-law, brought a burnt offering and other sacrifices to God, and Aaron came with all the elders of Israel to eat bread with Moses' father-in-law in the presence of God.

We remember from our study of chapter 2 how Moses tended sheep for Jethro, the priest of Midian, in this same area where the Israelites had now come. It was here that Moses married Zipporah, Jethro's daughter, a marriage blessed with two sons, Gershom and Eliezer.

Upon hearing that Moses and the Israelites were in this vicinity, Jethro came to Moses and arranged for the reuniting of Moses' family. The Bible does not tell us when Moses sent his wife and sons back to Jethro. Perhaps Moses felt that Zipporah was not yet strong enough in her faith to experience all the unusual events connected with Israel's departure from Egypt.

The two men, Moses and Jethro, greeted each other with respect. Moses told Jethro all that had happened to him and to the Israelites, especially "how the Lord had saved them."

The result of this meeting was that Jethro praised the Lord and confessed him as the true God, "greater than all other gods." Together Moses and Jethro brought sacrifices to God in which they expressed their fellowship of faith. Jethro has been referred to as one of the firstfruits among true gentile believers.

It is interesting to note how the Amalekites fought against the Israelites while Jethro, a Midianite priest, became a believer in the true God, the God of Israel. Both the Amalekites and the Midianites were descendants of Abraham. Amalek came from the family of Esau, Abraham's grandson. The Midianites were the descendants of Abraham and Keturah. We recall how God had said to Abraham,

> I will bless those who bless you,
>   and whoever curses you I will curse;
> and all peoples on earth
>   will be blessed through you. (Genesis 12:3)

In later Old Testament history, we are told how the Amalekites were finally doomed to destruction after having troubled the Israelites for many years. The Midianites, however, were received into Israel's fellowship and dwelt among them in the land of Canaan. Above all, they came to a knowledge of the Savior-God.

This twofold attitude of the heathen world toward the gospel is evident today too. Christianity is spreading more rapidly on the continent of Africa than anywhere else in the world. But the Far East, particularly China and India, remains for the most part hostile toward the gospel of Christ.

Jethro advises Moses

¹³The next day Moses took his seat to serve as judge for the people, and they stood around him from morning till evening. ¹⁴When his father-in-law saw all that Moses was doing for the people, he said, "What is this you are doing for the people? Why do you alone sit as judge, while all these people stand around you from morning till evening?"

¹⁵Moses answered him, "Because the people come to me to seek God's will. ¹⁶Whenever they have a dispute, it is brought to me, and I decide between the parties and inform them of God's decrees and laws."

¹⁷Moses' father-in-law replied, "What you are doing is not good. ¹⁸You and these people who come to you will only wear yourselves out. The work is too heavy for you; you cannot handle it alone. ¹⁹Listen now to me and I will give you some advice, and may God be with you. You must be the people's representative before God and bring their disputes to him. ²⁰Teach them the decrees and laws, and show them the way to live and the duties they are to perform. ²¹But select capable men from all the people—men who fear God, trustworthy men who hate dishonest gain—and appoint them as officials over thousands, hundreds, fifties and tens. ²²Have them serve as judges for the people at all times, but have them bring every difficult case to you; the simple cases they can decide themselves. That will make your load lighter, because they will share it with you. ²³If you do this and God so commands, you will be able to stand the strain, and all these people will go home satisfied."

²⁴Moses listened to his father-in-law and did everything he said. ²⁵He chose capable men from all Israel and made them leaders of the people, officials over thousands, hundreds, fifties and tens. ²⁶They served as judges for the people at all times. The difficult cases they brought to Moses, but the simple ones they decided themselves.

²⁷Then Moses sent his father-in-law on his way, and he returned to his own country.

These verses offer good advice for anyone who wants to administer a large organization. As Jethro observed how Moses was trying to settle cases and disputes that arose among the people of Israel by himself, he counseled Moses for the people's sake and for Moses' own sake to choose capable men to help him in this task. Moses could see at once that this was good practical advice and acted accordingly. The people were divided systematically into groups of "thousands, hundreds, fifties and tens." Each group had its leaders to help see to it that justice was properly administered according to orderly procedure.

In his farewell addresses Moses later refers to this organized system that was started here and which he carried out through his entire time of leadership. The many cases that needed settlement could be handled more quickly and efficiently, and the major problems could receive more attention by Moses himself.

It has often been said that a good administrator knows how to delegate authority. This also applies to the work of the church. Pastors who feel that they must do everything that needs to be carried out in a Christian congregation, or who feel that others can't perform certain tasks properly, are hurting themselves as well as the work of the church. Every congregation has capable laypeople who can share in taking care of many of the practical affairs so that the pastor can deal primarily with the spiritual needs of his people. We note how this principle was also instituted in the first New Testament congregation at Jerusalem so that the twelve apostles did not have to "neglect the ministry of the word of God in order to wait on tables" (Acts 6:2). Our laypeople can also help in spiritual tasks under the pastor's guidance—teaching Sunday school classes, admonishing fellow members in cases involving church discipline, helping to bring others to Christ in evangelism programs, and the like. A congregation that is doing the Lord's business will involve its laypeople!

With this chapter we bring Part One of the book of Exodus to a close. The theme of the entire book, we recall, is "Jehovah's covenant with the people of Israel." The first 18 chapters have presented the deliverance of the covenant people out of Egypt. What we have considered thus far—the birth and call of Moses, the negotiations between Moses and Pharaoh concerning Israel's release from bondage, the plagues, the Passover, the departure out of Egypt, the crossing of the Red Sea, and Israel's early experiences in the desert on their Journey to Mount Sinai—all this has been preparatory to the establishment of Jehovah's covenant with Israel.

We have come as far as "the Desert of Sinai . . . in front of the mountain" (19:1,2). What lies ahead is one of the most significant accounts in all Scripture.

PART TWO

The Establishment of Jehovah's Covenant with Israel
(19:1–24:18)

At Mount Sinai

19 In the third month after the Israelites left Egypt—on the very day—they came to the Desert of Sinai. ²After they set out from Rephidim, they entered the Desert of Sinai, and Israel camped there in the desert in front of the mountain.

³Then Moses went up to God, and the LORD called to him from the mountain and said, "This is what you are to say to the house of Jacob and what you are to tell the people of Israel: ⁴'You yourselves have seen what I did to Egypt, and how I carried you on eagles' wings and brought you to myself. ⁵Now if you obey me fully and keep my covenant, then out of all nations you will be my treasured possession. Although the whole earth is mine, ⁶you will be for me a kingdom of priests and a holy nation.' These are the words you are to speak to the Israelites."

⁷So Moses went back and summoned the elders of the people and set before them all the words the LORD had commanded him to speak. ⁸The people all responded together, "We will do everything the LORD has said." So Moses brought their answer back to the LORD.

⁹The LORD said to Moses, "I am going to come to you in a dense cloud, so that the people will hear me speaking with you and will always put their trust in you." Then Moses told the LORD what the people had said.

When Moses was tending the flock of Jethro "and came to Horeb, the mountain of God" (3:1), the Lord appeared to him in a burning bush. The Lord said to Moses, "Take off your sandals, for the place where you are standing is holy ground" (verse 5). After the Lord revealed himself there to Moses as the God of his fathers, calling Moses to lead the Israelites out of Egypt, he said to Moses, "When you have brought the people out of Egypt, you will worship God on this mountain" (verse 12).

The time for this promise to be fulfilled had now come. The entire nation of Israel was now approaching this holy mountain. In the third month after leaving Egypt, they camped in the desert in front of it. Some Bible scholars write page after page trying to describe the exact place where Israel camped and which mountain of the Horeb mountain range was Mount Sinai. The fact is, the Bible does not go into many details describing this place. The Lord apparently did not want people later on to point fingers at a definite spot and say, "Here God gave his Ten Commandments!" The place was too mysterious and too holy for that.

The words that God spoke here, however, are extremely important. God wants them to be remembered. They are words in which the Lord made a covenant, an agreement, with the entire nation of Israel. As a part of this covenant, he gave his people the Ten Commandments as the core, or center, of the entire code of laws given on Mount Sinai.

In this chapter we have the Lord's own introduction to this law code given on Mount Sinai. He spoke these words privately to Moses on the mountain, telling Moses to bring this message to the people. These introductory words are important since they outline the general principles upon which the entire Sinaitic law code is based. Let us examine God's introduction carefully.

"I carried you on eagles' wings and brought you to myself," the Lord declares. He reminds his people first of all how they got to this place. With the protecting care of an eagle teaching its little eaglets to fly, the Lord watched over his people every step of the way. Moses uses this same picture in his closing song to the Israelites, written toward the end of his life. He describes how the Lord guarded his people "like an eagle that stirs up its nest and hovers over its young, that spreads its wings to catch them and carries them on its pinions" (Deuteronomy 32:11). Israel needed guidance and protection in order to get from Egypt across the Red Sea through the desert to Mount Sinai; they would need continued guidance and training in the future.

"If you obey me fully and keep my covenant," the Lord continues, "then out of all nations you will be my treasured possession." Notice the "if" that the Lord places in this sentence. This covenant between the Lord and Israel made on Sinai would be conditional. It would also be two-sided. The Lord was choosing this people as his "treasured possession." He had just proved that to them by rescuing them from their slavery. He had given them the promise that they would be his very own nation, blessed above all other nations in the world. But in return for this, he would expect obedience from his people. He wanted them to demonstrate that they were his very own people by keeping the laws that he was about to give them.

We see a difference here between the covenant made four centuries before with Abraham (Genesis 12:1-3) and the covenant that would be made here on Sinai. The covenant with Abraham was all grace, pure grace, without any conditions connected with it. It contained promises and nothing but promises: "I will make you into a great nation and I will bless you; I will make your name great, . . . and all peoples on earth will be blessed through you." The Abrahamic covenant was a gospel covenant, an everlasting

113

covenant, a one-sided covenant in which the Lord came all the way to sinful mankind and made no demands, a covenant centered in a great blessing that the Lord himself would bring to Abraham, to his descendants, and to all the people on this earth. The sovereign, infinite God through this agreement actually placed himself under obligation to sinful mankind!

There are details about the covenant made on Sinai which we will consider later. From the very beginning, however, the Lord made it clear that this covenant would require obedience from the people of Israel, strict observance of rules and regulations given by God in order that they might show that they were his "treasured possession." "Although the whole earth is mine," the Lord concludes in this introduction, "you will be for me a kingdom of priests and a holy nation." What a blessing the Lord was granting his people in this covenant established on Sinai! Indeed, one might call this verse the theme of the entire Pentateuch.

The Lord chose the nation of Israel out of all the nations of this earth to be for him a kingdom of priests and a holy nation, so that through this nation he might accomplish his plan for the salvation of all people!

A wonderful blessing, yes, but at the same time a great responsibility to be a "kingdom of priests." Priests are mediators, go-betweens. Israel as a nation was to be a witness for the Lord to the nations of this world. They were to receive the Lord's promise of salvation and all his revelations pertaining to this. They were to protect and preserve these gifts of the Lord's grace. They were to bear witness to all the other nations that their God was the only true God, supreme Ruler of all, who in his mercy had planned a way of deliverance for all people.

In carrying out this service to God, they were to be a "holy nation." How to live as God's holy people would be reflected in all their laws. They were a nation set apart, different from the ungodly nations of this world because they were to show obedience to the rules and regulations that the Lord would give them. They would be dedicated completely to the Savior-God and his holy will in life and conduct.

By means of this introduction, the Lord prepared his people for the covenant that he would establish on Sinai.

We who live in New Testament times know that this covenant made with Israel as a nation applied until the coming of the Savior, Jesus Christ. When Christ, the promised Seed of woman, came, he was the perfect fulfillment of this law, which was like a shadow that foretold his coming (Colossians 2:16,17). Christ brought an end to this law, with its rites and ceremonies (Romans 10:4). By his perfect life and by his sacrifice on the cross, he accomplished eternal redemption for all people. In this New Testament time of grace, we are no longer spiritually immature like the people in the Old Testament, who were subject to the rules and regulations of this ceremonial and political law code given by God on Sinai. Christ has freed us from this and given us "full rights" as God's children under the Lord's covenant of grace, and grace alone (Galatians 3:23–4:7).

As the children of God by faith in Christ Jesus, we in New Testament times, as Peter reminds us, are also "a chosen people, a royal priesthood, a holy nation, a people belonging to God" (1 Peter 2:9). In thankful, loving obedience, we in word and deed are to "declare the praises of him who called [us] out of darkness into his wonderful light." Ceremonial rules and regulations such as the rite of circumcision or abstaining from certain sacrifices as prescribed in the Sinaitic law code no longer apply to us. The basic law of love to God and fellow man, as embedded in the Ten Commandments, is our rule and guide for living a life that is pleasing to God and according to his holy will.

The Ten Commandments will be treated more fully in the chapter that follows—there we will see how they were given by God on Mount Sinai. Here we have reviewed some of the basic principles of the covenant given by the Lord to his nation of Israel as he himself introduces this law code to them.

After Moses told the elders of the people the general terms of the covenant that the Lord was about to make with them, and after the elders conveyed this information to the people, the people voiced their agreement. "We will do everything the Lord has said," they declared. Their assent was unanimous. Moses immediately brought this answer back to the Lord.

We pause for a moment and think about this response of the people in the light of what happened not long after this, for it was at this very place that the people worshiped a golden calf. Perhaps we are inclined to wonder if this promise to "do everything the Lord has said" was hypocritical. But is the situation any different today? How many young people promise to be faithful to the Lord "even to death" at the time of their confirmation—before the Lord's very own altar, no less—only to fall away from the Lord not long after the promise is made? One must marvel at the patience of the Lord as he experiences such faithlessness again and again.

It surely is not the Lord's fault that people are so forgetful of their promises to him. Here the Lord tells Moses what is about to happen. He will come "in a dense cloud." The people will hear him speak from the dense cloud. An awesome event will take place. The time has come for them to prepare for this great event!

Final preparations

[10]And the LORD said to Moses, "Go to the people and consecrate them today and tomorrow. Have them wash their clothes [11]and be ready by the third day, because on that day the LORD will come down on Mount Sinai in the sight of all the people. [12]Put limits for the people around the mountain and tell them, 'Be careful that you do not go up the mountain or touch the foot of it. Whoever touches the mountain shall surely be put to death. [13]He shall surely be stoned or shot with arrows; not a hand is to be laid on him. Whether man or animal, he shall not be permitted to live.' Only when the ram's horn sounds a long blast may they go up to the mountain."

[14]After Moses had gone down the mountain to the people, he consecrated them, and they washed their clothes. [15]Then he said to the people, "Prepare yourselves for the third day. Abstain from sexual relations."

[16]On the morning of the third day there was thunder and lightning, with a thick cloud over the mountain, and a very loud trumpet blast. Everyone in the camp trembled. [17]Then Moses led the people out of the camp to meet with God, and they stood at the foot of the mountain. [18]Mount Sinai was covered with smoke, because the LORD descended on it in fire. The smoke billowed up from it like smoke from a furnace, the whole mountain trembled violently, [19]and the sound of the trumpet grew louder and louder. Then Moses spoke and the voice of God answered him.

[20]The LORD descended to the top of Mount Sinai and called Moses to the top of the mountain. So Moses went up [21]and the LORD said to him, "Go down and warn the people so they do not force their way through to see the LORD and many of them perish. [22]Even the priests, who approach the LORD, must consecrate themselves, or the LORD will break out against them."

[23]Moses said to the LORD, "The people cannot come up Mount Sinai, because you yourself warned us, 'Put limits around the mountain and set it apart as holy.'" [24]The LORD replied, "Go down and bring Aaron up with you. But the priests and the

people must not force their way through to come up to the LORD, or he will break out against them."

²⁵So Moses went down to the people and told them.

In order for the people to prepare themselves properly for the words of the Lord that they would soon hear from the mountaintop, God told Moses how they were to consecrate themselves. To consecrate means to set apart as holy. The people were to prepare themselves for taking part in a most holy act. They were to do this by washing their clothes, by erecting a barrier around the mountain so that they could not touch it, and by abstaining from all sexual relations.

After these preparations were completed, on the morning of the third day, "the LORD descended to the top of Mount Sinai." He made his presence known to his people in glorious ways. "There was thunder and lightning, with a thick cloud over the mountain." The whole mountain trembled violently. The Lord made known his glory in fire and sound and smoke, calling the people together with the sound of the trumpet. What an awesome experience this must have been for his people!

"Everyone in the camp trembled." You and I would have done the same under these circumstances. Who can stand before the presence of God's power and majesty and glory? Yet the Lord graciously veiled his glorious presence in a cloud so that the people might come close enough to hear his voice.

Once more the Lord issued a solemn warning through Moses that the people were not to go beyond the set boundaries. "Even the priests" were warned. (Before the consecration of the Levites, these "priests" were men who according to custom had taken care of religious duties for the people.)

Now the great moment has come. There is no further mention of thunder or lightning or the sound of the horn. All is in readiness to hear the voice of the Lord.

God introduces his covenant on Sinai

20 And God spoke all these words:

²"I am the LORD your God, who brought you out of Egypt, out of the land of slavery.

After the thunder and lightning, after the smoke and the blast of the trumpet, after the entire mount trembled violently, a stillness fell upon the area. Out of the stillness God spoke. Israel could hear his voice and understand what he said. God spoke "all these *words.*" By "words" the Bible means the Ten Commandments, also called the Decalog.

The Bible makes a distinction between the "words" given us in chapter 20 (the Ten Commandments) and the "laws" (the rules and regulations pertaining to the conduct of Israel as a nation) that are summarized for us in chapters 21 to 23. The Decalog contains chiefly the moral principles upon which the entire Sinaitic law code was based. In the "laws" these principles were explained and applied to Israel's situation through various civil and ceremonial regulations, also given by the Lord upon Mount Sinai. They are recorded in the rest of the Pentateuch.

God spoke the "words," the Ten Commandments, directly to all the people. The "laws" that follow he gave first of all to Moses privately on Mount Sinai.

The "words" were later written by God on two tablets of stone and given to Moses (31:18; 34:28). The "laws" were written by Moses upon scrolls after he came down from Mount Sinai (24:4).

We mention these things to emphasize the unique and prominent position that the "words," or the Ten Commandments, occupy in the giving of the law. They are given first; they are basic; they are spoken to all of the people. And God introduces them by saying, "I am the LORD your God, who brought you out of Egypt, out of the land of slavery."

"I am the LORD your God." This is the "I AM" God speaking, the Lord who appeared to Moses once before at this same place and revealed himself as the same God who had spoken to the patriarchs. He is a personal being, a God who moved with unlimited freedom, timeless, constant, unchangeable, and above all a covenant-Lord who promised to redeem his people. August Pieper, one of our church's venerable professors, used to say of this verse: "There is no purer, more heartwarming gospel in the whole Scripture than this verse with its promise."

God had kept his promise. He had brought his people out of the land of slavery. Israel had experienced his redeeming hand. Recognizing their complete dependence upon the mercy and grace of God, and trusting in his continued promise of help, Israel was now to respond obediently by following the commands they were about to receive.

It is important for us to understand the Ten Commandments in the light of this introductory statement by the Lord. He did not give the Decalog so that Israel should obey his commands and thereby earn a favorable relationship with him. God had already made clear what this relationship was. He was their Savior-God. He had proved that to them in many ways. In love he had adopted them as his chosen covenant people. He now showed them by these Commandments how they could respond to his grace by living according to his holy will. From this same moral code, they could determine in what ways they would still fall short of that perfect standard which he placed before them, how much they still transgressed his law, and how much they still needed the forgiving love that only a gracious Lord could freely grant them.

Keeping this gracious introduction of the Lord in mind, we turn to the Ten Commandments themselves.

The Ten Commandments

³"You shall have no other gods before me.

⁴"You shall not make for yourself an idol in the form of anything in heaven above or on the earth beneath or in the waters below. ⁵You shall not bow down to them or worship them; for I, the LORD your God, am a jealous God, punishing the children for the sin of the fathers to the third and fourth generation of those who hate me, ⁶but showing love to a thousand generations of those who love me and keep my commandments.

⁷"You shall not misuse the name of the LORD your God, for the LORD will not hold anyone guiltless who misuses his name.

⁸"Remember the Sabbath day by keeping it holy. ⁹Six days you shall labor and do all your work, ¹⁰but the seventh day is a Sabbath to the LORD your God. On it you shall not do any work, neither you, nor your son or daughter, nor your manservant or maidservant, nor your animals, nor the alien within your gates. ¹¹For in six days the LORD made the heavens and the earth, the sea, and all that is in them, but he rested on the seventh day. Therefore the LORD blessed the Sabbath day and made it holy.

¹²"Honor your father and your mother, so that you may live long in the land the LORD your God is giving you.

¹³"You shall not murder.

¹⁴"You shall not commit adultery.

¹⁵"You shall not steal.

¹⁶"You shall not give false testimony against your neighbor.

¹⁷"You shall not covet your neighbor's house. You shall not covet your neighbor's wife, or his manservant or maid-

servant, his ox or donkey, or anything that belongs to your neighbor."

In the Ten Commandments, God gave his people Israel a summary of the moral law. The Commandments offered a basic distinction between right and wrong. Their prohibitions did not merely apply to outward conduct. They began by pointing to the importance of reverence for the one true God, the only source of all good. They ended by calling attention to people's inner desires, their act of coveting, as the source of all evil. Moses later emphasized in his farewell addresses how true observance of the Commandments begins with the fear and love of God (Deuteronomy 5,6). Christ pointed to love as the fulfillment of the law. In his Sermon on the Mount, he emphasized again and again how true obedience to the Commandments begins in the heart.

Martin Luther uses the Ten Commandments as the basis of that chief part of the *Small Catechism* in which he taught the law of God. Luther's explanations to the Commandments draw upon the entire Scriptures to show what they mean. Since the Decalog is treated thoroughly in instruction courses that present the chief teachings of the Bible, we will not go into a detailed study of the individual Commandments here. Several questions, however, deserve our consideration.

Although the Bible speaks of *"Ten* Commandments" (34:28), they are not numbered here or elsewhere in Scripture. Various churches have followed different numbering systems. Most Protestant churches use verse 3 ("You shall have no other gods . . .") as the First Commandment, and verse 4 ("You shall not make for yourself an idol . . .") as the beginning of the Second Commandment. They consider verse 7 ("You shall not covet your neighbor's house.

You shall not covet your neighbor's wife. . . .") as one Commandment, namely, the Tenth. Thus where Jesus says that the law of God can be divided into two parts in Matthew 22:37-40, they say that "the first four commands concern men's relationship to God, the remaining six their relationship to one another" (Eerdmans' *Handbook to the Bible,* page 164).

The Lutheran church follows the arrangement that was first brought forward by the church father Augustine (354–430 A.D.), who argued that the words in verses 4 to 6 pertaining to idol worship were simply a fuller explanation of what it meant to have "other gods," making them a part of the First Commandment. Augustine then divided verse 17 into the Ninth and Tenth Commandments, the one referring to "house" and various items of personal property, and the other to "wife." Augustine claimed that coveting a person's property involved a different kind of sinful desire from that of coveting a person's wife. Luther appreciated the fact that a separate Commandment was not made out of idol worship, since a former coworker of his named Carlstadt made use of this division wrongfully in condemning all statues and pictures in the church.

The precise way of numbering the Ten Commandments cannot be decided on the basis of Scripture. Neither do we know exactly how many Commandments were written on each of the two stone tablets of the law given to Moses. Moreover, as Lutherans, we know that Luther in his *Small Catechism* placed the words "I, the LORD your God, am a jealous God . . ." as the conclusion to the Ten Commandments in answer to the question "What does God say of all these commandments?" Using these words as a conclusion to the Ten Commandments stresses how serious God is both in his threat to punish sin as well as in his promise of grace and mercy to all who show their thanks to him in loving obedience.

It should be noted, finally, that the wording of the Ten Commandments as we have here in chapter 20 is according to the Old Testament standards. We see this especially in the Commandment that refers to keeping the Sabbath Day holy. The Old Testament arrangement pertaining to the Sabbath was a part of the ceremonial code. It followed the pattern by which the Lord created all things in six days and rested on the seventh day. The Sabbath rest foreshadowed the rest for the soul that Christ would bring by his perfect work of redemption (Matthew 11:28,29). Christ is Lord "even of the Sabbath" (Mark 2:28). As New Testament Christians, we are not bound by this ceremonial regulation (Colossians 2:16,17).

The people of Israel's reaction

[18]When the people saw the thunder and lightning and heard the trumpet and saw the mountain in smoke, they trembled with fear. They stayed at a distance [19]and said to Moses, "Speak to us yourself and we will listen. But do not have God speak to us or we will die."

[20]Moses said to the people, "Do not be afraid. God has come to test you, so that the fear of God will be with you to keep you from sinning."

[21]The people remained at a distance, while Moses approached the thick darkness where God was.

After the Lord spoke the Ten Commandments, there was another vivid display of thunder and lightning, of smoke and fire and the blast of a trumpet on Mount Sinai. Moved by this awesome display of power, the people trembled with fear and pleaded with Moses to speak with God in their behalf.

Moses assured the people that God was using this display of power to put them to the test, to fill them with a true fear of God. They should have a high respect for God

Moses with the Ten Commandments

so that they would not disobey his commands. Moses agreed to serve as the people's mediator by going up into the mountain "where God was." The rest of the laws were given first of all by God to Moses privately on Mount Sinai.

Israel's worship in the desert

²²Then the Lord said to Moses, "Tell the Israelites this: 'You have seen for yourselves that I have spoken to you from heaven: ²³Do not make any gods to be alongside me; do not make for your-selves gods of silver or gods of gold.

²⁴'Make an altar of earth for me and sacrifice on it your burnt offerings and fellowship offerings, your sheep and goats and your cattle. Wherever I cause my name to be honored, I will come to you and bless you. ²⁵If you make an altar of stones for me, do not build it with dressed stones, for you will defile it if you use a tool on it. ²⁶And do not go up to my altar on steps, lest your nakedness be exposed on it.'

In these verses the Lord outlined the principles of wor-ship that the Israelites were to follow, especially as this applied to their situation in the desert. The Lord did not want them to make any images of him out of silver or gold. They should fashion a simple altar of earth and stones upon which they could bring their sacrifices to him. The Lord himself would show them where this was to be done: "Wherever I cause my name to be honored, I will come to you and bless you." Stones for the altar should not be cut, but left in their natural state. Steps up to the altar should be avoided in order to distinguish the Lord's altar from heathen altars and also to preserve a sense of modesty when offer-ing sacrifices upon it. A priest ascending steps would be in danger of exposing his "nakedness."

Some critics of the Bible claim that the Lord granted his people the right to worship him in different places when he said "wherever I cause my name to be honored. . . ."

Israel's religion at this time, they claim, was primitive. Later on, they say, Israel was told to worship God at one central place, which would show a higher development in their form of worship.

If we consider Israel's circumstances at this time, we can see how this argument of the critics is nothing but foolishness. Israel was wandering in the desert. They would be doing this for nearly 40 years. They would be camping at various places. God would show them where to camp and where to set up their place of worship: "wherever I cause my name to be honored." Later on, of course, as Moses directs them in the book of Deuteronomy, they would be settled in the land of Canaan. There the Lord wanted them to have one central place of worship in order to preserve their unity as his chosen people.

In the next chapter we will proceed to the Lord's regulations for his chosen people as applies to their civil and social relations.

Rights of Hebrew servants

21 "These are the laws you are to set before them:

²"If you buy a Hebrew servant, he is to serve you for six years. But in the seventh year, he shall go free, without paying anything. ³If he comes alone, he is to go free alone; but if he has a wife when he comes, she is to go with him. ⁴If his master gives him a wife and she bears him sons or daughters, the woman and her children shall belong to her master, and only the man shall go free.

⁵"But if the servant declares, 'I love my master and my wife and children and do not want to go free,' ⁶then his master must take him before the judges. He shall take him to the door or the doorpost and pierce his ear with an awl. Then he will be his servant for life.

⁷"If a man sells his daughter as a servant, she is not to go free as menservants do. ⁸If she does not please the master who has selected her for himself, he must let her be redeemed. He has no right

to sell her to foreigners, because he has broken faith with her. ⁹If he selects her for his son, he must grant her the rights of a daughter. ¹⁰If he marries another woman, he must not deprive the first one of her food, clothing and marital rights. ¹¹If he does not provide her with these three things, she is to go free, without any payment of money.

"These are the laws you are to set before them," the Lord said to Moses. Having set forth the principles that Israel was to follow in its worship, the Lord now instructed Moses as to the regulations that were to govern Israel in its national life as the people of God.

Our text uses the word "laws." This is a distinction from the "words," or the Ten Commandments, which we considered in chapter 20. As we read these "laws," we find that they are somewhat different from a book of laws as we think of them today. Although they call attention to specific situations, they are less precise than our laws as far as defining details pertaining to evidence required, jurisdiction, punishment of offenders, and the like. These Sinaitic "laws" point to the rights of people in various situations of life. The above text, for example, pertains to the rights of Hebrew servants.

We should not be surprised that this law code that God gave to Israel was written up in a different manner from present-day legal codes. God accommodated himself outwardly to the legal forms that people used at that time. Archeologists have found law codes of other nations from that period of history. A famous code they discovered, for example, is the code of Hammurabi, king of Babylon, who lived around 1700 B.C., several hundred years before Moses. In its outward form, Hammurabi's code is similar to that which God gave Moses. The differences lie in the content. The codes of heathen nations were made to praise the king. The code of Moses praises the works of the Lord. Heathen law codes reflect the wishes of an earthly ruler. The code of Moses expressed how Israel is to live as people of God. One can see these differences in all the regulations, whether pertaining to slavery, marriage, witchcraft, property, or whatever the case may be. Mosaic ordinances as given by God are far more considerate of the rights of people and far less cruel in the penalties for disobedience.

Slavery was commonly practiced by all nations in those days. Among other nations, a slave or a servant was treated just like any other piece of property. We see from the laws presented in the section before us how the rights of Hebrew servants, on the other hand, were carefully protected. Some of the situations pertaining to servants may seem strange to us, such as piercing a person's ear who wanted to be a servant for life or the situation where a manservant could go free but his wife and children would still belong to the master. This was an entirely different culture in another era of history. The people then understood the situation and knew what was meant much better than we can today. We notice also that some laws relate to the situation of a man having more than one wife, a situation we will discuss more fully later on as other cases arise.

Injuries relating to people

¹²"Anyone who strikes a man and kills him shall surely be put to death. ¹³However, if he does not do it intentionally, but God lets it happen, he is to flee to a place I will designate. ¹⁴But if a man schemes and kills another man deliberately, take him away from my altar and put him to death.

¹⁵"Anyone who attacks his father or his mother must be put to death.

¹⁶"Anyone who kidnaps another and either sells him or still has him when he is caught must be put to death.

¹⁷"Anyone who curses his father or mother must be put to death.

¹⁸"If men quarrel and one hits the other with a stone or with his fist and he does not die but is confined to bed, ¹⁹the one who struck the blow will not be held responsible if the other gets up and walks around outside with his staff; however, he must pay the injured man for the loss of his time and see that he is completely healed.

²⁰"If a man beats his male or female slave with a rod and the slave dies as a direct result, he must be punished, ²¹but he is not to be punished if the slave gets up after a day or two, since the slave is his property.

²²"If men who are fighting hit a pregnant woman and she gives birth prematurely but there is no serious injury, the offender must be fined whatever the woman's husband demands and the court allows. ²³But if there is serious injury, you are to take life for life, ²⁴eye for eye, tooth for tooth, hand for hand, foot for foot, ²⁵burn for burn, wound for wound, bruise for bruise.

²⁶"If a man hits a manservant or maidservant in the eye and destroys it, he must let the servant go free to compensate for the eye. ²⁷And if he knocks out the tooth of a manservant or maidservant, he must let the servant go free to compensate for the tooth.

In the first verses cited above, a difference is made between intentional (or premeditated) murder, which is punishable by death, and when a person is killed accidentally ("if he does not do it intentionally, but God lets it happen"). In the case of accidental manslaughter, the person could flee to the place that the Lord "will designate." This refers to the Levitical cities of refuge, for which provision was made after Israel was living in the land of Canaan, as recorded in Deuteronomy 4:41,42.

We notice how children who attacked or cursed their fathers or mothers were to be put to death. The Lord regarded parents as his representatives. That is why the punishment was so severe. Kidnappers also were to be put to death. Punishment for social crimes as regulated by God was much more severe than in our permissive society today.

A law that people often ask about is contained in verses 23 to 25: "If there is serious injury, you are to take life for life, eye for eye, tooth for tooth, hand for hand, foot for foot, burn for burn, wound for wound, bruise for bruise." This is the so-called *lex talionis* (law of retaliation), which states that the punishment should be proportionate to the crime. People often use this as an example of how harsh and primitive the Old Testament laws were when compared with our more compassionate and advanced laws of today. Let us note, however, that this law of retaliation was restricted to serious cases involving actual bodily harm. Let us note furthermore that in those days, when such cases were customarily dealt with through revenge, this law served to emphasize that the retaliation by revenge should not exceed whatever damage had been inflicted. In other words, it served to check passionate acts of vengeance, which could result in death. Finally, we need to remember that these laws were given by God to regulate decency and order in the society of that time. These were civil regulations, not moral decrees. Israel was governed as a theocracy, in which church and government were not separated as we experience under the constitution of the United States of America. We need to keep this difference in mind as we consider all the rules and regulations in this part of the Sinaitic law code. It might be added that there is no case on record where the "eye for eye" principle was actually carried out to the extent that a person who inflicted serious damage to another person's body was actually likewise inflicted with the same damage as punishment.

In verses 26 and 27, we see that a difference was made in cases involving bodily injury inflicted upon servants as opposed to free Israelites. In the case of servants who suffered bodily injury from their masters, the servants were compensated by being given their freedom.

Injuries relating to animals

[28]"If a bull gores a man or a woman to death, the bull must be stoned to death, and its meat must not be eaten. But the owner of the bull will not be held responsible. [29]If, however, the bull has had the habit of goring and the owner has been warned but has not kept it penned up and it kills a man or woman, the bull must be stoned and the owner also must be put to death. [30]However, if payment is demanded of him, he may redeem his life by paying whatever is demanded. [31]This law also applies if the bull gores a son or daughter. [32]If the bull gores a male or female slave, the owner must pay thirty shekels of silver to the master of the slave, and the bull must be stoned.

[33]"If a man uncovers a pit or digs one and fails to cover it and an ox or a donkey falls into it, [34]the owner of the pit must pay for the loss; he must pay its owner, and the dead animal will be his.

[35]"If a man's bull injures the bull of another and it dies, they are to sell the live one and divide both the money and the dead animal equally. [36]However, if it was known that the bull had the habit of goring, yet the owner did not keep it penned up, the owner must pay, animal for animal, and the dead animal will be his."

These rules govern situations relating to damages caused by animals to animals because of negligence on the part of the owner. You will notice that not only was the animal to be punished for wounding or killing someone, but the owner of the animal was responsible as well.

The laws relating to animals lead over into the subject of peoples' property that is damaged by animals. The subject of property damage is then continued in the next chapter.

Protection of property

22 "If a man steals an ox or a sheep and slaughters it or sells it, he must pay back five head of cattle for the ox and four sheep for the sheep.

[2]"If a thief is caught breaking in and is struck so that he dies, the defender is not guilty of bloodshed; [3]but if it happens after sunrise, he is guilty of bloodshed.

"A thief must certainly make restitution, but if he has nothing, he must be sold to pay for his theft.

⁴"If the stolen animal is found alive in his possession—whether ox or donkey or sheep—he must pay back double.

⁵"If a man grazes his livestock in a field or vineyard and lets them stray and they graze in another man's field, he must make restitution from the best of his own field or vineyard.

⁶"If a fire breaks out and spreads into thornbushes so that it burns shocks of grain or standing grain or the whole field, the one who started the fire must make restitution.

⁷"If a man gives his neighbor silver or goods for safekeeping and they are stolen from the neighbor's house, the thief, if he is caught, must pay back double. ⁸But if the thief is not found, the owner of the house must appear before the judges to determine whether he has laid his hands on the other man's property. ⁹In all cases of illegal possession of an ox, a donkey, a sheep, a garment, or any other lost property about which somebody says, 'This is mine,' both parties are to bring their cases before the judges. The one whom the judges declare guilty must pay back double to his neighbor.

¹⁰"If a man gives a donkey, an ox, a sheep or any other animal to his neighbor for safekeeping and it dies or is injured or is taken away while no one is looking, ¹¹the issue between them will be settled by the taking of an oath before the LORD that the neighbor did not lay hands on the other person's property. The owner is to accept this, and no restitution is required. ¹²But if the animal was stolen from the neighbor, he must make restitution to the owner. ¹³If it was torn to pieces by a wild animal, he shall bring in the remains as evidence and he will not be required to pay for the torn animal.

¹⁴"If a man borrows an animal from his neighbor and it is injured or dies while the owner is not present, he must make restitution. ¹⁵But if the owner is with the animal, the borrower will not have to pay. If the animal was hired, the money paid for the hire covers the loss.

The law of God given through Moses, as we see in the above verses, also contained regulations for the protection of property. As we read through this section with its references to livestock and fields and vineyards and houses, we can see that it looked forward to the time when God's people would be settled in the land of Canaan.

The situations set forth in these laws are quite simple and straightforward. Some cases may seem strange to us, as mentioned before, because they come out of a different time and a different culture. People living in less developed countries, such as in parts of Africa, find these situations and problems described here less difficult to understand than we do. Their own customary laws, which still are in force in rural areas, are very similar.

Those who have compared these laws with ancient law codes written in the same age of history find God's ordinances to be less harsh in the punishments prescribed for the guilty. Other codes, such as that of Hammurabi in ancient Babylon, demanded the death penalty for robbers and thieves in almost every instance. The opportunity to make restitution as found here was not provided in other codes. The Lord considered human life to be a sacred trust. He did require the death penalty, however, where his honor was openly desecrated, as we will see in the next section of laws.

Social responsibility

16"If a man seduces a virgin who is not pledged to be married and sleeps with her, he must pay the bride-price, and she shall be his wife. 17If her father absolutely refuses to give her to him, he must still pay the bride-price for virgins.

18"Do not allow a sorceress to live.

19"Anyone who has sexual relations with an animal must be put to death.

20"Whoever sacrifices to any god other than the LORD must be destroyed.

21"Do not mistreat an alien or oppress him, for you were aliens in Egypt.

22"Do not take advantage of a widow or an orphan. 23If you do and they cry out to me, I will certainly hear their cry. 24My anger will be aroused, and I will kill you with the sword; your wives will become widows and your children fatherless.

²⁵"If you lend money to one of my people among you who is needy, do not be like a moneylender; charge him no interest. ²⁶If you take your neighbor's cloak as a pledge, return it to him by sunset, ²⁷because his cloak is the only covering he has for his body. What else will he sleep in? When he cries out to me, I will hear, for I am compassionate.

²⁸"Do not blaspheme God or curse the ruler of your people.

²⁹"Do not hold back offerings from your granaries or your vats.

"You must give me the firstborn of your sons. ³⁰Do the same with your cattle and your sheep. Let them stay with their mothers for seven days, but give them to me on the eighth day.

³¹"You are to be my holy people. So do not eat the meat of an animal torn by wild beasts; throw it to the dogs.

A number of situations are presented in this section of laws that are of special interest.

Reference is made in verse 16 to a "bride-price." In Genesis we already saw in the arrangements made to obtain a wife for Isaac that many "costly gifts" were given by his father, Abraham, to Bethuel, the father of the bride (24:53); Jacob had arranged to "pay" Laban for the hands of his daughters in marriage by agreeing to work seven years for each one. The custom of arranging for a bride-price either in terms of earthly goods or years of service is still followed in other cultures today. The case presented in our text here deals with a man who seduces a virgin who is not pledged to be married. He was obligated by law to pay the bride-price and marry the girl. (Deuteronomy 22:23-27 presents the case of a man who sleeps with a virgin who is pledged to be married. In this latter case, the death penalty is required of both the man and the woman, unless the woman can prove that she was raped. In that situation, only the man was to be punished with death by stoning.)

Three situations are next presented in the above text where the law of God prescribed the death penalty.

Verse 18 states, "Do not allow a sorceress to live." A sorceress is a woman who claims to be able to use supernatural power in order to cast evil spells upon people, causing accidents, sickness, or death. A more familiar term for sorcery in those countries where it is still practiced, such as in Africa, is "witchcraft." The practice of sorcery is idolatry. It gives honor to the powers of Satan rather than to the true God. That is why the Lord demanded the death penalty, just as every form of open idolatry in Israel's theocracy was punished with death. In many cultures and societies in the world today, the power of witchcraft is still one of the greatest forces of evil. Africans, for example, are more troubled by superstitious practices than most people realize.

Verse 19 states, "Anyone who has sexual relations with an animal must be put to death." This sin is called bestiality. In many Canaanite societies, bestiality was connected with religious rites as a part of the worship of Baal. Hence God again demanded the death penalty.

Verse 20 states, "Whoever sacrifices to any god other than the LORD must be destroyed." The Hebrew term translated here as "destroyed" refers to the giving over of things or persons to the Lord by totally destroying them. God demanded that the same be done to entire cities when Israel conquered Canaan. They were "devoted" to the Lord, given over to him in an act of the total destruction of what was evil.

In the verses that follow, the Lord showed his compassion for widows, orphans, and the poor by requiring his people to show this same spirit of compassion in their lives. Those who failed to help the poor and needy would experience the Lord's anger. In the case of those who were destitute, the Israelites were to lend money without charging interest.

According to verse 28, blaspheming the name of the Lord was forbidden. In the book of Leviticus, a case is recorded of a man who uttered the Lord's name as a curse, and the entire assembly of Israel stoned him (24:10-16). The high priest Caiaphas condemned Jesus to death for blasphemy, because Jesus said under oath that he was the Christ, the Son of God. We know, of course, that Jesus spoke the truth.

Chapter 22 closes with several reminders to the Israelites that they were to honor the Lord as his holy people with their offerings and with the dedication of their firstborn sons and the firstborn of their cattle and sheep to him. "Do not eat the meat of an animal torn by wild beasts; throw it to the dogs," the Lord declared in conclusion. An animal torn by beasts hadn't been properly drained of blood, and God's Old Testament people were not to eat meat with blood in it. In every way, Israel was to demonstrate itself to be a holy people, consecrated to the Lord.

We in New Testament times are not bound by ceremonial regulations as the Israelites were in the Old Testament. Yet we should not forget the sense of dedication in which the grace of God should work in us. As the apostle Paul writes to the Romans, "I urge you, brothers, in view of God's mercy, to offer your bodies as living sacrifices, holy and pleasing to God—this is your spiritual act of worship. Do not conform any longer to the pattern of this world, but be transformed by the renewing of your mind. Then you will be able to test and approve what God's will is— his good, pleasing and perfect will" (12:1,2).

Laws of justice and mercy

23 "Do not spread false reports. Do not help a wicked man by being a malicious witness.

²"Do not follow the crowd in doing wrong. When you give testimony in a lawsuit, do not pervert justice by siding with the crowd, ³and do not show favoritism to a poor man in his lawsuit.

⁴"If you come across your enemy's ox or donkey wandering off, be sure to take it back to him. ⁵If you see the donkey of someone who hates you fallen down under its load, do not leave it there; be sure you help him with it.

⁶"Do not deny justice to your poor people in their lawsuits. ⁷Have nothing to do with a false charge and do not put an innocent or honest person to death, for I will not acquit the guilty.

⁸"Do not accept a bribe, for a bribe blinds those who see and twists the words of the righteous.

⁹"Do not oppress an alien; you yourselves know how it feels to be aliens, because you were aliens in Egypt.

In the previous section dealing with Israel's social responsibilities, the Lord emphasized the importance of compassion in dealing with widows and orphans, the poor and the needy. In this section before us now, the emphasis is upon justice, especially when testifying in court. There should be no malicious bearing of witness, no partiality in making decisions, no false charges, no bribery, no taking advantage of foreigners. Israel was to show itself as a holy people. A finer set of principles of justice and mercy cannot be found anywhere than in these few verses. If only one could find a dedication to such principles in our courts today, especially on the part of those who testify!

The Lord adds a significant comment here: "For I will not acquit the guilty." Israel was to remember that even though the sins warned against here might often escape human detection, there was still a higher court of justice that could not be deceived, namely, the Lord's. People today are still obliged to swear in a court of law that their testimony is true, a fitting reminder of that Judge who can "search the heart and examine the mind, to reward a man according to his conduct, according to what his deeds deserve" (Jeremiah 17:10). When people no longer have respect for the God before whom they take an oath in court, a breakdown of law and order will surely result. The final verdict, of course, will be rendered on that day when, as the apostle Paul declares, "we must all appear before the judgment seat of Christ, that each one may receive what is due him for the things done while in the body, whether good or bad" (2 Corinthians 5:10). May the Holy Spirit give us the spirit of Christ, so that our faith also is active in works of justice!

Sabbath laws

¹⁰**"For six years you are to sow your fields and harvest the crops, ¹¹but during the seventh year let the land lie unplowed and unused. Then the poor among your people may get food from it, and the wild animals may eat what they leave. Do the same with your vineyard and your olive grove.**

¹²**"Six days do your work, but on the seventh day do not work, so that your ox and your donkey may rest and the slave born in your household, and the alien as well, may be refreshed.**

¹³**"Be careful to do everything I have said to you. Do not invoke the names of other gods; do not let them be heard on your lips.**

Not only were the people to rest on the seventh day of the week, but every seventh year was also to be a year of rest for the fields. Here the idea of the "sabbatical year" is mentioned briefly. In Leviticus chapter 25 and Deuteronomy chapter 15, the details of this arrangement are explained.

The three annual festivals

¹⁴"Three times a year you are to celebrate a festival to me.

¹⁵"Celebrate the Feast of Unleavened Bread; for seven days eat bread made without yeast, as I commanded you. Do this at the appointed time in the month of Abib, for in that month you came out of Egypt.

"No one is to appear before me empty-handed.

¹⁶"Celebrate the Feast of Harvest with the firstfruits of the crops you sow in your field.

"Celebrate the Feast of Ingathering at the end of the year, when you gather in your crops from the field.

¹⁷"Three times a year all the men are to appear before the Sovereign Lord.

¹⁸"Do not offer the blood of a sacrifice to me along with anything containing yeast.

"The fat of my festival offerings must not be kept until morning.

¹⁹"Bring the best of the firstfruits of your soil to the house of the Lord your God.

"Do not cook a young goat in its mother's milk.

We have here a brief outline of the three great festivals according to which the church year of the Israelites was arranged. Leviticus chapter 23 and Deuteronomy chapter 16 give us a much more complete description of this arrangement. After their arrival in the land of Canaan, the Israelites were to celebrate these three festivals in a central place of worship. After the temple was built in Jerusalem under Solomon, that place was Jerusalem. Three times a year all the men of Israel were to "appear before the Sovereign Lord."

We have already heard about the *Feast of Unleavened Bread* in connection with the institution of the Passover. However, this is the first time that mention is made in the Bible of the other two festivals, the Feast of Harvest and the Feast of Ingathering.

The *Feast of Harvest* was also called the Feast of Weeks. It was celebrated 50 days after the Passover festival, with its Feast of Unleavened Bread. At this occasion the people would be able to celebrate by enjoying the produce of the firstfruits of the grain harvest.

The *Feast of Ingathering,* as we see in Leviticus, was celebrated in connection with the great Day of Atonement and was later also associated with the Feast of Tabernacles. This came at the time when the final gathering of the year's produce of fruit, oil, and wine took place.

It is interesting to note that the church year of the Israelites had three major festivals, even as we in our Christian church year have the three great celebrations: Christmas, Easter, and Pentecost. The Old Testament Feast of Unleavened Bread occurs at about the time of our Easter. Their Feast of Harvest, 50 days later, comes at the time of our Pentecost. Their Feast of Ingathering can be compared to our Harvest Festival or Thanksgiving, where we thank the Lord for his bountiful blessings.

The final regulation mentioned in this section dealing with social and ceremonial laws is this: "Do not cook a young goat in its mother's milk." At first reading, this may seem like a very strange statement to give in such a prominent place. That this statement has a special meaning is clear from the fact that it is given elsewhere in the laws of Moses in places that are equally important.

But what does it mean? What is its special significance? Bible scholars have come up with a variety of answers. Luther comments that while the meat of a young goat cooked in milk was a special treat in those days, Israel was warned not to do this until the goat had been weaned. To break this regulation, Luther claimed, would be inhumane. Another scholar adds the comment that to cook a kid in its own mother's milk would show contempt for the relation that God established between a parent and its young. Still others have commented that to eat milk and meat together

141

was contrary to Israelite kosher, or dietary, laws. We fail to find such a law in Scripture, however, other than the remote possibility of this passage.

Archeological discoveries of more recent years, particularly the Ras Shamra tablets at ancient Ugarit, show that the Canaanites prepared such a dish at their festal ceremonies, which were a part of their pagan fertility rites. The heathen Canaanites believed that boiling a baby goat in its own mother's milk was a way of persuading Baal to grant the blessings of fertility. This discovery probably sheds the best light upon this passage. The Lord is speaking here of religious festivals and various rites that were to be observed in their celebration. He is warning his people not to celebrate as the pagans did, but to bring their thankofferings according to his direction. Even the suggestion or appearance of honoring foreign gods is to be strictly avoided.

The words of the Lord that follow are concluding words, offering encouragement to his people as they follow his precepts.

God's angel to prepare the way

[20]"See, I am sending an angel ahead of you to guard you along the way and to bring you to the place I have prepared. [21]Pay attention to him and listen to what he says. Do not rebel against him; he will not forgive your rebellion, since my Name is in him. [22]If you listen carefully to what he says and do all that I say, I will be an enemy to your enemies and will oppose those who oppose you. [23]My angel will go ahead of you and bring you into the land of the Amorites, Hittites, Perizzites, Canaanites, Hivites and Jebusites, and I will wipe them out. [24]Do not bow down before their gods or worship them or follow their practices. You must demolish them and break their sacred stones to pieces. [25]Worship the LORD your God, and his blessing will be on your food and water. I will take away sickness from among you, [26]and none will miscarry or be barren in your land. I will give you a full life span.

²⁷"I will send my terror ahead of you and throw into confusion every nation you encounter. I will make all your enemies turn their backs and run. ²⁸I will send the hornet ahead of you to drive the Hivites, Canaanites and Hittites out of your way. ²⁹But I will not drive them out in a single year, because the land would become desolate and the wild animals too numerous for you. ³⁰Little by little I will drive them out before you, until you have increased enough to take possession of the land.

³¹"I will establish your borders from the Red Sea to the Sea of the Philistines, and from the desert to the River. I will hand over to you the people who live in the land and you will drive them out before you. ³²Do not make a covenant with them or with their gods. ³³Do not let them live in your land, or they will cause you to sin against me, because the worship of their gods will certainly be a snare to you."

The "angel" that the Lord is sending ahead of his people in their journey is the Lord himself. Israel is to listen to him alone and to honor his Name alone. He will fight their battles for them. He will bring them into their promised inheritance.

"I will send the hornet ahead of you," the Lord declares. The same picture is given in Deuteronomy 7:20 and Joshua 24:12 to describe the Lord who brings terror and calamities of all kinds to Israel's enemies so that they can conquer them. Anyone who has been attacked by a swarm of hornets will appreciate the force of this picture. In the story of Israel's conquest of the land of Canaan, we read how their enemies were overcome by overwhelming fear, by surprise attacks, by storms, floods, and natural disasters. This would not all happen at once, but in gradual steps, as the Lord foretells, so that the land would not become desolate or the wild animals too numerous.

After giving the broad outlines of their borders in Canaan, the Lord concludes this portion with a final warning that the Israelites should not make a covenant with the Canaanites. They should be driven out, lest their heathen worship become a snare to God's people. How repeatedly and urgently the Lord warned his people against foreign entanglements. If only Israel had listened!

Israel was not alone in their failure to heed God's warnings. God warns his New Testament Christians to keep away from evil associations, both socially as well as religiously. Many don't seem to see the need for this, thinking that they can play with fire without being burned, much as Peter in his overconfidence warmed himself in the company of Christ's enemies. Christians sometimes resent being told to "be different" in their manner of life and in the ways in which they are to reflect their whole purpose of life. May Israel's example serve us as a warning! God has called us not only to be his own; he has called us to be different.

Instructions to Moses

24 Then he said to Moses, "Come up to the LORD, you and Aaron, Nadab and Abihu, and seventy of the elders of Israel. You are to worship at a distance, ²but Moses alone is to approach the LORD; the others must not come near. And the people may not come up with him."

³When Moses went and told the people all the LORD's words and laws, they responded with one voice, "Everything the LORD has said we will do." ⁴Moses then wrote down everything the LORD had said.

After having given the basic provisions of his Sinaitic covenant with Israel, the Lord asks Moses, Aaron, Aaron's sons Nadab and Abihu, and seventy elders to ascend Mount Sinai. Moses alone, however, is to approach the Lord to receive instructions concerning the ratification of the covenant.

Moses then returns and tells the people "all the LORD's words and laws." Although there are various interpretations concerning what is meant by "all the LORD's words and laws," we understand the "words" to be the Ten Commandments stated in chapter 20 and the "laws" to be the regulations pertaining to the social and ceremonial life of Israel as recorded from 20:22 to 23:32. Moses was also directed to record these "words and laws" in writing, known as the "Book of the Covenant" (24:7).

After voicing their agreement with the contents of the Book of the Covenant, the people are ready for its solemn ratification.

The covenant ratified

He got up early the next morning and built an altar at the foot of the mountain and set up twelve stone pillars representing the twelve tribes of Israel. ⁵Then he sent young Israelite men, and they offered burnt offerings and sacrificed young bulls as fellowship offerings to the LORD. ⁶Moses took half of the blood and put it in bowls, and the other half he sprinkled on the altar. ⁷Then he took the Book of the Covenant and read it to the people. They responded, "We will do everything the LORD has said; we will obey."

⁸Moses then took the blood, sprinkled it on the people and said, "This is the blood of the covenant that the LORD has made with you in accordance with all these words."

The following morning Moses "built an altar at the foot of the mountain and set up twelve stone pillars representing the twelve tribes of Israel." The altar indicated the Lord's presence in the ceremony that was to take place; the 12 stone pillars were no doubt placed somewhere around the altar. The covenant was between the Lord and his people. Young Israelite men served as priests, since the Levitical priesthood had not as yet been organized. "Burnt offerings," in which the bulls were burned entirely upon the altar, and "fellowship offerings," by which the people expressed their fellowship with the Lord at special occasions, were brought. The fellowship offerings included a common meal to express thanksgiving and fellowship. This eating and drinking in the presence of the Lord took place later on in the service. (When the Lord some time afterwards gave Moses the regulations for the blood sacrifices, as we find recorded in the book of Leviticus, both burnt offerings and fellowship offerings were included.)

Because of the special occasion, half the blood from the animals was sprinkled on the altar and the other half on the people. This was sacrificial blood, offered as an expiation, a price for sin. Sin destroyed the fellowship between God and man. The price of atonement was in the shedding of blood. We see how this thought was impressed upon God's Old Testament people through the many blood sacrifices. All the Old Testament animal sacrifices, we know, foreshadowed the one great sacrifice brought on Golgotha by the Savior Jesus Christ. It was only through his perfect sacrifice that these animal sacrifices which pointed to him were effective (Hebrews 9:11-14). John writes, "He [Jesus Christ] is the atoning sacrifice for our sins, and not only for ours but also for the sins of the whole world" (1 John 2:2).

After the sprinkling of blood on the altar, the people once more solemnly promised to live according to the terms of the covenant. Then Moses sprinkled the blood upon the people.

The well-known Bible scholar Alfred Edersheim has this to say about the ratification ceremony described in our text: "This transaction was the most important in the whole history of Israel. By this one sacrifice, never renewed, Israel was formally set apart as the people of God; and it lay at the foundation of all the sacrificial worship which followed" (*Old Testament Bible History*, page 120).

The writer of the book of Hebrews explains the significance of this ratification ceremony for us as New Testament Christians: "When Moses had proclaimed every commandment of the law to all the people, he took the blood of calves, together with water, scarlet wool and branches of hyssop, and sprinkled the scroll and all the people. He said, 'This is the blood of the covenant, which God has commanded you to keep.' In the same way, he sprinkled with the blood both the tabernacle and everything used in its ceremonies. In fact, the law requires that nearly everything be cleansed with blood, and without the shedding of blood there is no forgiveness" (9:19-22).

With the poet of old, we sing in a Lenten hymn,

> Thousand, thousand thanks shall be,
> Dearest Jesus, unto thee. (CW 114)

An audience with God

⁹Moses and Aaron, Nadab and Abihu, and the seventy elders of Israel went up ¹⁰and saw the God of Israel. Under his feet was something like a pavement made of sapphire, clear as the sky itself. ¹¹But God did not raise his hand against these leaders of the Israelites; they saw God, and they ate and drank.

After the solemn ceremony whereby fellowship was established between the Lord and Israel through the sprinkling of blood, this relationship was expressed in a meal that the leaders of Israel experienced in the presence of God. God granted these representatives of Israel an unusual vision of himself. We read that they "saw the God of Israel." Not in the fullness of his glory, of course, since the Lord said to Moses some time after this, "You cannot see my face, for no one may see me and live" (33:20). Whether the use of the word "God" here instead of LORD (Yahweh) has any significance is difficult to say. In any case, the Lord graciously dimmed his absolute glory in some way. This vision, with its "pavement made of sapphire," reminds us of the vision described by the prophet Ezekiel recorded in Ezekiel 1:25-28.

Again we are reminded of those beautiful pictures in the book of Revelation, of when that great multitude of the redeemed—which no one can count, from every nation, tribe, people, and language—will be standing before the throne of God and in front of the Lamb, of when "they will see his face, and his name will be on their foreheads. . . . They will not need the light of a lamp or the light of the sun, for the Lord God will give them light. And they will reign for ever and ever" (22:4,5).

Moses' ascent

[12]The LORD said to Moses, "Come up to me on the mountain and stay here, and I will give you the tablets of stone, with the law and commands I have written for their instruction."

[13]Then Moses set out with Joshua his aide, and Moses went up on the mountain of God. [14]He said to the elders, "Wait here for us until we come back to you. Aaron and Hur are with you, and anyone involved in a dispute can go to them."

[15]When Moses went up on the mountain, the cloud covered it, [16]and the glory of the LORD settled on Mount Sinai. For six days the cloud covered the mountain, and on the seventh day the LORD called to Moses from within the cloud. [17]To the Israelites the glory of the LORD looked like a consuming fire on top of the mountain. [18]Then Moses entered the cloud as he went on up the mountain. And he stayed on the mountain forty days and forty nights.

As a fitting close to this ratification of the covenant between the Lord and Israel at Mount Sinai, Moses now at the Lord's own request ascends the mountain to receive the tablets of stone with the Ten Commandments, as well as detailed instructions concerning the building of the tabernacle, the place of the covenant.

"The glory of the LORD settled on Mount Sinai," we read. Again we note this expression "glory of the LORD." The Lord assures Israel of his presence as a cloud covers the mountain. As the Israelites behold this "glory of the LORD," it looks like a "consuming fire on top of the mountain." It reminds the people of the holiness, the majesty, and the power of their Lord. Yet we see how "Moses entered the cloud as he went up on the mountain." Holy and majestic, yes, like a consuming fire. Yet at the same time gracious and forgiving, receiving Moses as a mediator of his covenant with his people!

There Moses remained 40 days and 40 nights. It was a miracle that he could do this without eating and drinking. The number 40 occurs here as well as in Elijah's journey to Horeb (1 Kings 19:1-9), Christ's temptation in the desert (Matthew 4:1-11), and Israel's wandering in the wilderness (Numbers 14). In each case it involves a time of testing as well as of strengthening by a merciful Lord.

These last verses of chapter 24 bring the second chief part of the book of Exodus to a close. In part one we were told about the deliverance of the covenant people out of Egypt. Part two presented to us the establishing of the covenant with Israel. We are now ready for part three, the entry into the place of the covenant, the tabernacle.

The Entry into the Place of the Covenant, the Tabernacle
(25:1–40:38)

The Lord had made a covenant with his people Israel on Mount Sinai. He was the only true God, and he was their Lord, their covenant-Lord. They were his people, set apart to glorify his name. A bond of fellowship existed between the Lord and Israel. The Lord wanted his people to be assured that he was present when they worshiped him. The tabernacle was to serve this purpose. The Lord wanted this people to know that he dwelled in their midst. He also traveled with them from place to place. The tabernacle was the meeting place where the Lord manifested his presence among them and where they could draw near to him as their Savior-God.

But how could sinful people come into the presence of a holy and righteous God? It was only by an act of grace on the Lord's part that a bond of fellowship between the two could even be considered in the first place. Already hundreds of years before this, the Lord in his mercy made this choice. He had told Abraham that through his descendants all the nations of this earth would be blessed. God had promised that he would carry out his plan of salvation for all mankind through Abraham's seed. After Abraham's descendants had developed into the nation of Israel, the

Lord was faithful to this promise. He delivered them from their bondage in Egypt. He was now leading them to the land he had promised to Abraham. He had reassured them that they would be his kingdom of priests and his holy nation by establishing his covenant with them on Mount Sinai. The fact that Israel could consider itself to be the Lord's treasured possession was entirely due to an act of the Lord's grace.

The covenant that the Lord had made on Sinai, however, was not a one-sided covenant. It also expected Israel to demonstrate its faithfulness to the Lord as the people of his possession. The Lord revealed his holy law to them to show them what it meant to be truly holy before him in all their ways. He also gave them certain principles whereby they could guide their social lives and civic responsibilities as a nation dedicated to his service. Israel, however, could not fulfill the requirements that God's law demanded. His moral law, revealed in his Ten Commandments, showed them their sin. God's holiness demanded perfection, and their lives were far from perfect. In carrying out the social and civic requirements that set them apart as the people of God's possession, they often failed. And so the Lord provided a way through the services performed in the tabernacle for a sinful people to remain in fellowship with a holy God.

Again, these arrangements were made by a gracious and forgiving Lord. Israel could approach God through mediators. God would provide a priesthood through whom this mediation would take place. The priests, and especially the high priest, would be the go-betweens. The mediation that the priests would perform on behalf of the people would take place through the sacrifices that would be brought at the tabernacle. The people would be told what animals and grain to bring to be offered as sacrifices to the Lord.

Through these sacrifices the relationship between a sinful people and a just God could be restored and maintained. (The book of Leviticus explains in detail the various kinds of sacrifices that the priests would offer for the people.)

The construction of the tabernacle with its furnishings, as well as the priestly garments that were to be made, picture this relationship between a gracious Lord and his chosen people, Israel. The instructions that the Lord gave Moses concerning these matters as found in the next seven chapters indicate how Israel's worship was to be symbolic of its covenant relationship with the Lord. The Lord would dwell in the midst of his people. They were to approach him through mediators. It was by way of sacrifice that the people were to express their relationship to him and make atonement for their many sins and failings. It was through their offerings that they were to show their thanks and praise to the glory of his name. As we consider the construction of the tabernacle with its various appointments, we want to keep this manner of Israel's worship as the Lord's covenant people in mind. This was the Lord's own arrangement during the many centuries while God's people waited for the promised Savior.

At the same time, we want to remember that Israel's Old Testament form of worship, with all its ceremonial regulations, was a type, a picture, a shadow of that perfect restoration of fellowship between sinful mankind and a holy God, which the Lord himself would accomplish through the gift of his only begotten Son. When Jesus came, the eternal "Word became flesh and made his dwelling among us" (John 1:14). The expression that John uses here literally means that the Lord "tabernacled among us." Israel's tabernacle is a picture of Christ's saving presence in the world of sin. In the tabernacle in the desert, God revealed his glory by appearing in a cloud. John writes of the Word who became flesh: "We have seen his glory, the glory of the One and Only, who came from the Father, full of grace and truth." Israel's approach to God through the mediation of priests and by way of blood sacrifices was "an illustration for the present time," the writer of the book of Hebrews tells us (9:9). The holy writer continues, "When Christ came as high priest of the good things that are already here, he went through the greater and more perfect tabernacle that is not man-made, that is to say, not a part of this creation. He did not enter by means of the blood of goats and calves; but he entered the Most Holy Place once for all by his own blood, having obtained eternal redemption" (verses 11,12). The Old Testament sacrifices were an effective means of atoning for sin only through the fulfillment accomplished by Christ's perfect sacrifice on Calvary's cross, as the writer of Hebrews explains throughout his epistle, especially in chapters 8, 9, and 10. Finally, Israel's earthly tabernacle was a picture of our heavenly tabernacle, where God will dwell with his holy people in perfect fellowship for all eternity. John writes in the book of Revelation, "I heard a loud voice from the throne [of God in heaven] saying, 'Now the dwelling of God is with men, and he will live with them'" (21:3). The word translated as "dwelling" in this verse is again the word that literally means "tabernacle." As John continues in this passage, he portrays the redeemed in heaven: "They will be his people, and God himself will be with them and be their God. He will wipe every tear from their eyes. There will be no more death or mourning or crying or pain, for the old order of things has passed away" (verses 3,4).

We will want to keep this symbolism in mind as we consider the directions that the Lord gave Moses upon Mount Sinai concerning the tabernacle. Its construction and arrangement was prescribed by the Lord himself in every detail. The Lord left nothing to man's invention. Everything about this tabernacle, or "Tent of Meeting" (27:21; 40:2), was to express this covenant relationship between the Lord and his chosen people. It was to be a visible pledge of his invisible presence in their midst and their means of expressing their trust in his mercy as they dedicated themselves to him as his holy people.

Offerings for the tabernacle

25 **The LORD said to Moses, ²"Tell the Israelites to bring me an offering. You are to receive the offering for me from each man whose heart prompts him to give. ³These are the offerings you are to receive from them: gold, silver and bronze; ⁴blue, purple and scarlet yarn and fine linen; goat hair; ⁵ram skins dyed red and hides of sea cows; acacia wood; ⁶olive oil for the light; spices for the anointing oil and for the fragrant incense; ⁷and onyx stones and other gems to be mounted on the ephod and breastpiece.**

⁸"Then have them make a sanctuary for me, and I will dwell among them. ⁹Make this tabernacle and all its furnishings exactly like the pattern I will show you.

"Tell the Israelites to bring me an offering," the Lord directed Moses. The Hebrew word used here for "offering" literally means "a gift which is lifted up." Students of the Bible are not sure whether this means that the gift was "lifted up" from one's possessions, or actually lifted up by the priest when it was brought to the Lord. Whatever the case, this was to be a freewill offering, "from each man whose heart prompts him to give." Let us keep this in mind when we later note the response to this appeal from the Lord for freewill offerings.

The various items that the people were to bring were specified. God later directed how these items were to be used. Was the Lord asking for something too difficult to fulfill? Where could the Israelites obtain these items? Certain things such as precious metals, cloth, and gems they had received from the Egyptians. Goat hair and ram skins they had in abundance. Hides of sea cows could be obtained from the Red Sea, which was not too far away. Acacia trees grew in the area where they were camped. Oil, spices, and incense could be purchased from caravans passing through the area.

The purpose of this offering was for a sanctuary where the Lord promised to dwell among his people. According to our text, the Lord himself would show Moses a picture or model of the tabernacle and its furniture. Much later, Stephen refers to this in his speech before the Jewish Supreme Council: "It [the tabernacle of Testimony] had been made as God directed Moses, according to the pattern he had seen" (Acts 7:44). The writer of the book of Hebrews mentions the same pattern that God showed Moses in the mountain, stating that the sanctuary was to be "a copy and shadow of what is in heaven" (8:5). The tabernacle, in other words, was to picture in an earthly form the perfect dwelling place of believers with their Lord in their eternal home.

Our Christian churches today are not built according to the same Old Testament pattern that the Lord gave Moses. In the New Testament we are no longer bound by the many ceremonial regulations that the Israelites were commanded to observe when approaching the Lord in their worship. Christ abolished these ceremonial regulations by his all-atoning sacrifice on the cross. And yet our churches with their appointments also picture to us the place where the Lord comes to his people. He does this today through his holy Word and precious sacraments. In most of our churches, our attention is directed to a cross. Before the Lord's altar the congregation brings all its requests to him in prayer and receives the Lord's own body and blood in the Lord's Supper. We too should want that place that we call our "house of God" to reflect the place where his honor dwells.

We sometimes hear people say that we "can pray to God in a barn" and that "it's foolish to waste so much money on our places of worship." To this we reply that our churches should be a true reflection of our love and respect for our God. They should demonstrate visibly the appreciation Christians have for those priceless gifts of grace that the Lord has so freely granted them and continues to bestow on them. When people love the Lord, their freewill offerings will suffice to provide a place where they can honor the Lord with their wealth and with their firstfruits.

The ark

[10]"Have them make a chest of acacia wood—two and a half cubits long, a cubit and a half wide, and a cubit and a half high. [11]Overlay it with pure gold, both inside and out, and make a gold molding around it. [12]Cast four gold rings for it and fasten them to its four feet, with two rings on one side and two rings on the other. [13]Then make poles of acacia wood and overlay them with gold. [14]Insert the poles into the rings on the sides of the chest to carry it. [15]The poles are to remain in the rings of this ark; they are not to be removed. [16]Then put in the ark the Testimony, which I will give you.

[17]"Make an atonement cover of pure gold—two and a half cubits long and a cubit and a half wide. [18]And make two cherubim out of hammered gold at the ends of the cover. [19]Make one cherub on one end and the second cherub on the other; make the cherubim of one piece with the cover, at the two ends. [20]The cherubim are to have their wings spread upward, overshadowing the cover with them. The cherubim are to face each other, looking toward the cover. [21]Place the cover on top of the ark and put in the ark the Testimony, which I will give you. [22]There, above the cover between the two cherubim that are over the ark of the Testimony, I will meet with you and give you all my commands for the Israelites.

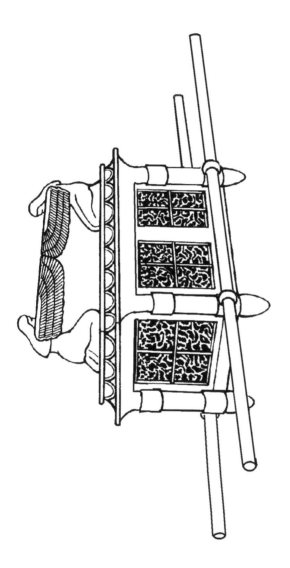

The ark of the covenant

Plans for a building usually begin with the structure itself and then proceed to the furnishings contained in it. The Lord's plans concerning the tabernacle reverse this order. They begin with *the ark of the covenant,* the central feature of the tabernacle. Everything else was planned around it, since the ark emphasized the Lord's own presence among his people.

The ark itself was an oblong box of acacia wood overlaid with gold. It measured about 3¾ feet in length, 2¼ feet wide, and 2¼ feet high (2½ cubits long, 1½ cubits wide, and 1½ cubits high). Two gold rings were fastened to the ark on each side, near the bottom. Poles of acacia wood overlaid with gold were inserted into these rings so that the ark could be carried. The poles were to remain in the rings at all times so that those who carried the ark would not touch it.

Into this ark Moses was instructed to place "the Testimony." This is the name given to the two tablets of stone upon which the Lord himself inscribed the Ten Commandments.

The cover of the ark is referred to as "an atonement cover." The King James translation of the Bible calls this the "mercy seat." The Hebrew word means "to cover." The translation "atonement cover" is a fitting one, since it was upon this place that the high priest sprinkled the blood of atonement on the great Day of Atonement (Leviticus 16:11-17). This act signified that the sins of the people were covered, that is, removed from God's sight. The transgressions against the Ten Commandments, which were lying under this cover, were atoned for.

The cover itself was to be made of pure gold, with the figures of two golden cherubim mounted upon it. Cherubim are angelic creatures. God placed cherubim at the Garden of

Eden to "guard the way to the tree of life" (Genesis 3:24). Here the two cherubim faced each other, looking toward the cover, with their wings spread out to overshadow it.

The ark of the covenant together with its atonement cover became Jehovah's throne in the midst of his people, the footstool of the God of Israel. Here was kept the holy will of God as revealed in his Commandments, a God who punished sin. Here was also the throne of God's grace, where he supplied a way for his people to have their sins taken away.

David called the ark of the covenant "the footstool of our God" (1 Chronicles 28:2; see also Psalm 132:7). Here the high priest would make "atonement for himself, his household and the whole community of Israel" (Leviticus 16:17). What a beautiful type of our Great High Priest, Jesus Christ, who "when [he] came as high priest of the good things that are already here, he went through the greater and more perfect tabernacle that is not man-made, that is to say, not a part of this creation. He did not enter by means of the blood of goats and calves; but he entered the Most Holy Place once for all by his own blood, having obtained eternal redemption" (Hebrews 9:11,12).

The pattern of the tabernacle

The table

²³"Make a table of acacia wood—two cubits long, a cubit wide and a cubit and a half high. ²⁴Overlay it with pure gold and make a gold molding around it. ²⁵Also make around it a rim a handbreadth wide and put a gold molding on the rim. ²⁶Make four gold rings for the table and fasten them to the four corners, where the four legs are. ²⁷The rings are to be close to the rim to hold the poles used in carrying the table. ²⁸Make the poles of acacia wood, overlay them with gold and carry the table with them. ²⁹And make its plates and dishes of pure gold, as well as its pitchers and bowls for the pour-

ing out of offerings. ³⁰Put the bread of the Presence on this table to be before me at all times.

The next furnishing for the sanctuary described by the Lord to Moses was a table, referred to in some translations as the "table of shewbread" or the "table of the bread of the Presence." This table was 3 feet long, 1½ feet wide, and 2¼ feet high (2 cubits long, 1 cubit wide, and 1½ cubits high), also made of acacia wood overlaid with gold. Rings were to be placed in the four legs for the poles by which the table was to be carried. Vessels of gold to be used for bread and gold pitchers for pouring out drink offerings were to be placed upon this table.

In the book of Leviticus instructions were given concerning the bread that should be placed upon this table: "Take fine flour and bake twelve loaves of bread. . . . Set them in two rows, six in each row, on the table of pure gold before the LORD. Along each row put some pure incense as a memorial portion to represent the bread and to be an offering made to the LORD by fire. This bread is to be set out before the LORD regularly, Sabbath after Sabbath, on behalf of the Israelites, as a lasting covenant. It belongs to Aaron and his sons, who are to eat it in a holy place, because it is a most holy part of their regular share of the offerings made to the LORD by fire" (24:5-9).

The 12 loaves of bread represented the 12 tribes of Israel. As we are told in Leviticus, the bread was to be "set out before the LORD" regularly, a grain offering presented by Israel as a "lasting covenant." There are various interpretations of this passage. Some of these are rather complicated. The simplest meaning would be that the bread on the table assured Israel of the Lord's presence among his people and represented Israel's continual offering of thanks to him for their daily bread. Thus these things were symbols of constant fellowship between the two parties of the covenant.

The lampstand

[31]"Make a lampstand of pure gold and hammer it out, base and shaft; its flower-like cups, buds and blossoms shall be of one piece with it. [32]Six branches are to extend from the sides of the lampstand—three on one side and three on the other. [33]Three cups shaped like almond flowers with buds and blossoms are to be on one branch, three on the next branch, and the same for all six branches extending from the lampstand. [34]And on the lampstand there are to be four cups shaped like almond flowers with buds and blossoms. [35]One bud shall be under the first pair of branches extending from the lampstand, a second bud under the second pair, and a third bud under the third pair—six branches in all. [36]The buds and branches shall all be of one piece with the lampstand, hammered out of pure gold.

[37]"Then make its seven lamps and set them up on it so that they light the space in front of it. [38]Its wick trimmers and trays are to be of pure gold. [39]A talent of pure gold is to be used for the lampstand and all these accessories. [40]See that you make them according to the pattern shown you on the mountain.

The only light in the tabernacle itself came from the lampstand described in these verses. This consisted of a central shaft, with three branches extending outward and upward from each side, providing a place for seven lamps in all. Both the stem and the branches were decorated with cup-shaped almond flowers. Four of these flowers were on the central shaft and three on each branch.

The seven lamps set on top of the stem and branches consisted of containers for oil, with a protruding wick that gave light as it burned. Instruments for the use of the lamps—wick trimmers, tweezers for removing used wicks, trays—were to be made of pure gold, as was the lampstand itself. The size of the lampstand is not given. The ancient historian Josephus stated that it was five feet in height with its branches extending out nearly two feet on each side.

In 27:21 we are told that Aaron and his sons were to "keep the lamps burning before the LORD from evening till morning" and that this was to be "a lasting ordinance among the Israelites for the generations to come." (We will discuss the position in the tabernacle of these furnishings later.)

Light is often used in Scripture as a symbol for Christ, the true Light of the world, as indicated in Isaiah 9:2 and John 8:12. Believers in Christ are to reflect his light (Isaiah 60:3; Matthew 5:14; Acts 13:47). Israel, as the Lord's covenant people, was to let its spiritual light shine before all the nations of the earth.

The number 7 is used frequently in Scripture. The prophet Zechariah sees a golden lampstand with seven lamps as representative of God's holy people (Zechariah 4). In the book of Revelation the seven churches of the New Testament are pictured in the form of seven lampstands (Revelation 1:20). Israel's function as a light in a world of darkness has been passed on to the church of Jesus Christ.

The curtains of the tabernacle

26 "Make the tabernacle with ten curtains of finely twisted linen and blue, purple and scarlet yarn, with cherubim worked into them by a skilled craftsman. ²All the curtains are to be the same size—twenty-eight cubits long and four cubits wide. ³Join five of the curtains together, and do the same with the other five. ⁴Make loops of blue material along the edge of the end curtain in one set, and do the same with the end curtain in the other set. ⁵Make fifty loops on one curtain and fifty loops on the end curtain of the other set, with the loops opposite each other. ⁶Then make fifty gold clasps and use them to fasten the curtains together so that the tabernacle is a unit.

⁷"Make curtains of goat hair for the tent over the tabernacle—eleven altogether. ⁸All eleven curtains are to be the same size—thirty cubits long and four cubits wide. ⁹Join five of the curtains together into one set and the other six into another set. Fold the sixth curtain double at the front of the tent. ¹⁰Make fifty loops along the edge of the end curtain in one set and also along the edge of the end curtain in the other set. ¹¹Then make fifty bronze clasps and put them in the loops to fasten the tent together as a unit. ¹²As for the additional length of the tent curtains, the half curtain that is left over is to hang down at the rear of the tabernacle. ¹³The tent curtains will be a cubit longer on both sides; what is left will hang over the sides of the tabernacle so as to cover it. ¹⁴Make for the tent a covering of ram skins dyed red, and over that a covering of hides of sea cows.

The tabernacle, which was to contain the furnishings described in the foregoing chapter, was only a temporary residence. The Hebrew word for "tabernacle" is also used for the dwellings of desert nomads, people who moved from place to place. Since the Israelites were on a journey in the desert and were moving from place to place, the tabernacle had to be constructed in such a way that it could be dismantled, carried in parts from one place to another, and set up again. It is necessary to keep this in mind as we consider the instructions that are given in this chapter.

As we consider these instructions, detailed as they are, we note that Bible students find it difficult to agree on a number of details about the tabernacle's exact specifications. Of the models one sees either in pictures or in small replicas, no two are the same in all details. Was the ornamental curtain hung *inside* the frame or over the outside, so that only the top of this curtain was visible? Was the frame formed of hollow squares so that the ornamental curtain, if hung over the outside, could be seen in part at least on the sides? Or was the frame formed of solid partitions? Were the outer coverings suspended over a ridgepole so as to form a peak or gable? Or were they simply stretched flat over the top of the frame? What kind of pattern was woven into the ornamental curtain? These are but a few of the questions which puzzle the experts.

The instructions were sufficiently clear to Moses, however, since the Lord had showed him an exact pattern on the mountain. The own brief description here will be based on our own understanding of the instructions given by the Lord to Moses, realizing that some readers may prefer a different explanation.

The first curtain described in this chapter is the ornamental curtain. This was pieced together out of ten curtains, each 42 feet long and 6 feet wide. Fastened together, they formed one hanging that was 60 by 42 feet in size. The cloth for this hanging was a beautiful tapestry made of white linen together with blue, purple, and scarlet fabrics, with figures of cherubim woven into the fabric. White symbolizes holiness; blue is the color of the sky; purple stands for royalty; crimson is the color of blood, in which there is life. The cherubim picture God's heavenly hosts of angels.

This curtain was the first to be mounted over the framework, forming the tabernacle. We are inclined to believe that the walls of the framework fit together as a solid piece so that only the ceiling of the ornamental curtain was visible from the inside of the tabernacle. Of all the experts on this subject, a man by the name of Umberto Cassuto seems to speak with the most authority in his *Commentary on the Book of Exodus* (page 351), and this is his explanation. The ten curtains forming this ornamental curtain were fastened together by means of loops coupled together with gold clasps. The 60-foot curtain must have hung down at the back of the tabernacle, leaving the front open, as far as this curtain was concerned. Cassuto favors the explanation that the top had a flat appearance instead of gabled.

Over this ornamental curtain were stretched several additional roof coverings. The first was made of goats' hair, the usual material for tents in those days. This too was pieced together of smaller curtains and held together by bronze clasps, forming one great covering of 66 by 45 feet. This curtain completely covered the ornamental curtain and could also hang down in front as a protecting screen. It was firmly held on the outside by ropes and pegs. Over this covering of goats' hair were two more outer coverings, one of ram skins dyed red and another of sea cow hides.

Next in this chapter is a description of the framework over which these curtains were to be suspended.

The framework of the tabernacle

¹⁵"Make upright frames of acacia wood for the tabernacle. ¹⁶Each frame is to be ten cubits long and a cubit and a half wide, ¹⁷with two projections set parallel to each other. Make all the frames of the tabernacle in this way. ¹⁸Make twenty frames for the south side of the tabernacle ¹⁹and make forty silver bases to go under them—two bases for each frame, one under each projection. ²⁰For the other side, the north side of the tabernacle, make twenty frames ²¹and forty silver bases—two under each frame. ²²Make six frames for the far end, that is, the west end of the tabernacle, ²³and make two frames for the corners at the far end. ²⁴At these two corners they must be double from the bottom all the way to the top, and fitted into a single ring; both shall be like that. ²⁵So there will be eight frames and sixteen silver bases—two under each frame.

²⁶"Also make crossbars of acacia wood: five for the frames on one side of the tabernacle, ²⁷five for those on the other side, and five for the frames on the west, at the far end of the tabernacle. ²⁸The center crossbar is to extend from end to end at the middle of the frames. ²⁹Overlay the frames with gold and make gold rings to hold the crossbars. Also overlay the crossbars with gold.

³⁰**"Set up the tabernacle according to the plan shown you on the mountain.**

The framework was made of acacia wood plated with gold. Each board was 15 feet long and 2¼ feet wide. Each board had projections at the bottom that fit into silver bases. These silver bases weighed about 95 pounds each, enough to secure the frame in solid fashion. Twenty such boards formed each side, and six boards were at the back—with none at the front, which was to serve as the entrance to the Holy Place. The number of boards provides us with the information concerning the overall dimensions of the tabernacle itself, namely 45 feet long, 15 feet wide, and 15 feet high. (Measured in biblical terms, this would be 30 by 10 by 10 cubits.) It is only from the size and number of the boards described here in this chapter that we can calculate the overall dimensions of the tabernacle. In overall length and width, the tabernacle was half the size of Solomon's temple. Part of the temple also had walls that were proportionately higher.

Extra boards were fashioned at the corners of the tabernacle to give the structure added strength. Five bars made of acacia wood overlaid with gold ran horizontally along each side and back, fitting into gold rings attached to the boards. "The manner in which the bars were arranged is a moot question," Cassuto declares (*Commentary on the Book of Exodus,* page 358). We have not found two commentators who agree as to whether the bars were placed on the inside or the outside of the tabernacle or who seem to know exactly where they were positioned on the framework. Again, we can rest assured that Moses knew, having seen an exact model of the finished product.

Since reference is made in these verses to the sides being at the north and south and the back at the west end of the tabernacle, we know that the open side without boards was at the east end.

The information that we do have beautifully conveys the thought intended by the holy writer. We have the description of a structure which was solid, dignified, and at the same time designed in a practical way so that it could be readily transported from place to place. One has to marvel at the wisdom of its entire concept, surely according to a plan devised by God and not by man.

The curtains

[31]**"Make a curtain of blue, purple and scarlet yarn and finely twisted linen, with cherubim worked into it by a skilled craftsman. [32]Hang it with gold hooks on four posts of acacia wood overlaid with gold and standing on four silver bases. [33]Hang the curtain from the clasps and place the ark of the Testimony behind the curtain. The curtain will separate the Holy Place from the Most Holy Place. [34]Put the atonement cover on the ark of the Testimony in the Most Holy Place. [35]Place the table outside the curtain on the north side of the tabernacle and put the lampstand opposite it on the south side.**

[36]**"For the entrance to the tent make a curtain of blue, purple and scarlet yarn and finely twisted linen—the work of an embroiderer. [37]Make gold hooks for this curtain and five posts of acacia wood overlaid with gold. And cast five bronze bases for them.**

A curtain was to divide the tabernacle interior into two parts. This curtain was to be made of the same material and design as the first curtain described in verse 1, with its beautiful colors and figures of cherubim worked into the material. It was to hang on gold hooks at a place where four pillars would separate the two compartments. These pillars were stationed at a distance of 30 feet (20 cubits) from the entrance to the tent, thus dividing the tabernacle into an inner room, which was a perfect cube (15 by 15 by 15 feet—in biblical terms, 10 by 10 by 10 cubits), and an outer room, which was rectangular (30 by 15 by 15 feet high—in biblical terms, 20 by 10 by 10 cubits).

The proportions of these two rooms are not given in these verses. They must be determined from a statement in verse 33: "Hang the [dividing] curtain from the clasps. . . ." Umberto Cassuto explains, "Since there were to be five curtains in front of the clasps (on the first of the coverings—cf. Exodus 26:1-6), and each one was to be four cubits wide, it will thus be seen that behind the veil there would remain a space ten cubits by ten cubits and ten cubits high" *(Commentary on the Book of Exodus,* page 360). Other scholars agree as to the size of these two rooms without explaining how they arrive at this conclusion. The proportions agree with those of Solomon's temple, which was twice the size.

The inner curtain separated the Holy Place from the Most Holy Place. The Most Holy Place contained the ark of the covenant; the Holy Place, the table of the bread of the Presence on the north side and the lampstand on the south side.

At the entrance to the tabernacle on its east side there was another veil of less elaborate workmanship. This was also hung on gold hooks. Five pillars were to be placed at this entrance.

The Most Holy Place (literally, "holy of holies") was that part of the tabernacle which the high priest entered once a year on the great Day of Atonement to make "atonement for himself, his household and the whole community of Israel" (Leviticus 16:17). The curtain between the Holy Place and the Most Holy Place signified that a sinful man was not to approach the most holy God except through the blood of atonement. When Christ died on the cross, this curtain in the temple at Jerusalem "was torn in two from top to bottom" (Matthew 27:51). Through his atoning sacrifice we have "peace with God" and "access by faith into this grace in which we now stand" (Romans 5:1,2). "He himself is our peace, who has made the two one and has destroyed the barrier, the dividing wall of hostility, by abolishing in his flesh the law with its commandments and regulations" (Ephesians 2:14,15). "Brothers, since we have confidence to enter the Most Holy Place by the blood of Jesus, by a new and living way opened for us through the curtain, that is, his body, and since we have a great priest over the house of God, let us draw near to God with a sincere heart in full assurance of faith" (Hebrews 10:19-22). How beautifully the Bible portrays the symbolical meaning of Old Testament worship and at the same time expresses our advantages as New Testament Christians!

The dimensions of the Most Holy Place are significant. The number 10 symbolizes completeness. As a perfect cube (10 by 10 by 10 cubits), the Most Holy Place is a picture of the heavenly Jerusalem, a "city . . . laid out like a square, as long as it was wide" (Revelation 21:16). This city of God is "the dwelling of God . . . with men" (verse 3). In olden times, the square was also a type of the world. Likewise the church of God was planted in Israel to embrace the entire world. Scripture complements Scripture. The Old Testament presents the type, or the shadow. The New Testament gives us the fulfillment, or the body itself. To the redeemed in Christ, the Lord says, "You have come to Mount Zion, to the heavenly Jerusalem, the city of the living God. You have come to thousands upon thousands of angels in joyful assembly, to the church of the firstborn, whose names are written in heaven" (Hebrews 12:22,23). Truly, also Old Testament believers were given a foretaste of their heavenly home!

The Holy Place, with its table and lampstand—and, as we will see later, also its altar of incense—was restricted to the priests for the performance of their duties. Here the lights of the lampstand were kept burning. Here the bread of the Presence was placed every Sabbath. Here the priests burned incense every morning and evening, symbolic of the prayers of believers. This was also separated from outside view and access by an ornamental curtain.

As we consider the provisions that the Lord gave Old Testament believers in their worship, we marvel at how graciously the Lord pictured for them their way to him as his very own covenant people. At the same time, we can't help being reminded of the unrestricted access we in New Testament times have through our Great High Priest, the Lord Jesus Christ, through whom we have been brought near to God and "have access to the Father by one Spirit" (Ephesians 2:18). "Through Jesus," as the writer of Hebrews encourages us, "let us continually offer to God a sacrifice of praise—the fruit of lips that confess his name. And do not forget to do good and to share with others, for with such sacrifices God is pleased" (13:15,16).

The altar of burnt offering

27 "Build an altar of acacia wood, three cubits high; it is to be square, five cubits long and five cubits wide. ²Make a horn at each of the four corners, so that the horns and the altar are of one piece, and overlay the altar with bronze. ³Make all its utensils of bronze—its pots to remove the ashes, and its shovels, sprinkling bowls, meat forks and firepans. ⁴Make a grating for it, a bronze network, and make a bronze ring at each of the four corners of the network. ⁵Put it under the ledge of the altar so that it is halfway up the altar. ⁶Make poles of acacia wood for the altar and overlay them with bronze. ⁷The poles are to be inserted into the rings so they will be on two sides of the altar when it is carried. ⁸Make the altar hollow, out of boards. It is to be made just as you were shown on the mountain.

The altar described in these verses was to stand in the courtyard, before the tabernacle entrance on the east side.

Basically, it was a hollow frame of acacia wood plated with bronze, 7½ feet square and 4½ feet in height (5 cubits square and 3 cubits high). A horn projected at each of the four corners.

Halfway up the altar was a network of bronze. Bronze rings were attached at the four corners of this network. Halfway up the altar was also a ledge that went around the altar on all sides.

Again scholars disagree as to the exact meaning of the verse that describes the network. We interpret this to mean that this item was not a grate inside the altar upon which the sacrifice rested, but rather a bronze network that was fastened vertically below the ledge, which extended around the altar. In other words, the grating supported the ledge and rested on the ground on all four sides. This network construction permitted air to enter from below and provided a draft for the fire on the altar. Thus the lower half of the altar was broader on every side than the upper half. The purpose of the ledge was to make it easier for the priests to perform their sacrificial duties at the altar.

Poles were specified for transporting the altar, to be inserted in the bronze rings. Various bronze utensils such as shovels, meat forks, sprinkling bowls, and fire pans were also mentioned. The altar was to be hollow for easy transport, but it could be filled with earth, gravel and stones when the altar was in use.

From the very beginning of worship as we find it reported in Scripture, altars play a significant role. Cain and Abel, we know, brought offerings to the Lord. Some type of altar must have served as the place for their offerings. After coming out of the ark, Noah's first act was to build an altar to the Lord and sacrifice burnt offerings on it as his expression of worship. Of Abram we read that "he built an altar to the Lord and called on the name of the Lord" (Genesis 12:8). In the tabernacle courtyard, the altar was the place where the many animal sacrifices outlined in the book of Leviticus were to be offered: burnt offerings for their daily worship, offerings for special occasions, thanksgiving and fellowship offerings, sin offerings for expiation and purification, and trespass offerings for specific sins requiring restitution (see Leviticus 1–7). According to Leviticus 6:12, the fire was kept burning on the altar continuously. It never went out while Israel was in an encampment and the tabernacle was erected for worship.

The horns on the altar had a special meaning. The Scriptures refer to the Lord as a rock, a shield, and a horn of salvation (Psalm 18:2). As Hannah, the mother of Samuel, rejoiced in the Lord, she sang, "In the Lord my horn is lifted high" (1 Samuel 2:1). As Zechariah, the father of John the Baptist, praised the Lord, he declared, "He has raised up a horn of salvation for us in the house of his servant David" (Luke 1:69). Just as the horn was used by certain animals as a weapon of defense against an enemy, so the horn was a symbol of the Lord's protecting care. One who accidentally killed another person could flee to the horns of the altar, cling to them, and find there a place of protection against the custom of revenge.

As Israel's altar provided a place for continual sacrifice to assure the people of the Lord's constant mercy and forgiveness, so we as New Testament Christians find assurance in our Savior Jesus Christ, who "loved us and gave himself up for us as a fragrant offering and sacrifice to God" (Ephesians 5:2). As the people of Israel demonstrated their thanks to God in bringing offerings to the Lord's altar, so Paul encourages the Christians in Rome, "Do not offer the parts of your body to sin, as instruments of wickedness, but rather offer yourselves to God, as those who have been brought from death to life; and offer the parts of your body to him as instruments of righteousness. For sin shall not be your master, because you are not under law, but under grace" (Romans 6:13,14).

The altar of sacrifice reminded Israel of atoning blood and a dedication of firstfruits, of God's grace and the believer's response to that grace. The cross of Christ reminds us of the precious price of our redemption through the blood of Christ and encourages us to live for him who died for us.

The courtyard

⁹"Make a courtyard for the tabernacle. The south side shall be a hundred cubits long and is to have curtains of finely twisted linen, ¹⁰with twenty posts and twenty bronze bases and with silver hooks and bands on the posts. ¹¹The north side shall also be a hundred cubits long and is to have curtains, with twenty posts and twenty bronze bases and with silver hooks and bands on the posts.

¹²"The west end of the courtyard shall be fifty cubits wide and have curtains, with ten posts and ten bases. ¹³On the east end, toward the sunrise, the courtyard shall also be fifty cubits wide. ¹⁴Curtains fifteen cubits long are to be on one side of the entrance, with three posts and three bases, ¹⁵and curtains fifteen cubits long are to be on the other side, with three posts and three bases.

¹⁶"For the entrance to the courtyard, provide a curtain twenty cubits long, of blue, purple and scarlet yarn and finely twisted linen—the work of an embroiderer—with four posts and four bases. ¹⁷All the posts around the courtyard are to have silver bands and hooks, and bronze bases. ¹⁸The courtyard shall be a hundred cubits long and fifty cubits wide, with curtains of finely twisted linen five cubits high, and with bronze bases. ¹⁹All the other articles used in the service of the tabernacle, whatever their function, including all the tent pegs for it and those for the courtyard, are to be of bronze.

²⁰"Command the Israelites to bring you clear oil of pressed olives for the light so that the lamps may be kept burning. ²¹In the

Tent of Meeting, outside the curtain that is in front of the Testimony, Aaron and his sons are to keep the lamps burning before the LORD from evening till morning. This is to be a lasting ordinance among the Israelites for the generations to come.

The courtyard surrounding the tabernacle was rectangular, 150 feet long by 75 feet wide (100 cubits long by 50 cubits wide). For purposes of comparison, it was about half as long as an American football field. The courtyard was enclosed by hangings of white linen, 5½ feet high, suspended on pillars. There were 20 pillars for each of the longer sides and 10 for the shorter ones. The pillars were made of bronze and set into bronze sockets. Silver hooks, cords, and bronze pins fastened the hangings securely. The court's entrance was on the east side, where a 30-foot place of entry was screened off with tapestry of blue, purple, and scarlet yarn and finely twisted linen. Clear olive oil of finest quality was to be provided by the people to keep the lamps in the tabernacle burning from evening till morning.

In the courtyard itself, toward the east entrance, was the place for the altar of burnt offering described in the first part of this chapter, as well as the bronze basin where the priests were to wash themselves before entering the tabernacle. Only people of the covenant were permitted to enter the courtyard as they brought their offerings and sacrifices to the Lord. Only the priests could enter the Holy Place in the tabernacle. And only the high priest could enter the Most Holy Place, and this only once a year, on the great Day of Atonement.

The following is a free translation of a German work. It is interesting because it draws a comparison between three great eras as pictured in the tabernacle and its courtyard.

> The tabernacle was the Lord's dwelling in the
> midst of his people. The Israelites were pre-

ferred before all other nations in that they, as the covenant people, had access to the courtyard of the tabernacle and were thereby especially close to God. Yet even not all Israelites could enter the tabernacle itself. Only through the mediation of priests was a closer access to the Lord permitted.

Although the priests could enter the Holy Place, only once a year could their high priest pass beyond the curtain into the Most Holy Place. When he sprinkled the blood on the atonement cover, he typified the reconciliation with God that was to be perfectly accomplished in the New Testament through the atoning blood of Christ.

Thus we see the tabernacle picturing a threefold division, with three steps, or ranks, of progression. First, there is the courtyard, representing the Old Testament congregation, which still needed a priesthood to mediate between itself and the Lord's blessings. The Holy Place represents the New Testament church, where because of Christ's finished work, all Christians are priests and can approach the Lord directly. Finally, the Most Holy Place pictures the heavenly congregation, which has reached its complete fulfillment in perfect fellowship with the Lord forever.

This is certainly an interesting comparison. As we worship the Lord in the beauty of his holiness and are reassured through Word and sacrament of his abiding presence with us, we recall the words of the writer of the book of Revelation in the Bible's closing verses: "He who testifies to these things says, 'Yes, I am coming soon.' Amen. Come, Lord Jesus. The grace of the Lord Jesus be with God's people. Amen" (22:20,21).

The priestly garments

28 "Have Aaron your brother brought to you from among the Israelites, along with his sons Nadab and Abihu, Eleazar and Ithamar, so they may serve me as priests. ²Make sacred garments for your brother Aaron, to give him dignity and honor. ³Tell all the skilled men to whom I have given wisdom in such matters that they are to make garments for Aaron, for his consecration, so he may serve me as priest. ⁴These are the garments they are to make: a breastpiece, an ephod, a robe, a woven tunic, a turban and a sash. They are to make these sacred garments for your brother Aaron and his sons, so they may serve me as priests. ⁵Have them use gold, and blue, purple and scarlet yarn, and fine linen.

The Lord had chosen Israel out of all nations to be his very own. He wanted the Israelites to be his holy people. They should live in fellowship with himself, a holy God. Israel, however, feared to approach the Lord directly. As the Lord gave the Ten Commandments on Mount Sinai, we read, "When the people saw the thunder and lightning and heard the trumpet and saw the mountain in smoke, they trembled with fear" (20:18). They asked Moses to be their mediator, their go-between.

While Moses agreed to serve as mediator to receive the law from the Lord, this very same law provided another way of mediation for the people in their Old Testament worship. That was through the institution of the priesthood. This was to be carried out by the tribe of Levi under the leadership of Aaron's family. In this chapter the Lord instructs Moses to bring forward Aaron and his four sons, Nadab, Abihu, Eleazar, and Ithamar to serve as priests. Aaron was to be the high priest, and this office was to be carried on through his family.

This chapter deals chiefly with instructions concerning the garments that the priests were to wear in their office. These garments were to be made by skilled men and woven of gold, blue, purple, and scarlet yarn together with fine linen.

The individual items of the high priest's clothing are described in the verses that follow.

The ephod

⁶"Make the ephod of gold, and of blue, purple and scarlet yarn, and of finely twisted linen—the work of a skilled craftsman. ⁷It is to have two shoulder pieces attached to two of its corners, so it can be fastened. ⁸Its skillfully woven waistband is to be like it—of one piece with the ephod and made with gold, and with blue, purple and scarlet yarn, and with finely twisted linen.

⁹"Take two onyx stones and engrave on them the names of the sons of Israel ¹⁰in the order of their birth—six names on one stone and the remaining six on the other. ¹¹Engrave the names of the sons of Israel on the two stones the way a gem cutter engraves a seal. Then mount the stones in gold filigree settings ¹²and fasten them on the shoulder pieces of the ephod as memorial stones for the sons of Israel. Aaron is to bear the names on his shoulders as a memorial before the LORD. ¹³Make gold filigree settings ¹⁴and two braided chains of pure gold, like a rope, and attach the chains to the settings.

The ephod was the most distinctive part of the high priest's clothing. In later Old Testament writings, whenever the "ephod" is referred to, it is associated with the high priest's special power to "inquire of the Lord," that is, to receive an answer from the Lord concerning some question or problem that was troubling Israel. The ephod had this significance because the Urim and Thummim was in the breastpiece attached to it. We will discuss these items later.

The ephod was a waistcoat or apron, made of the same material used to make the curtain in the sanctuary. Instead of figures of cherubim woven into it, however, it was worked through with gold thread. The ephod consisted of two pieces, front and back, joined at the shoulders by shoulder pieces. A waistband bound it together around the waist.

On each shoulder strap was an onyx stone, mounted in gold, upon which were engraved the names of the 12 tribes of Israel, 6 on each stone. This showed that the priest represented the people before the Lord. The names were engraved in the order of their birth. The historian Josephus takes this to mean that the names of the six elder sons were upon the right shoulder and the six younger sons on the left.

Attached to the shoulder pieces were two "braided chains of pure gold," woven like rope. Their purpose was to attach the breastpiece to the ephod from above. The breastpiece is described next.

The breastpiece

¹⁵"Fashion a breastpiece for making decisions—the work of a skilled craftsman. Make it like the ephod: of gold, and of blue, purple and scarlet yarn, and of finely twisted linen. ¹⁶It is to be square—a span long and a span wide—and folded double. ¹⁷Then mount four rows of precious stones on it. In the first row there shall be a ruby, a topaz and a beryl; ¹⁸in the second row a turquoise, a sapphire and an emerald; ¹⁹in the third row a jacinth, an agate and an amethyst; ²⁰in the fourth row a chrysolite, an onyx and a jasper. Mount them in gold filigree settings. ²¹There are to be twelve stones, one for each of the names of the sons of Israel, each engraved like a seal with the name of one of the twelve tribes.

²²"For the breastpiece make braided chains of pure gold, like a rope. ²³Make two gold rings for it and fasten them to two corners of the breastpiece. ²⁴Fasten the two gold chains to the rings at the cor-

ners of the breastpiece, ²⁵and the other ends of the chains to the two settings, attaching them to the shoulder pieces of the ephod at the front. ²⁶Make two gold rings and attach them to the other two corners of the breastpiece on the inside edge next to the ephod. ²⁷Make two more gold rings and attach them to the bottom of the shoulder pieces on the front of the ephod, close to the seam just above the waistband of the ephod. ²⁸The rings of the breastpiece are to be tied to the rings of the ephod with blue cord, connecting it to the waistband, so that the breastpiece will not swing out from the ephod.

²⁹"Whenever Aaron enters the Holy Place, he will bear the names of the sons of Israel over his heart on the breastpiece of decision as a continuing memorial before the LORD. ³⁰Also put the Urim and the Thummim in the breastpiece, so they may be over Aaron's heart whenever he enters the presence of the LORD. Thus Aaron will always bear the means of making decisions for the Israelites over his heart before the LORD.

The breastpiece was made of the same material as the ephod, but folded double to give it extra strength and provide a pouch. Its dimensions were 9 by 9 inches (a span measures about 9 inches). Twelve precious stones, four rows of three each, were fastened onto this breastpiece. Upon each stone was engraved the name of one of the twelve tribes of Israel. The types of precious stones to be used were individually specified, indicating the great care that the Lord required in making this breastpiece. Authorities differ as to the meaning of some of the words used to designate the types of stones.

The breastpiece, as mentioned before, was attached to the shoulder pieces by means of braided gold chains. At the bottom of the breastpiece, the same method was used to attach it to the waistband around the priest's waist.

According to the text, "the Urim and the Thummim" were put in the breastpiece so that they could be in a position "over Aaron's heart whenever he enters the presence of the LORD." To this day, Bible scholars don't know what

the Urim and Thummim really were. The words themselves seem to be plural forms of the Hebrew words *light*
and *right,* although there is not complete agreement upon
these interpretations. No description is given of them other
than that they were part of the breastpiece. The opinion
that makes the most sense was that these objects were
possibly stones which were to be kept in the pouch-like
pockets of the breastpiece. At times it seems that the
answer from the Lord through the Urim and Thummim
involved casting lots.

The text also states, "Thus Aaron will always bear the
means of making decisions for the Israelites over his heart
before the LORD." Although much concerning the procedure of how the Urim and Thummim were used is a mys-
tery, certain bits of information can be gathered from later
references in Scripture concerning its use:

- Only the person at the head of the people
  was able to make inquiry of the Lord through
  the priest (Joshua, Numbers 27:21; Saul,
  1 Samuel 14:37; David, 1 Samuel 23:2).

- The question had to be formulated in such a
  way as to make only a yes or no answer possible. The Lord's answer was given only to
  one question at a time.

- In some circumstances, when things were
  not in order, the Lord refused to give answer
  through the Urim and Thummim (1 Samuel
  14:37).

At times, no specific reference is made to the Urim and
Thummim but only to the use of the ephod or to "inquiring
of the Lord" through the priest. After David's time, we do
not find any further references to their use.

Other priestly garments

³¹"Make the robe of the ephod entirely of blue cloth, ³²with an opening for the head in its center. There shall be a woven edge like a collar around this opening, so that it will not tear. ³³Make pomegranates of blue, purple and scarlet yarn around the hem of the robe, with gold bells between them. ³⁴The gold bells and the pomegranates are to alternate around the hem of the robe. ³⁵Aaron must wear it when he ministers. The sound of the bells will be heard when he enters the Holy Place before the LORD and when he comes out, so that he will not die.

³⁶"Make a plate of pure gold and engrave on it as on a seal: HOLY TO THE LORD. ³⁷Fasten a blue cord to it to attach it to the turban; it is to be on the front of the turban. ³⁸It will be on Aaron's forehead, and he will bear the guilt involved in the sacred gifts the Israelites consecrate, whatever their gifts may be. It will be on Aaron's forehead continually so that they will be acceptable to the LORD.

³⁹"Weave the tunic of fine linen and make the turban of fine linen. The sash is to be the work of an embroiderer. ⁴⁰Make tunics, sashes and headbands for Aaron's sons, to give them dignity and honor. ⁴¹After you put these clothes on your brother Aaron and his sons, anoint and ordain them. Consecrate them so they may serve me as priests.

⁴²"Make linen undergarments as a covering for the body, reaching from the waist to the thigh. ⁴³Aaron and his sons must wear them whenever they enter the Tent of Meeting or approach the altar to minister in the Holy Place, so that they will not incur guilt and die.

"This is to be a lasting ordinance for Aaron and his descendants.

The priest's robe worn underneath the ephod was woven of one piece of blue cloth, having armholes but no sleeves. It reached only to the knees. On the lower hem were small golden bells alternating with pomegranates made of twisted yarn. (The pomegranate fruit is about the size of an apple, yellow or pink in color, and was commonly grown in that area.) Only Aaron as high priest could wear this attire. Aaron was not to appear before the Lord without this robe and its sound of bells. Failure to wear this garment would result in his death.

There are various interpretations about the symbolical meaning of these bells and pomegranates. The simplest meaning is, no doubt, the best. The high priest was to approach the presence of the Lord with the sound of bells— that is, with all due respect, not suddenly or irreverently— wearing the exact attire prescribed by the Lord himself. These things were a constant reminder to him of his high office and responsibility as the representative of the Lord's people. Similarly, every Israelite was to wear a fringe on the border of his garment to remember the Commandments of the Lord and keep them.

As a headdress the high priest was to wear a turban of fine white linen. Affixed to the front of this turban was a gold plate with the words "HOLY TO THE LORD" engraved upon it. The purpose of this sign upon his forehead was that Aaron should "bear the guilt involved in the sacred gifts the Israelites consecrate." The high priest was the atoning mediator between the people and the Lord. Whatever gifts and sacrifices the sinful people brought to the Lord in their acts of worship were made acceptable through his mediation.

By way of contrast, we remember that Christ, our Great High Priest, wore as his headdress a crown of thorns as he bore the guilt of all mankind. His was a perfect atonement for the sins of the world.

A tunic of fine linen was to complete the high priest's outer garments. This was a long-sleeved garment reaching to the ankles, worn beneath the robe. The ordinary priests were also to wear this white tunic, with a sash and headband not otherwise described. Their clothing was simple yet dignified.

Beneath the tunic, Aaron and the priests were to wear linen breeches as undergarments. They were not to enter the sanctuary or approach the altar to perform sacrificial acts without these garments. Failure to do so would bring the death penalty. Their nakedness should be covered. Among the surrounding heathen nations, it was customary to perform religious rites in a state of nakedness. In the service of the true God, absolute modesty was a strict requirement.

This brings to a close the ordinances pertaining to the priestly garments in the Old Testament service of worship. We note the rich symbolism of their inscribed shoulder pieces, their gem-filled breastpiece, their mysterious Urim and Thummim, their bells and pomegranates, and their golden engraved headpiece. With their finely woven fabrics, their braided chains, and their overall design, these garments were beautiful and dignified at the same time. The Lord himself designed them so that his people could ascribe to him the glory due his name and worship him in the splendor of his holiness.

Our pastoral garments in New Testament times are less elaborate. Our way of dispensing the Lord's gifts of grace is surrounded with far less ceremony and symbolism. Some pastors prefer to hide their person by wearing a simple black robe. Others cover this robe with a white surplice, stole, or a long, narrow scarf with fringed ends, often colored according to the church's seasons. Pastors use these differing garments in Christian liberty and according to the wishes of the congregation served. Whatever is used should reflect the dignity of our worship and be to the glory of God.

Consecration of the priests

29 "This is what you are to do to consecrate them, so they may serve me as priests: Take a young bull and two rams without defect. ²And from fine wheat flour, without yeast, make bread, and cakes mixed with oil, and wafers spread with oil. ³Put them in a basket and present them in it—along with the bull and the two rams. ⁴Then bring Aaron and his sons to the entrance to the Tent of Meeting and wash them with water. ⁵Take the garments and dress Aaron with the tunic, the robe of the ephod, the ephod itself and the breastpiece. Fasten the ephod on him by its skillfully woven waistband. ⁶Put the turban on his head and attach the sacred diadem to the turban. ⁷Take the anointing oil and anoint him by pouring it on his head. ⁸Bring his sons and dress them in tunics ⁹and put headbands on them. Then tie sashes on Aaron and his sons. The priesthood is theirs by a lasting ordinance. In this way you shall ordain Aaron and his sons.

In this chapter we are told how the priests were to be consecrated for their special service in the tabernacle. The ceremony as it is described is very elaborate and impressive. In Leviticus chapter 8 we are told how every one of these directions was carried out as the priests were inducted into their office. From Leviticus we can also gain further insight into the significance of each kind of sacrifice.

The first verses here list the items that were to be in the ceremony: a young bull, two rams, bread without yeast, cakes mixed with oil, wafers spread with oil.

The next verses explain how Aaron and his sons were to be brought forward to the entrance of the tabernacle, washed with water, and clothed in their holy garments (as described in the previous chapter). Aaron was to be anointed with oil as a token of his office as high priest. This part of the ceremony was symbolic of the spiritual cleansing of the priests, especially the figurative imparting of the Lord's Holy Spirit upon the high priest by anointing him with oil.

The sin offering

¹⁰"Bring the bull to the front of the Tent of Meeting, and Aaron and his sons shall lay their hands on its head. ¹¹Slaughter it in the

LORD's presence at the entrance to the Tent of Meeting. ¹²Take some of the bull's blood and put it on the horns of the altar with your finger, and pour out the rest of it at the base of the altar. ¹³Then take all the fat around the inner parts, the covering of the liver, and both kidneys with the fat on them, and burn them on the altar. ¹⁴But burn the bull's flesh and its hide and its offal outside the camp. It is a sin offering.

After the cleansing of Aaron and his sons and the anointing of Aaron, the bull was to be brought forward as the next part of the consecration ceremony. Aaron and his sons were to place their hands on the bull's head to show how their sins were transferred to the animal that was to be sacrificed. The bull was then slaughtered "in the LORD's presence at the entrance to the Tent of Meeting." Some of the blood was put on the horns of the altar of burnt offering, which was in the courtyard. The rest of the blood was dashed against the base of the altar.

The purpose of this bloody sacrifice was to show that the Lord accepted the death of the animal for the atonement of Aaron's sins. In Leviticus we are told the significance of the use of blood: "The life of a creature is in the blood, and I have given it to you to make atonement for yourselves on the altar; it is the blood that makes atonement for one's life" (17:11).

The fat, the covering of the liver, and the kidneys were to be burned on the altar. The bull's flesh, its hide, and its offal were to be burned outside the camp. Thus the better parts were to be part of the sacrifice for sin to be offered to the Lord as a fragrance pleasing to him.

The writer of Hebrews calls attention to the fact that Jesus, our Great High Priest, "suffered outside the city gate [of Jerusalem] to make the people holy through his own blood" (13:12). He then encourages his people, "Let us, then, go to him outside the camp, bearing the disgrace he bore. For here we do not have an enduring city, but we are looking for the city that is to come" (verses 13,14). Jesus, as our perfect sacrifice for sin, did not need to offer sacrifices first for his own sins, as required of the Old Testament high priests. His sacrifice was offered once for all when he offered himself on the cross of Calvary. He suffered shame and disgrace as he bore upon himself the sins of the world.

The ram of dedication

[15]"**Take one of the rams, and Aaron and his sons shall lay their hands on its head. **[16]**Slaughter it and take the blood and sprinkle it against the altar on all sides. **[17]**Cut the ram into pieces and wash the inner parts and the legs, putting them with the head and the other pieces. **[18]**Then burn the entire ram on the altar. It is a burnt offering to the LORD, a pleasing aroma, an offering made to the LORD by fire.**

One of the two rams was to be used at the consecration service as a whole burnt offering. The ritual of the preparation and the use of blood for this offering was according to the rules prescribed later in Leviticus chapter 1. This offering, in which the entire flesh of the animal was burned on the altar, signified an act of complete dedication to the Lord and to his service. Thus the Old Testament priests were to be entirely dedicated to the service of the Lord.

This type of sacrifice reminds us of the words of Paul, who encourages Christians to dedicate themselves as the Lord's New Testament priests in the following way: "I urge you, brothers, in view of God's mercy, to offer your bodies as living sacrifices, holy and pleasing to God—this is your spiritual act of worship. Do not conform any longer to the pattern of this world, but be transformed by the renewing of your mind. Then you will be able to test and approve what God's will is—his good, pleasing and perfect will" (Romans 12:1,2).

An act of dedication meant devoting oneself entirely to the Lord's service. It was not to be a half-hearted kind of service. How well this type of sacrifice in the Old Testament pictured such total dedication!

The ram of ordination

¹⁹"Take the other ram, and Aaron and his sons shall lay their hands on its head. ²⁰Slaughter it, take some of its blood and put it on the lobes of the right ears of Aaron and his sons, on the thumbs of their right hands, and on the big toes of their right feet. Then sprinkle blood against the altar on all sides. ²¹And take some of the blood on the altar and some of the anointing oil and sprinkle it on Aaron and his garments and on his sons and their garments. Then he and his sons and their garments will be consecrated.

²²"Take from this ram the fat, the fat tail, the fat around the inner parts, the covering of the liver, both kidneys with the fat on them, and the right thigh. (This is the ram for the ordination.) ²³From the basket of bread made without yeast, which is before the LORD, take a loaf, and a cake made with oil, and a wafer. ²⁴Put all these in the hands of Aaron and his sons and wave them before the LORD as a wave offering. ²⁵Then take them from their hands and burn them on the altar along with the burnt offering for a pleasing aroma to the LORD, an offering made to the LORD by fire. ²⁶After you take the breast of the ram for Aaron's ordination, wave it before the LORD as a wave offering, and it will be your share.

²⁷"Consecrate those parts of the ordination ram that belong to Aaron and his sons: the breast that was waved and the thigh that was presented. ²⁸This is always to be the regular share from the Israelites for Aaron and his sons. It is the contribution the Israelites are to make to the LORD from their fellowship offerings.

The ram specified in this service as the "ram for the ordination" was used in a very special way. Some of the animal's blood was put on the lobes of the right ears of Aaron and his sons, on the thumbs of their right hands, and on the toes of their right feet. With the ear the priest was to hear the word of the Lord; with the hand he was to perform his tasks properly; with the foot he was to walk correctly in the sanctuary. These items of the priest's body, therefore, were especially sanctified for service to the Lord. The rest of the blood, together with the oil, was dashed against the altar and sprinkled on Aaron and his sons and their garments. Oil was a symbol of the Spirit of God. Thus in body, soul, and spirit, these men were sanctified for the Lord's spiritual service. Even their garments were set apart for the service of the Lord.

The fat parts of this ram, the covering of the liver, the kidneys, and the right thigh were taken together with the unleavened bread, the cake made with oil, and the wafers and were waved before the Lord "as a wave offering." Then these items were to be burned on the altar "for a pleasing aroma to the LORD." The breast of the ram was also to be waved before the Lord, and the breast and the right thigh to be given to Aaron and his sons as their share.

This type of offering is later referred to in Leviticus chapter 3 as a "fellowship offering," or also a "peace offering." It was used to give glory to the Lord on special occasions of dedication and thanksgiving, and the giving of a part to the priest signified God's fellowship with his people through their representatives.

The expression "wave offering" has been explained by the Jews in their Talmud as an act of moving back and forth, first toward the Lord and again back toward the priest, signifying fellowship between the two parties in this sacrificial act. In this case a part of the "wave offering" was given back to the priest to indicate that the Lord shared his gifts with the officiating priests, also in an act of fellowship. The breast was "waved" and the thigh was "presented" (lifted up and returned) as the priest's share of the fellowship offering.

The sacrificial meal

[29]"Aaron's sacred garments will belong to his descendants so that they can be anointed and ordained in them. [30]The son who succeeds him as priest and comes to the Tent of Meeting to minister in the Holy Place is to wear them seven days.

[31]"Take the ram for the ordination and cook the meat in a sacred place. [32]At the entrance to the Tent of Meeting, Aaron and his sons are to eat the meat of the ram and the bread that is in the basket. [33]They are to eat these offerings by which atonement was made for their ordination and consecration. But no one else may eat them, because they are sacred. [34]And if any of the meat of the ordination ram or any bread is left over till morning, burn it up. It must not be eaten, because it is sacred.

[35]"Do for Aaron and his sons everything I have commanded you, taking seven days to ordain them. [36]Sacrifice a bull each day as a sin offering to make atonement. Purify the altar by making atonement for it, and anoint it to consecrate it. [37]For seven days make atonement for the altar and consecrate it. Then the altar will be most holy, and whatever touches it will be holy.

The Lord adds a number of regulations here.

Aaron's priestly garments were to be passed on from generation to generation. (We note how carefully this was observed at the time of Aaron's death, recorded in Numbers 20:22-29, when Aaron's garments were passed on to his son Eleazar on Mount Hor.)

The ordination ceremony of priests was to take seven days, and on each successive day the entire service as previously described was to be repeated. On each of the seven days, the altar also was to be consecrated to the service of the Lord. How could Israel ever forget the solemnity of this occasion as well as its significance!

An added feature in these verses in connection with the ordination service for the priests was the sacrificial meal. The part of the ram received by Aaron, that is, the breast and the thigh, together with the unleavened bread brought in the basket, were to be eaten by Aaron and his sons at the entrance to the tabernacle. This too was a token of fellowship, a common meal in the presence of the Lord. As New Testament Christians, we have a "communion," a fellowship meal, as we celebrate the Lord's Supper. As we receive the true body and blood of Christ for the forgiveness of our sins, we have the assurance of fellowship with our Savior-God as well as with our fellow Christians. The apostle Paul writes, "Is not the cup of thanksgiving for which we give thanks a participation in the blood of Christ? And is not the bread that we break a participation in the body of Christ? Because there is one loaf, we, who are many, are one body, for we all partake of the one loaf" (1 Corinthians 10:16,17).

With these verses the part of the chapter describing the ordination service of the priests is brought to a close.

The daily sacrifice

³⁸"This is what you are to offer on the altar regularly each day: two lambs a year old. ³⁹Offer one in the morning and the other at twilight. ⁴⁰With the first lamb offer a tenth of an ephah of fine flour mixed with a quarter of a hin of oil from pressed olives, and a quarter of a hin of wine as a drink offering. ⁴¹Sacrifice the other lamb at twilight with the same grain offering and its drink offering as in the morning—a pleasing aroma, an offering made to the LORD by fire.

⁴²"For the generations to come this burnt offering is to be made regularly at the entrance to the Tent of Meeting before the LORD. There I will meet you and speak to you; ⁴³there also I will meet with the Israelites, and the place will be consecrated by my glory.

⁴⁴"So I will consecrate the Tent of Meeting and the altar and will consecrate Aaron and his sons to serve me as priests. ⁴⁵Then I will dwell among the Israelites and be their God. ⁴⁶They will know that I am the LORD their God, who brought them out of Egypt so that I might dwell among them. I am the LORD their God.

The directions concerning the daily offerings to be brought at the tabernacle are attached here, immediately after the instructions for the consecration of the priests, because these offerings were a part of the tabernacle service, which was constantly repeated.

Every morning and every evening, a lamb was to be offered together with a grain offering. More exact instructions concerning these offerings are given in the book of Leviticus. These offerings were to be "a pleasing aroma, an offering made to the Lord by fire." The entire offering of these items was to be consumed by fire on the altar. These daily offerings signified that Israel was to consecrate its daily life to the Lord. The Lord, in turn, promised his abiding presence with his people. Here the Lord would also manifest his glorious presence to his people.

For Israel, service to the Lord as his covenant people was a daily matter. How clearly this morning and evening service should have served to impress upon them this constant, daily rededication to the Lord! The Lord was not only to be remembered in time of special need or at special occasions. His presence among them was never failing, just as their service to him was a daily expression of their devotion to him.

If this was true of Israel in Old Testament times, how much more should this be true of us today! Our morning and evening prayers are not prescribed by law. They should be a free expression of our constant dependence upon that gracious Lord, in whom we live and move and have our being. One of our hymns expresses this for us so well:

> With the Lord begin your task; Jesus will direct it.
> For his aid and counsel ask; Jesus will perfect it.
> Ev'ry morn with Jesus rise, and, when day is
>   ended,
> In his name then close your eyes;
>   be to him commended. (CW 478:1)

The altar of incense

30 "Make an altar of acacia wood for burning incense. ²It is to be square, a cubit long and a cubit wide, and two cubits high—its horns of one piece with it. ³Overlay the top and all the sides and the horns with pure gold, and make a gold molding around it. ⁴Make two gold rings for the altar below the molding— two on opposite sides—to hold the poles used to carry it. Make the poles of acacia wood and overlay them with gold. ⁶Put the altar in front of the curtain that is before the ark of the Testimony—before the atonement cover that is over the Testimony—where I will meet with you.

⁷"Aaron must burn fragrant incense on the altar every morning when he tends the lamps. ⁸He must burn incense again when he lights the lamps at twilight so incense will burn regularly before the LORD for the generations to come. ⁹Do not offer on this altar any other incense or any burnt offering or grain offering, and do not pour a drink offering on it. ¹⁰Once a year Aaron shall make atonement on its horns. This annual atonement must be made with the blood of the atoning sin offering for the generations to come. It is most holy to the LORD."

The altar described in these verses is also called the "gold altar" in 39:38. It was small in size, 1½ feet square and 3 feet high (1 cubit square and 2 cubits high). It was to be made of acacia wood overlaid with pure gold. There were to be four horns on each upper corner, a gold molding around the top, and gold rings on each side to facilitate carrying it with poles. Its position was to be in the Holy Place, in front of the curtain that separated the Holy Place from the Most Holy Place. Thus it stood in close relation to the ark of the covenant—so close, in fact, that it is referred to in several passages as belonging to the inner sanctuary. Its position could not have been in the Most Holy Place, however, since it was used daily.

Every morning and evening, Aaron was to burn fragrant incense upon this altar. Although no other type of sacrifice was to be burned on it, Aaron was to "make atonement on its horns" once a year, on the great Day of Atonement. This act was performed in order to "cleanse it [the altar] and to consecrate it from the uncleanness of the Israelites" (Leviticus 16:19).

Many of us are acquainted with the following response from the Order of Vespers, or evening service, of our churches:

> Let my prayer rise before you as incense,
> the lifting up of my hands as the evening sacrifice.
>
> (CW, page 55)

This response is based upon Psalm 141:2, which relates the use of incense as being symbolic of prayer. The book of Revelation also speaks of the 24 elders failing down before the Lamb: "Each one had a harp and they were holding golden bowls full of incense, which are the prayers of the saints" (5:8). As the smoke from the incense rises to the Lord, so the prayers of his people are to rise continually to him as a fragrant aroma.

The Bible in 1 Thessalonians 5:17,18 encourages Christians to "pray continually" and to "give thanks in all circumstances." Moreover, 1 Timothy 2:1 encourages us that "requests, prayers, intercession and thanksgiving be made for everyone." Finally, Paul declares that "in everything, by prayer and petition, with thanksgiving" we should present our requests to God (Philippians 4:6). An appropriate time for this is every morning and evening, as the Lord directed his Old Testament people to do every day at the altar of incense.

Atonement money

¹¹Then the LORD said to Moses, ¹²"When you take a census of the Israelites to count them, each one must pay the LORD a ransom for his life at the time he is counted. Then no plague will come on them when you number them. ¹³Each one who crosses over to those

already counted is to give a half shekel, according to the sanctuary shekel, which weighs twenty gerahs. This half shekel is an offering to the LORD. ¹⁴All who cross over, those twenty years old or more, are to give an offering to the LORD. ¹⁵The rich are not to give more than a half shekel and the poor are not to give less when you make the offering to the LORD to atone for your lives. ¹⁶Receive the atonement money from the Israelites and use it for the service of the Tent of Meeting. It will be a memorial for the Israelites before the LORD, making atonement for your lives.

Each Israelite male of 20 years and older was required to pay a half shekel to the Lord whenever a census was taken. This was looked upon as "a ransom for his life." Israel was thus reminded of its sinfulness by nature, and that it could remain as God's covenant people only by the Lord's grace, which covered its sin. In order to cover this sin, the Lord directed how payment was to be made.

At age 20 Israelite males were considered ready for military service. Rich and poor alike were to pay the same amount. The offering was to be used for the tabernacle service. The amount paid, a half shekel, comes to about ⅕ ounce, probably of silver.

We hear of an unauthorized census that was taken by David in 2 Samuel chapter 24, and because of it, a terrible plague as threatened in these verses came upon the people. Although no explanation is given as to why God punished Israel so severely on that occasion, it is possible that David overlooked some regulation pertaining to this law.

We in New Testament times were redeemed, as Peter reminds us, "not with perishable things such as silver or gold . . . but with the precious blood of Christ" (1 Peter 1:18,19).

Basin for washing

¹⁷Then the LORD said to Moses, ¹⁸"Make a bronze basin, with its bronze stand, for washing. Place it between the Tent of Meeting

and the altar, and put water in it. ¹⁹Aaron and his sons are to wash their hands and feet with water from it. ²⁰Whenever they enter the Tent of Meeting, they shall wash with water so that they will not die. Also, when they approach the altar to minister by presenting an offering made to the LORD by fire, ²¹they shall wash their hands and feet so that they will not die. This is to be a lasting ordinance for Aaron and his descendants for the generations to come."

The basin described here was placed in the courtyard between the altar for burnt offering and the tabernacle. No description of the size or shape is given. Here the priests were to wash their hands and their feet whenever they performed their sacred duties or entered the tabernacle. Those who neglected to do this would die.

Anointing oil and incense

²²Then the LORD said to Moses, ²³"Take the following fine spices: 500 shekels of liquid myrrh, half as much (that is, 250 shekels) of fragrant cinnamon, 250 shekels of fragrant cane, ²⁴500 shekels of cassia—all according to the sanctuary shekel—and a hin of olive oil. ²⁵Make these into a sacred anointing oil, a fragrant blend, the work of a perfumer. It will be the sacred anointing oil. ²⁶Then use it to anoint the Tent of Meeting, the ark of the Testimony, ²⁷the table and all its articles, the lampstand and its accessories, the altar of incense, ²⁸the altar of burnt offering and all its utensils, and the basin with its stand. ²⁹You shall consecrate them so they will be most holy, and whatever touches them will be holy.

³⁰"Anoint Aaron and his sons and consecrate them so they may serve me as priests. ³¹Say to the Israelites, 'This is to be my sacred anointing oil for the generations to come. ³²Do not pour it on men's bodies and do not make any oil with the same formula. It is sacred, and you are to consider it sacred. ³³Whoever makes perfume like it and whoever puts it on anyone other than a priest must be cut off from his people.'"

³⁴"Then the LORD said to Moses, "Take fragrant spices—gum resin, onycha and galbanum—and pure frankincense, all in equal amounts, ³⁵and make a fragrant blend of incense, the work of a per-

fumer. **It is to be salted and pure and sacred. ³⁶Grind some of it to powder and place it in front of the Testimony in the Tent of Meeting, where I will meet with you. It shall be most holy to you. ³⁷Do not make any incense with this formula for yourselves; consider it holy to the LORD. ³⁸Whoever makes any like it to enjoy its fragrance must be cut off from his people."**

Notice the special formula for oil to be used when anointing the tabernacle and its furnishings as well as the priests. Myrrh is resin from a tree not native to Palestine. Liquid myrrh as specified here was a very precious substance. Mixed with the other sweet-smelling and highly aromatic items (cinnamon, cane, and cassia), some of which came from Arabia and India, the resulting oil must have been difficult to prepare and very costly, indeed. It was not to be used for any other purpose, such as anointing the human body, under penalty of death.

Anointing with oil in the Old Testament was always symbolic of bestowing the gift of the Holy Spirit or setting something aside for a highly spiritual purpose in the Lord's service. Prophets, priests, and kings were inducted into office by anointing them with oil.

The incense to be used in Old Testament worship was also carefully prescribed. Its private use was also forbidden. This was to be burned on the altar of incense described at the beginning of this chapter. Some of the items mentioned (such as frankincense) were obtainable only in southern Arabia. Onycha came from a sea animal along the coasts of the Red Sea.

The fragrance of the oil and the incense was to give the tabernacle a distinctive odor, one which was a constant reminder of the Lord's presence. No detail of the tabernacle, not even the kind of oil and incense used, was left to the imagination of people.

Bezalel and Oholiab

31 Then the Lord said to Moses, ²"See, I have chosen Bezalel son of Uri, the son of Hur, of the tribe of Judah, ³and I have filled him with the Spirit of God, with skill, ability and knowledge in all kinds of crafts—⁴to make artistic designs for work in gold, silver and bronze, ⁵to cut and set stones, to work in wood, and to engage in all kinds of craftsmanship. ⁶Moreover, I have appointed Oholiab son of Ahisamach, of the tribe of Dan, to help him. Also I have given skill to all the craftsmen to make everything I have commanded you: ⁷the Tent of Meeting, the ark of the Testimony with the atonement cover on it, and all the other furnishings of the tent—⁸the table and its articles, the pure gold lampstand and all its accessories, the altar of incense, ⁹the altar of burnt offering and all its utensils, the basin with its stand—¹⁰and also the woven garments, both the sacred garments for Aaron the priest and the garments for his sons when they serve as priests, ¹¹and the anointing oil and fragrant incense for the Holy Place. They are to make them just as I commanded you."

The directions for the construction of the tabernacle were now complete. But the Lord's instructions to Moses were not finished. The Lord also told Moses which two men were to supervise the building of the tabernacle, its furnishings, and all its appointments. The Lord promised that he had given these men and their helpers special skills to carry out the work just as he had commanded Moses.

Bezalel of the tribe of Judah was chosen by the Lord to be the master builder; Oholiab of the tribe of Dan, his chief helper.

Once again we see how nothing that had to do with the building of the tabernacle and all its contents was left to chance. The craftsmen also were endowed by the Lord with special skills to do the work just as the Lord had prescribed it. This was the Lord's house. He would dwell there with his people. Everything connected with this place should therefore be dignified, meaningful, and made exactly according to the Lord's specifications.

The Lord was serious also about preserving the beauty of his dwelling place. We know how angry the Lord Jesus became when the beauty of the temple in Jerusalem was marred by those who conducted business in its courtyard. He drove such people out with a whip, and upset the tables of those exchanging money there.

Our places of worship are less elaborate in their design. We do not have to observe all the ceremonial laws of the Old Testament. And yet we want our churches to be dignified, expressing our love to the Lord. We too are privileged to give glory to his holy name for his bountiful gifts of grace.

The Sabbath

¹²Then the LORD said to Moses, ¹³"Say to the Israelites, 'You must observe my Sabbaths. This will be a sign between me and you for the generations to come, so you may know that I am the LORD, who makes you holy.

¹⁴"Observe the Sabbath, because it is holy to you. Anyone who desecrates it must be put to death; whoever does any work on that day must be cut off from his people. ¹⁵For six days, work is to be done, but the seventh day is a Sabbath of rest, holy to the LORD. Whoever does any work on the Sabbath day must be put to death. ¹⁶The Israelites are to observe the Sabbath, celebrating it for the generations to come as a lasting covenant. ¹⁷It will be a sign between me and the Israelites forever, for in six days the LORD made the heavens and the earth, and on the seventh day he abstained from work and rested.'"

At the close of these directions concerning the building of the tabernacle, the Lord once more impresses upon the Israelites through Moses the importance of careful observance of the Sabbath regulations. The Sabbath, on the seventh day of the week, was to be kept as a "sign" between the Lord and his people "for the generations to come."

The word *sabbath* is a Hebrew word meaning "rest." No work, as we remember from chapter 20, was to be done on that day. Anyone who broke this law was to be put to death. In Numbers 15:32-36 we are told of a man who gathered firewood on the Sabbath Day. He was taken outside the camp of the Israelites and stoned to death.

We read that the Sabbath law was to be a "lasting covenant." It was to be a sign between the Lord and the Israelites "forever." Do these words state that we in our day should still observe these Sabbath regulations? Are the Seventh-Day Adventists right when they condemn us for worshiping on a Sunday? When Jesus came, he declared himself to be the Lord of the Sabbath Day. He abolished all the ceremonial regulations of the Old Testament by his work of redemption. "Therefore do not let anyone judge you by what you eat or drink, or with regard to a religious festival, a New Moon celebration or a Sabbath day," Paul writes to the Colossians. "These are a shadow of the things that were to come; the reality, however, is found in Christ" (Colossians 2:16,17).

In what sense, then, are we to understand the Sabbath law as a "lasting covenant" that should endure "forever"? Simply in the light of Christ's perfect fulfillment of the Sabbath. After the completion of his work of redemption, the Lord also rested on the Sabbath. But he rose again on the following day as a pledge to the world that his work was finished. In remembrance of his mighty victory over sin, death and hell, we celebrate his resurrection day as our "Lord's day" until we can enjoy that eternal Sabbath rest in heaven, as described in Hebrews chapter 4.

The tablets of the Testimony

[18]**When the LORD finished speaking to Moses on Mount Sinai, he gave him the two tablets of the Testimony, the tablets of stone inscribed by the finger of God.**

When all the instructions concerning the tabernacle were received by Moses, the Lord gave him "the two tablets of the Testimony." These were the two tablets of stone upon which the Ten Commandments were written. According to 32:15,16 God himself supplied the tablets and inscribed them on both sides. These Commandments were the holy law of God. The Lord wanted them to be preserved. The tablets were "inscribed by the finger of God." The writing upon the tablets, in other words, was by a divine miracle.

We have previously discussed the numbering of the Commandments, under chapter 20, and how church bodies have different opinions concerning this. We speak of those Commandments which refer to our love to God as being on the first of these two tablets and the Commandments which refer to our love to our neighbor as being on the second tablet. We do this because Moses sums up the Commandments in this way in Deuteronomy 6:5 and Leviticus 19:18, and because Christ himself makes this distinction in Matthew 22:37-40. According to our numbering of the Commandments in the Lutheran church, we place the first three Commandments on the first tablet and the last seven on the second tablet.

While Moses was on Mount Sinai 40 days and 40 nights receiving all these instructions from the Lord, the Israelites became impatient and rebelled against the one who had been so gracious to them.

The golden calf

32 **When the people saw that Moses was so long in coming down from the mountain, they gathered around Aaron and said, "Come, make us gods who will go before us. As for this fellow Moses who brought us up out of Egypt, we don't know what has happened to him."**

²**Aaron answered them, "Take off the gold earrings that your wives, your sons and your daughters are wearing, and bring them to me." ³So all the people took off their earrings and brought them to Aaron. ⁴He took what they handed him and made it into an idol cast in the shape of a calf, fashioning it with a tool. Then they said, "These are your gods, O Israel, who brought you up out of Egypt."**

⁵**When Aaron saw this, he built an altar in front of the calf and announced, "Tomorrow there will be a festival to the LORD." ⁶So the next day the people rose early and sacrificed burnt offerings and presented fellowship offerings. Afterward they sat down to eat and drink and got up to indulge in revelry.**

In his *Bible History Commentary,* Werner Franzmann refers to Israel's worship of the golden calf as "the incredible sin"—truly incredible, taking place just after the Lord had made a covenant with his chosen people. Franzmann comments, "The greatest sin is possible for sin-corrupted men. . . . What is truly incredible in this story is the grace of the Lord" (page 264).

We appreciate Franzmann's forthright way of calling a sin by its right name and not attempting to excuse Israel's guilt in any way. Many Bible scholars try to excuse Israel by claiming that the people still imagined that they were worshiping the true God, except in another form. Even if this were true, it would still be breaking God's express command given in 20:4,5. Perhaps Aaron tried to cover the seriousness of Israel's sin by saying, "Tomorrow there will be a festival to the *LORD*" after he made the golden calf.

Yes, Aaron used the name "LORD" (Yahweh). But the Israelites leave no question in our minds concerning their desires in the story that follows. We see this in their eating and drinking and in their indulgence in revelry as a part of their "worship" of this idol. When referring to this incident in 1 Corinthians 10:7, the apostle Paul clearly calls the Israelites "idolaters." Stephen does the same in his speech to the Jewish court, recorded in Acts 7:41. The psalmist has this to say in Psalm 106:19-21:

> At Horeb they made a calf
>> and worshiped an idol cast from metal.
> They exchanged their Glory
>> for an image of a bull, which eats grass.
> They forgot the God who saved them,
>> who had done great things in Egypt.

As their revelry reached its height, as we see later on when Moses came down from Mount Sinai, their behavior went out of control. Incredible? Yes, especially in the light of the amazing grace that these people had experienced at the hand of their Savior-God, who had rescued them from slavery, who had manifested his glory to them in so many ways. He had even made a covenant with them and was at that very moment explaining to Moses the way in which they were to worship him as the kings and priests of this covenant. Yet as Scripture so often reminds us, sin strikes when it is least expected, and it is committed also by those who have experienced the Lord's abundant mercy. We think of people like David or Solomon or Judas Iscariot. Using this same example of the Israelites at Mount Sinai, Paul warns, "So, if you think you are standing firm, be careful that you don't fall!" (1 Corinthians 10:12).

Scholars disagree as to whether the Israelites requested Aaron to make "gods" or "a god" for them to serve. The translation of the Bible that we are following has "gods" in this verse. While generally speaking we find the New International Version to offer an excellent translation, in this passage we would prefer the translation "Come, make us a god. . . ." Aaron yielded to their request by asking for their gold earrings. If he did this in order to discourage them from pursuing their wishes further, Aaron miscalculated badly. If people are serious about committing idolatry, nothing will stop them. People will spend any amount of money to satisfy their cravings for indulging in vice of every kind, as we see in our society today.

Aaron's choice of making a calf to serve as Israel's idol was in keeping with Israel's experience in Egypt. The Egyptian god Apis was a young bull, a symbol of power and sex. No doubt the Israelites had often seen the wild celebrations in Egypt connected with the so-called worship of this god. This was just what they wanted! Certainly far more enjoyable than to be bound by a strict moral code! Once those who have been trained to follow a strict way of life break out of this discipline, they often lose all restraint.

But this kind of pleasure—if it can be called that—is short-lived indeed. The time of reckoning must come. In Israel's case, it came when Moses came down from the mountain. For God knew what was going on. The next verses give us the Lord's reaction to Israel's worship of the golden calf.

Moses the mediator

⁷Then the LORD said to Moses, "Go down, because your people, whom you brought up out of Egypt, have become corrupt. ⁸They have been quick to turn away from what I commanded them and have made themselves an idol cast in the shape of a calf. They have bowed down to it and sacrificed to it and have said, 'These are your gods, O Israel, who brought you up out of Egypt.'

⁹"I have seen these people," the LORD said to Moses, "and they are a stiff-necked people. ¹⁰Now leave me alone so that my anger may burn against them and that I may destroy them. Then I will make you into a great nation."

¹¹But Moses sought the favor of the LORD his God. "O LORD," he said, "why should your anger burn against your people, whom you brought out of Egypt with great power and a mighty hand? ¹²Why should the Egyptians say, 'It was with evil intent that he brought

them out, to kill them in the mountains and to wipe them off the face of the earth'? Turn from your fierce anger; relent and do not bring disaster on your people. [13]Remember your servants Abraham, Isaac and Israel, to whom you swore by your own self: 'I will make your descendants as numerous as the stars in the sky and I will give your descendants all this land I promised them, and it will be their inheritance forever.'" [14]Then the LORD relented and did not bring on his people the disaster he had threatened.

The Lord's reaction to Israel's idolatry was expressed in words of just anger. "Your people," he says to Moses on the mountain, "have become corrupt." Not "*my* people . . ." but "*your* people, whom *you* brought out of Egypt." How could a holy and righteous God have anything to do with a nation that had made itself filthy with sin! The Lord, who knows all things at all times, then told Moses just exactly what these corrupt Israelites had done.

Moreover, the Lord continues to point out to Moses what a "stiff-necked" people he had chosen as his own. Like cattle that simply will not be led in the way they should go— that was Israel. God expresses himself in even stronger terms: "Now leave me alone so that my anger may burn against them and that I may destroy them. Then I will make you into a great nation."

With these words the Lord put Moses to the test. Would God actually go so far in his anger as to destroy Israel? Would Moses really be the one to carry on God's plans of salvation for the human race? Although these questions occur to us, we note that the Lord does not immediately destroy Israel. "Now leave me alone . . ." he declares. By making another proposal to Moses, the Lord for the moment at least places the matter into Moses' hands.

And Moses stands the test! He serves as a true mediator between an angry God and a sinful people. "Why should your anger burn against your people," Moses replies, "whom *you* brought out of Egypt with great power and a mighty hand?" Moses calls to the Lord's attention the fact that he is dealing with his very own covenant people, not Moses' people. Then Moses continues, What will the Egyptians say? Would they then accuse God of bringing this nation out into the wilderness merely to destroy them? The honor of the Lord, the God of Israel, was at stake. Finally Moses uses his most telling argument: "Remember your servants Abraham, Isaac and Israel. . . ." Remember the promises you made to the fathers of this nation!

The Lord, who is faithful to all his promises, "relented" and did not carry out his threat to destroy Israel. The Lord did not change his mind. The God of all grace, who has promised to hear the prayers of his children, wants them to hold him to his word of promise. He wants us to do the same in our times of need. In 1 Kings 8:56,57 Solomon prayed at the dedication of the temple in Jerusalem, "Praise be to the LORD, who has given rest to his people Israel just as he promised. Not one word has failed of all the good promises he gave through his servant Moses. May the LORD our God be with us as he was with our fathers; may he never leave us nor forsake us." We too can pray as Solomon did. The apostle Paul declares in 2 Corinthians 1:20, "No matter how many promises God has made, they are 'Yes' in Christ. And so through him the 'Amen' is spoken by us to the glory of God." What a comfort for us that we can turn to the same Lord in our troubles and simply hold him to his word, remembering, above all, the words of John: "This is what he promised us—even eternal life" (1 John 2:25).

In this act of Moses' mediation lies another comforting thought for us. Many times Moses acted as a mediator between a sinful Israel and a righteous God—at Taberah when the people complained about their food, at Kadesh Barnea when the people cried out against the report of the 12 men who had come back from Canaan with their report, recorded in Numbers chapter 14; at the time when the Lord sent venomous snakes to punish his impatient people. In Psalm 106:23 the psalmist says of Moses:

> He [God] said he would destroy them [Israel]—
> > had not Moses, his chosen one,
> stood in the breach before him
> > to keep his wrath from destroying them.

We have a mediator who is greater than Moses: Jesus Christ, who "bore the sin of many, and made intercession for the transgressors," as Isaiah tells us (53:12). Of him the writer of Hebrews says, "He is able to save completely those who come to God through him, because he always lives to intercede for them" (7:25). Let us ask the Father in Christ's name, praying with confidence that the Lord will keep every promise made to us in his Word.

Moses takes action

[15]**Moses turned and went down the mountain with the two tablets of the Testimony in his hands. They were inscribed on both sides, front and back. [16]The tablets were the work of God; the writing was the writing of God, engraved on the tablets.**

[17]**When Joshua heard the noise of the people shouting, he said to Moses, "There is the sound of war in the camp."**

[18]**Moses replied:**

> **"It is not the sound of victory,**
> > **it is not the sound of defeat;**
> > **it is the sound of singing that I hear."**

[19]**When Moses approached the camp and saw the calf and the dancing, his anger burned and he threw the tablets out of his hands, breaking them to pieces at the foot of the mountain. [20]And he took the calf they had made and burned it in the fire; then he**

ground it to powder, scattered it on the water and made the
Israelites drink it.

²¹He said to Aaron, "What did these people do to you, that you
led them into such great sin?"

²²"Do not be angry, my lord," Aaron answered. "You know
how prone these people are to evil. ²³They said to me, 'Make us
gods who will go before us. As for this fellow Moses who brought
us up out of Egypt, we don't know what has happened to him.' ²⁴So
I told them, 'Whoever has any gold jewelry, take it off.' Then they
gave me the gold, and I threw it into the fire, and out came this
calf!"

²⁵Moses saw that the people were running wild and that Aaron
had let them get out of control and so become a laughingstock to
their enemies. ²⁶So he stood at the entrance to the camp and said,
"Whoever is for the LORD, come to me." And all the Levites rallied
to him.

²⁷Then he said to them, "This is what the LORD, the God of
Israel, says: 'Each man strap a sword to his side. Go back and forth
through the camp from one end to the other, each killing his
brother and friend and neighbor.'" ²⁸The Levites did as Moses commanded, and that day about three thousand of the people died.
²⁹Then Moses said, "You have been set apart to the LORD today, for
you were against your own sons and brothers, and he has blessed
you this day."

After hearing from the Lord on Mount Sinai of the
Israelites' sin of idolatry, and after first interceding for the
people, Moses went down the mountain carrying the stone
tablets inscribed by the Lord with the Ten Commandments.
He met Joshua on the way, and as they approached the
camp, they heard the sounds of those singing and dancing
around the golden calf. The account that follows is told in
short sentences and without much detail, reflecting the burning anger of Moses as he promptly dealt with the situation.

Moses threw down the tablets, breaking them to pieces.
He ground the golden calf to powder, scattered it on the
water of a stream flowing down the mountain, and made
the Israelites drink it. He didn't even stop to reply to Aaron's

miserable excuses, as Aaron blamed the people and made it seem that he simply threw some gold into the fire and "out came this calf." Seeing the confusion of those who were out chasing about and out of control, Moses called out for helpers to restore order. The Levites, his own tribespeople, rallied to the Lord's cause. Going through the camp, the Levites put three thousand Israelites to the sword. The idolatry was stopped.

A few questions arise in connection with this brief account that are not fully answered in the Bible itself. Why did Moses make the people drink the water mixed with the material of the golden calf? Was this to demonstrate to the people how weak their idol-god was? Did he want to humiliate them by having them drink a god whom they had worshiped? Was this a punishment to show that they had desecrated their only true source of life, just as water is a source of life? Was a result of this drinking the plague mentioned in verse 35, which the Lord caused to come upon the people? Was this simply the result of Moses' burning anger, without any special meaning attached to it? The Bible doesn't say. There may be some truth in all of the above opinions, which have been expressed by Bible scholars.

Another question has been raised: If all the people were involved, how was it possible for just one tribe to overpower all the rest of them as the Levites did? Since only three thousand of the people died, were perhaps only a part of the Israelites involved in this sin of idolatry?

Even if only part of the nation had been directly involved, the entire nation was held responsible. God dealt with Israel as a community. We see this later in the case of one man, Achan, who was guilty of stealing a few items from the conquered city of Ai, contrary to the Lord's express command. On that occasion the Lord held all the people

The golden calf

accountable for this sin, as we see in Joshua chapter 7. In this case of worshiping the golden calf, the anger of Moses was directed against the entire nation.

A happy development arising out of this incident was the behavior of the Levites. When Jacob spoke prophetic words to each of his sons at the end of his life, he cursed Simeon and Levi because they had dealt violently with the Shechemites and had killed them in their anger. As recorded in Genesis 49:7, Jacob said, "I will scatter them [the descendants of Simeon and Levi] in Jacob and disperse them in Israel." Here Moses says to his fellow tribespeople who answered his call for help, "You have been set apart to the LORD today, for you were against your own sons and brothers, and he has blessed you this day." As Moses neared the end of his life, he had this to say in Deuteronomy 33:9 about Levi and his descendants:

> He said of his father and mother,
>   "I have no regard for them."
> He did not recognize his brothers
>   or acknowledge his own children,
> but he watched over your word
>   and guarded your covenant.

As the Levites followed Moses' command at this occasion at Sinai, it was necessary for them to disregard family ties and tribal relationships to defend the Lord's honor. In this way they demonstrated that they were truly fit to serve as priests and mediators for the entire nation. In accordance with Jacob's prophecy, they were indeed scattered after they arrived in Canaan. They received no separate inheritance of land. But they were the Lord's inheritance. They lived in 48 Levitical cities throughout the Land of Promise, serving as priests who were to instruct the people in the teachings of the law of God.

Moses intercedes again

³⁰The next day Moses said to the people, "You have committed a great sin. But now I will go up to the LORD; perhaps I can make atonement for your sin."

³¹So Moses went back to the LORD and said, "Oh, what a great sin these people have committed! They have made themselves gods of gold. ³²But now, please forgive their sin—but if not, then blot me out of the book you have written."

³³The LORD replied to Moses, "Whoever has sinned against me I will blot out of my book. ³⁴Now go, lead the people to the place I spoke of, and my angel will go before you. However, when the time comes for me to punish, I will punish them for their sin."

³⁵And the LORD struck the people with a plague because of what they did with the calf Aaron had made.

At the time of Moses' first intercession on behalf of the Israelites (32:11-13), the Lord had not given him a direct reply as to how he would deal with the Israelites. Moses in the meantime had gone down from the mountain and chastised the people severely for their sin of worshiping the golden calf. Moses therefore announced to the people that he would go back up to the Lord. "Perhaps I can make atonement for your sin," he told them.

In order to "make atonement," or pay the price, for the people's sin so that the wrath of God could be averted, Moses not only pleaded for Israel's forgiveness. He offered himself as payment. If the Lord would not listen to this plea for forgiveness, Moses declared, "then blot me out of the book you have written."

With these words Moses referred to the book of life, in which are listed the names of the righteous. They are the people who will enjoy everlasting life in heaven. The book of Revelation in various places refers to those written in the book of life as the redeemed saints in heaven (3:5; 13:8). To be blotted out of this book would mean to be cut off forever from fellowship with the Lord.

In making this proposition to the Lord, was Moses being carried away by his emotions so that he didn't realize what he was saying? Or was this offer one of the greatest examples of self-sacrificing love that we find in all Scripture—as many Bible scholars claim? Whatever the case, no mere man can atone for sin. Only the sinless blood of Christ could accomplish that. The apostle Paul also had great sorrow in his heart when he thought of how many of his own people had rejected Christ and thereby sealed their eternal doom. "I could wish that I myself were cursed and cut off from Christ," Paul declared in Romans 9:3,4, "for the sake of my brothers, those of my own race, the people of Israel." Paul knew, however, that "no man can redeem the life of another or give to God a ransom for him," as Psalm 49:7 truly says.

The Lord clearly indicated as much in his reply to Moses: "Whoever has sinned against me I will blot out of my book." Judgment belonged to the Lord alone. At the same time, the Lord assured Moses that his "angel" would still go before them. (What the Lord meant by this we will see in the following chapter.) As a further punishment for their idolatry, however, the Lord struck the people with a plague.

With this act the chapter that reports the tragic sin of Israel's worship of the golden calf is brought to a close. One might say that there was now a truce between the Lord and his rebellious people. Israel, however, had in a most serious manner broken the covenant relationship with the Lord. This had happened very soon after God had established it. Would the covenant be fully restored to Israel? The next two chapters bring us the answer to this important question.

"I will send an angel"

33 Then the LORD said to Moses, "Leave this place, you and the people you brought up out of Egypt, and go up to the land I promised on oath to Abraham, Isaac and Jacob, saying, 'I will give it to your descendants.' ²I will send an angel before you and drive out the Canaanites, Amorites, Hittites, Perizzites, Hivites and Jebusites. ³Go up to the land flowing with milk and honey. But I will not go with you, because you are a stiff-necked people and I might destroy you on the way."

⁴When the people heard these distressing words, they began to mourn and no one put on any ornaments. ⁵For the LORD had said to Moses, "Tell the Israelites, 'You are a stiff-necked people. If I were to go with you even for a moment, I might destroy you. Now take off your ornaments and I will decide what to do with you.'" ⁶So the Israelites stripped off their ornaments at Mount Horeb.

In reply to Moses' intercession, as we heard in the previous verses, the Lord had stated that his angel would go before the people as they would continue their journey. What did these words mean? Would this be "the angel of the Lord," namely, the Lord himself? Or would this be a created angel?

In the above verses the Lord clarified this statement. Again he said, "I will send an angel before you." He would keep his promise to the patriarchs. He would drive out the inhabitants of Canaan. He would give them "the land flowing with milk and honey." "But I will not go with you," the Lord declared. He added his reason for this changed situation:

"Because you are a stiff-necked people and I might destroy you on the way." The people had shown themselves to be hard-hearted. If they would continue this course, the Lord in his just anger might be compelled to destroy them. That is why the Lord said he would send an angel before them instead of going with them himself.

The reaction of the people to this declaration of the Lord was an act of repentance. They mourned. They removed their ornaments to show their sorrow. The Lord repeated his threat. But he also added a statement indicating a ray of hope that the situation still could be changed: "Now take off your ornaments and I will decide what to do with you."

Likewise the Lord graciously deals with his people in every age. Through his Word he points us to our sin and the just punishment we deserve. But lest we despair, he also extends the sure promises of his grace. It is a training in repentance and instruction in righteousness that we need as long as we live.

The Tent of Meeting

⁷**Now Moses used to take a tent and pitch it outside the camp some distance away, calling it the "tent of meeting." Anyone inquiring of the LORD would go to the tent of meeting outside the camp. ⁸And whenever Moses went out to the tent, all the people rose and stood at the entrances to their tents, watching Moses until he entered the tent. ⁹As Moses went into the tent, the pillar of cloud would come down and stay at the entrance, while the LORD spoke with Moses. ¹⁰Whenever the people saw the pillar of cloud standing at the entrance to the tent, they all stood and worshiped, each at the entrance to his tent. ¹¹The LORD would speak to Moses face to face, as a man speaks with his friend. Then Moses would return to the camp, but his young aide Joshua son of Nun did not leave the tent.**

The fellowship relationship between the Lord and Israel was in a state of suspension as a result of their sin of worshiping the golden calf. The Lord had not only said to Moses, as we heard in the preceding verses, "I will not go with you"; the Lord actually refused to demonstrate his close relationship with his people in the same way as he had in the past. The Lord still communicated with Moses, but in a tent that Moses pitched outside the camp. There the pillar of cloud would come. There the Lord would "speak to Moses face to face, as a man speaks with his friend."

With Moses, in other words, the Lord continued to communicate as he had in the past. But the people were still to be tested, to reawaken in their hearts a longing that the covenant relationship might be fully restored. This purpose, we see, was also being achieved, as from their own tents the people anxiously watched how Moses would go to his own tent outside the camp and how the Lord would come to Moses' tent in the pillar of cloud.

This assurance that the Lord extended to Moses encouraged him to see if the former relationship between the Lord and Israel could again be fully restored.

Moses and the glory of the Lord

¹²Moses said to the LORD, "You have been telling me, 'Lead these people,' but you have not let me know whom you will send with me. You have said, 'I know you by name and you have found favor with me.' ¹³If you are pleased with me, teach me your ways so I may know you and continue to find favor with you. Remember that this nation is your people."

¹⁴The LORD replied, "My Presence will go with you, and I will give you rest."

¹⁵Then Moses said to him, "If your Presence does not go with us, do not send us up from here. ¹⁶How will anyone know that you are pleased with me and with your people unless you go with us? What else will distinguish me and your people from all the other people on the face of the earth?"

¹⁷And the LORD said to Moses, "I will do the very thing you have asked, because I am pleased with you and I know you by name."

¹⁸Then Moses said, "Now show me your glory."

¹⁹And the LORD said, "I will cause all my goodness to pass in front of you, and I will proclaim my name, the LORD, in your presence. I will have mercy on whom I will have mercy, and I will have compassion on whom I will have compassion. ²⁰But," he said, "you cannot see my face, for no one may see me and live."

²¹Then the LORD said, "There is a place near me where you may stand on a rock. ²²When my glory passes by, I will put you in a cleft in the rock and cover you with my hand until I have passed by.

215

²³Then I will remove my hand and you will see my back; but my face must not be seen."

Moses had received the promise from the Lord that an angel would continue to guide the Israelites on the way to the land of Canaan. The Lord's assurance, as we saw, was qualified. The Lord himself would not do the guiding as he had in the past, but a created angel would serve to lead the way. Moreover, the preceding verses showed how Moses had experienced the people's expression of repentance as they stripped themselves of their ornaments and showed a sincere desire for their bond of fellowship with the Lord to be reestablished. Finally, Moses was reassured by the fact that his own personal bond of fellowship with the Lord had remained as close as ever. The Lord had continued to communicate "face to face" with Moses as he had in the past (33:11).

And so Moses now courageously decides to take matters in hand and press his case further in behalf of Israel. The conversation between himself and the Lord that is recorded in the verses before us show Moses wrestling with the Lord in prayer as Jacob had once done, not wanting to let the Lord go without first receiving a blessing.

Moses first of all reminds the Lord of the close relationship existing between them. Moses then pleads for greater information concerning the Lord's intentions as far as Israel is concerned: "Teach me your ways. . . . Remember that this nation is your people." If I am to be your leader of this your people, Moses pleads, please let me know your intentions concerning them. We see how Moses approaches the throne of the Lord's grace "boldly and confidently," as Luther encourages us in his explanation of the Lord's Prayer in his Small Catechism.

The Lord reassures Moses, "My Presence will go with you, and I will give you rest." Moses receives what he asks for! The Lord promises that his own personal Presence will continue to be with his people. They will have more than a created angel to guide them! Moses holds the Lord firmly to this word of assurance. "If your Presence does not go with us, do not send us up from here. How will anyone know that you are pleased with me and with your people unless you go with us? What else will distinguish me and your people from all the other people on the face of the earth?'" These words of Moses, although stated as questions, are actually the words of a believer who clings to the Word and promise of God. He approaches the Lord in the spirit of the psalmist who declares, "Whom have I in heaven but you? And earth has nothing I desire besides you. My flesh and my heart may fail, but God is the strength of my heart and my portion forever" (Psalm 73:25,26).

Once more the Lord reassures Moses: "I will do the very thing you have asked, because I am pleased with you and I know you by name." Moses is overcome with joy. In this joyful mood he proceeds to make one more daring request. He says to the Lord, "Now show me your glory." Although Moses had communicated with the Lord "face to face" (33:11), he had seen no more than an outward manifestation of the Lord's glory. He had not seen the Lord's glory in its total splendor. Moses wants to see God in *all* his holiness, his majesty and perfection. Did Moses really know what he was asking? Was his request a sudden impulsive act? Various reasons have been given for this desire on the part of Moses. Some say it was because of the seriousness of Israel's sin. Others give the extreme pressure resting upon Moses as mediator between the Lord and the people as the cause for his wanting to see the Lord in all his glory. Still others say he was simply overcome with joy.

Whatever Moses' reason may have been, the Lord could not comply with Moses' request, as he himself states: "You cannot see my face, for no one may see me and live." As a human being cannot look into the light of the sun without being blinded by its brilliance, so likewise sinful people living here on this earth cannot behold the glory of a holy God without being destroyed. Believers also are sinful human beings. They cannot know God fully or comprehend his ways. They cannot dwell in his holy light. Only in eternity will the veil between a believer and the holy God be removed, and "we shall see him as he is" (1 John 3:2).

The Lord, however, does not become angry with Moses because of his unusual request. He rather says to him, "I will cause all my goodness to pass in front of you, and I will proclaim my name, the LORD, in your presence. I will have mercy on whom I will have mercy, and I will have compassion on whom I will have compassion." What a beautiful reminder lies in these words! For us human beings here on this earth, the Lord's glory rests in that name by which he has revealed himself to us—the I AM WHO I AM, the LORD of the covenant, the God who in his Word has revealed himself to us above all in his mercy, his compassion, his free and faithful grace!

The Lord then grants Moses an unusual experience. On the summit of Mount Sinai, the Lord himself puts Moses into the cleft of a rock. While passing by, the Lord covers Moses with his "hand," that is, with his protecting power. After passing by, the Lord lets Moses see his "back," that is, the reflection of his glory. What Moses actually sees here is difficult to put into words. Moses himself says no more about it. Even the words that the Lord himself uses are beyond our understanding. The Lord reveals to his servant Moses as much as he can in the circumstances. The important revelation as far as Moses is concerned is the proclaiming of the Lord's name; we hear more about this in the chapter that follows.

There are times in our own lives as Christians when the pressures of this earthly existence weigh heavily upon us. Life's problems and disappointments mount with increasing fury. Our own responsibilities never seem to lessen in intensity. "How much more can we be expected to carry?" we ask. We wrestle with the Lord in prayer. We long for some kind of added reassurance that he is truly there, according to his promise.

With Peter we declare, "Lord, to whom shall we go? You have the words of eternal life" (John 6:68). Yes, "the words of eternal life." But isn't there more for us than mere words? Heaven seems so far away. "Oh, that we were there!" we sing in a Christmas hymn. "Show us your glory," we say with Moses. We want the Lord to give some tangible sign of his glorious presence.

Moses wanted this. Elijah, another of the Lord's Old Testament prophets, desired the same reassurance. At the point of despair, Elijah came to this very same mountain of God, we are told. "I am the only one left," he cried out, "and now they are trying to kill me too" (1 Kings 19:10). The Lord also granted Elijah unusual experiences on this mountain as he caused a great and powerful wind to tear the mountain apart, an earthquake to shatter the rocks, and also a fire. But the Lord, we are told, "was not in the wind . . . not in the earthquake . . . not in the fire." He came to Elijah in "a gentle whisper." The Lord also demonstrated to Elijah that he should look for reassurance from the Lord not in outward signs of the Lord's majesty and power. To us, as believers, the Lord comes in the gentle whisper of the his strengthening Word, in his gospel message of life and salvation. That is strong enough to sustain us, the Lord reassures us, until we see the fullness of our Lord's glory in heaven.

In the chapter that follows, the Lord once more emphasizes this truth by proclaiming his name to Moses and also reconfirming his covenant with his people.

The sermon on the name of the Lord

34 The LORD said to Moses, "Chisel out two stone tablets like the first ones, and I will write on them the words that were on the first tablets, which you broke. ²Be ready in the morning, and then come up on Mount Sinai. Present yourself to me there on top of the mountain. ³No one is to come with you or be seen anywhere on the mountain; not even the flocks and herds may graze in front of the mountain."

⁴So Moses chiseled out two stone tablets like the first ones and went up Mount Sinai early in the morning, as the LORD had commanded him; and he carried the two stone tablets in his hands. ⁵Then the LORD came down in the cloud and stood there with him and proclaimed his name, the LORD. ⁶And he passed in front of Moses, proclaiming, "The LORD, the LORD, the compassionate and gracious God, slow to anger, abounding in love and faithfulness, ⁷maintaining love to thousands, and forgiving wickedness, rebellion and sin. Yet he does not leave the guilty unpunished; he punishes the children and their children for the sin of the fathers to the third and fourth generation."

After Moses had experienced the passing by of the glory of the Lord while he was in a cleft in the rock, the Lord instructed him to "chisel out two stone tablets like the first ones" and bring them back upon Mount Sinai the following morning. We note that this time the Lord did not supply the stone tablets as he had previously done. Since Moses had broken the tablets that the Lord had supplied, it was natural that Moses himself should replace them with new ones. The Lord promised that he would again write on these tablets the words of the Ten Commandments.

Early the following morning, Moses once more ascended Mount Sinai. This time there was no thunder, no sound of trumpets, not even Joshua to accompany him. Alone he went up with the two tablets to meet the Lord in the cloud and to hear the Lord's words, which Luther called "the sermon on the name of the Lord." Again we are told that the Lord himself "passed in front of Moses" and personally proclaimed this sermon that was centered on his name, the LORD: "The LORD, the LORD, . . ." are the first words of this sermon. We recall how it was on this same mountain that the Lord had revealed his glory to Moses in a burning bush. We remember how at that time, as the Lord called Moses to lead his people out of Egypt, the Lord had revealed himself as "I AM" and "the LORD," the personal, eternal, unchangeable God of grace. This is the great truth that the Lord once more emphasizes in this sermon: "The LORD, the LORD, the compassionate and gracious God, slow to anger."

"Only One can be truly gracious," August Pieper explains, "he who alone is exalted almighty, absolutely independent, who needs to seek no one's favor or to fear anyone else, from whom grace flows forth out of unselfishness, out of the pure goodness, love, and mercy of his heart" (*The Wauwatosa Theology,* Volume 2, page 480).

The Lord describes himself as long-suffering, actually "slow to anger." In his inner being we know God is love, not wrath. He can indeed become angry when his love and mercy are despised, but he is *slow* to anger, "abounding in love and faithfulness." God does not waver. His grace and faithfulness go together. He keeps his promises.

"Maintaining love to thousands, and forgiving wickedness, rebellion and sin," the Lord continues in this sermon. By "thousands" we simply understand an unlimited number of people and generations. The grace of God, like God himself, is boundless. And this is the greatness of his glory! He forgives sins of all kinds—sins of wickedness, sins of rebellion against his law, daily sins.

But the Lord proclaims another side of himself in the closing words of this same sermon: "Yet he does not leave the guilty unpunished; he punishes the children and their children for the sin of the fathers to the third and fourth generation." Although the Lord's grace is boundless, this does not mean that he disregards the seriousness of sin. Every sin is an abuse of God's glory since it breaks his holy law. No sin, therefore, goes unpunished!

How can these two sides of the Lord agree? August Pieper writes,

> For us Christians all the mysteries in God's essence and will are solved—not in our understanding but in faith. We know no bare God, no abstract Deity, but only a God who is called Jehovah, the Lord, the Redeemer and Holy One of Israel. . . . In this Jehovah-God his law and his Gospel, his infinite grace and his dreadful wrath, are harmonized in such a glorious manner as no other two opposites are harmonized in this world and the next, in time and eternity. Both are at the same time true. He forgives iniquity and transgression and sin for a thousand generations, and thereby still lets no one be wholly innocent and go unpunished, but visits the guilt of the fathers upon the children and the children's children.

And the Man in whom this contradiction in
God and in all his ways finds its solution is
called *Jesus Christ,* the Jehovah-God, the
embodiment and revelation of all mysteries
in heaven and on earth, of eternity and time:
God manifest in the flesh, 1 Timothy 3:16.
(pages 484,485)

Professor Pieper goes on to explain how Jesus, in our
stead, was punished under the law of sinners for our sins,
so that grace might reign and that we sinners might have
peace forevermore. As we stand in this saving grace, the
Lord still chastens us, sometimes severely. But he does this
as a loving Father in order to rescue us from final destruction. "This is the true and blessed harmonization of the
grace and wrath of God our Savior," Professor Pieper concludes (page 486).

And so we as Christians walk by faith and not by
sight. "We cannot comprehend God," as Professor Pieper
reminds us, "beyond the earnestness of his law and the
faithfulness of his Gospel promise." Like Moses, we desire
to see the glory of the Lord. Someday we will. In the
meantime, we know that God has revealed to us all that
we need to know concerning himself so that we can
someday enjoy life in his presence forever. In this hope,
we sing with the psalmist in Psalm 16:9-11:

My heart is glad and my tongue rejoices;
   my body also will rest secure,
because you will not abandon me to the grave,
   nor will you let your Holy One see decay.
You have made known to me the path of life;
   you will fill me with joy in your presence,
   with eternal pleasures at your right hand.

The covenant restored

⁸Moses bowed to the ground at once and worshiped. ⁹"O Lord, if I have found favor in your eyes," he said, "then let the Lord go with us. Although this is a stiff-necked people, forgive our wickedness and our sin, and take us as your inheritance."

¹⁰Then the LORD said: "I am making a covenant with you. Before all your people I will do wonders never before done in any nation in all the world. The people you live among will see how awesome is the work that I, the LORD, will do for you. ¹¹Obey what I command you today. I will drive out before you the Amorites, Canaanites, Hittites, Perizzites, Hivites and Jebusites. ¹²Be careful not to make a treaty with those who live in the land where you are going, or they will be a snare among you. ¹³Break down their altars, smash their sacred stones and cut down their Asherah poles. ¹⁴Do not worship any other god, for the LORD, whose name is Jealous, is a jealous God.

¹⁵"Be careful not to make a treaty with those who live in the land; for when they prostitute themselves to their gods and sacrifice to them, they will invite you and you will eat their sacrifices. ¹⁶And when you choose some of their daughters as wives for your sons and those daughters prostitute themselves to their gods, they will lead your sons to do the same.

¹⁷"Do not make cast idols.

¹⁸"Celebrate the Feast of Unleavened Bread. For seven days eat bread made without yeast, as I commanded you. Do this at the appointed time in the month of Abib, for in that month you came out of Egypt.

¹⁹"The first offspring of every womb belongs to me, including all the firstborn males of your livestock, whether from herd or flock. ²⁰Redeem the firstborn donkey with a lamb, but if you do not redeem it, break its neck. Redeem all your firstborn sons.

"No one is to appear before me empty-handed.

²¹"Six days you shall labor, but on the seventh day you shall rest; even during the plowing season and harvest you must rest.

²²"Celebrate the Feast of Weeks with the firstfruits of the wheat harvest, and the Feast of Ingathering at the turn of the year. ²³Three times a year all your men are to appear before the Sovereign LORD, the God of Israel. ²⁴I will drive out nations before you and enlarge your territory, and no one will covet your land

when you go up three times each year to appear before the Lord your God.

²⁵"Do not offer the blood of a sacrifice to me along with anything containing yeast, and do not let any of the sacrifice from the Passover Feast remain until morning.

²⁶"Bring the best of the firstfruits of your soil to the house of the Lord your God.

"Do not cook a young goat in its mother's milk."

²⁷Then the Lord said to Moses, "Write down these words, for in accordance with these words I have made a covenant with you and with Israel." ²⁸Moses was there with the Lord forty days and forty nights without eating bread or drinking water. And he wrote on the tablets the words of the covenant—the Ten Commandments.

After hearing the sermon on the name of the Lord from the Lord himself, Moses bowed down to the ground and worshiped this Savior-God. He was emboldened once more to ask the Lord to accompany his people with his divine Presence. "Although this is a stiff-necked people," Moses prayed, "forgive our wickedness and our sin, and take us as your inheritance."

The Lord replied by once more confirming the covenant that he had established upon Mount Sinai, which Israel had broken by its worship of the golden calf. In the above verses, the Lord summarized the chief points of the Sinaitic covenant. He warned especially against making any kind of treaty with the people in the land of Canaan. All signs of idol worship—heathen altars, monuments, poles dedicated to the goddess Asherah—were to be destroyed. The Lord then briefly repeated his instructions concerning the true worship of Jehovah. Laws concerning the Sabbath, special festivals, and the dedication of the firstborn were once more referred to. All these laws look forward with hope to the day when Israel would enter the promised land of Canaan, giving Moses and the people assurance that the covenant is fully restored. The Lord's summary of the Sinaitic law closes with the same statement with which he closed the first giving of the covenant on Mount Sinai: "Do not cook a young goat in its mother's milk."

Again Moses was required to write down all the words of the covenant as he had done previously, remaining on Mount Sinai for 40 days and nights without bread or water. The regulations of the covenant were the same. The Ten Commandments were restored on the two stone tablets with the same words. Through Moses' 40-day absence, the people were again tested. This time they stood the test and waited patiently for Moses to return.

The radiant face of Moses

²⁹**When Moses came down from Mount Sinai with the two tablets of the Testimony in his hands, he was not aware that his face was radiant because he had spoken with the LORD. ³⁰When Aaron and all the Israelites saw Moses, his face was radiant, and they were afraid to come near him. ³¹But Moses called to them; so Aaron and all the leaders of the community came back to him, and he spoke to them. ³²Afterward all the Israelites came near him, and he gave them all the commands the LORD had given him on Mount Sinai.**

³³**When Moses finished speaking to them, he put a veil over his face. ³⁴But whenever he entered the LORD's presence to speak with him, he removed the veil until he came out. And when he came out and told the Israelites what he had been commanded, ³⁵they saw that his face was radiant. Then Moses would put the veil back over his face until he went in to speak with the LORD.**

The reflection of the glory of the Lord upon the face of Moses was to serve as a sign to the people that the covenant had been reinstated. The glory of the Lord was again present among his people, through Moses. Moses, however, was not even aware that his face was shining. But Aaron and the Israelites were afraid to go near Moses because of the brightness of his face. Out of concern for this fear, Moses therefore covered his face with a veil when speaking to the people and when giving them all the commands the Lord had given him on Mount Sinai.

Unfortunately, the King James English translation of the Bible, as well as Luther's German translation, conveys the idea that the chief purpose of the veil on Moses' face was to *hide* the Lord's glory so that the people would not be afraid of Moses. The fact of the matter is, as the New International Version and other translations correctly convey, that Israel *did* see the Lord's glory reflected on Moses' face. Moses put the veil on his face not only because the people were afraid but, as Paul writes in 2 Corinthians 3:13, "to keep the Israelites from gazing at it while the radiance was fading away."

Moses' face reflected the glory of the Sinaitic law. That glory, as Paul calls to our attention in 2 Corinthians chapter 3, was a fading glory. "In Christ is it taken away," Paul declares (verse 14). The glory of our New Testament ministry, Paul emphasizes with this comparison, is greater than that of Moses. The New Testament ministry, centered in Christ, who fulfilled the law, is a ministry of the Spirit that will never fade away. It is a ministry that reflects the glory of the gospel, which has no conditions or limitations and which endures forever. In our New Testament ministry, we, as Christians, should therefore convey above all the unending joy that our message brings to lost sinners. What an undeserved privilege our gracious Lord has bestowed upon us!

An interesting sidelight to these verses lies in Michelangelo's famous statue of Moses in the city of Genoa, Italy. In verse 29 we read that the face of Moses "was radiant because he had spoken with the LORD." The Hebrew word for "radiant" is derived from the same word in Hebrew which means "horn." When the church father Jerome translated the Bible into the Latin language, he conveyed the idea that as Moses came down from Mount Sinai with the two tablets of stone, his head appeared as though horns were projecting from it. Michelangelo's statue of Moses therefore portrays Moses' head with horns instead of rays of light.

With these verses, chapter 34 is brought to a close. The covenant had been restored. Because of Israel's sin of calf-worship, a serious interruption had occurred. Because of the Lord's mercy, the break that Israel had caused in fellowship relations with the Lord had been healed. The people were now ready to proceed with the business at hand, the erection of the tabernacle according to the Lord's plans.

Sabbath regulations

35 Moses assembled the whole Israelite community and said to them, "These are the things the LORD has commanded you to do: ²For six days, work is to be done, but the seventh day shall be your holy day, a Sabbath of rest to the LORD. Whoever does any work on it must be put to death. ³Do not light a fire in any of your dwellings on the Sabbath day."

After the covenant between the Lord and the Israelites had been restored, Moses assembled the Israelites in order to announce the divine command to proceed with the building of the tabernacle. First of all, however, he emphasized to the people the instructions that had been given concerning the regulations of the Sabbath Day. No work was to be done on the seventh day of the week; no fire was to be kindled. The penalty for breaking these Sabbath regulations was death.

The Sabbath reminder was given at this time to restrain the people when undertaking this building program. True, the work was to be done for the Lord, and it was important work. More important as far as the Lord was concerned, however, was a strict observance of the Sabbath laws. No building of the tabernacle was to be done on the Sabbath Day.

Why was the observance of the Sabbath so important? It was not a means of meriting the Lord's favor. The Sabbath rest was rather a symbol of that perfect rest which the Lord has promised his people through the sending of the Savior, a rest which would be accomplished through his coming and which would last forever. It was a shadow of Christ. When Jesus, the fulfillment of the Sabbath, came, he declared, "Come to me, all you who are weary and burdened, and I will give you rest. Take my yoke upon you and learn from me, for I am gentle and humble in heart, and you will find rest for your souls" (Matthew 11:28,29). Jesus offers this rest for the soul through the assurance of the forgiveness of sins. He won this rest for all people through his saving work. He offers this rest to all today through the proclaiming of his gospel.

The writer of the book of Hebrews refers to this Sabbath rest that remains for the people of God. He does so in connection with the preaching of the gospel and encourages his people to be attentive to the preaching of the gospel at every opportunity. "Today, if you hear his voice," he declares, "do not harden your hearts" (3:7,8).

It is good for us New Testament Christians to take this encouragement to heart. The Old Testament Sabbath regulations pertaining to complete rest on a certain day of the week no longer apply to us. Christ was the perfect fulfillment of the Old Testament Sabbath. This does not give us license, as many seem to think, to despise the Word of that Savior, which strengthens us on our way to eternal life. By neglecting the opportunity to hear his Word and to praise his name in our worship, we become the slaves of our own selfish desires, destined to merit eternal doom rather than to inherit eternal rest.

May our worship on the Lord's day be a foretaste of that perfect rest and fellowship with the Lord of which John writes in the book of Revelation: "I heard a loud voice from the throne saying, 'Now the dwelling of God is with men, and he will live with them. They will be his people, and God himself will be with them and be their God. He will wipe every tear from their eyes. There will be no more death or mourning or crying or pain, for the old order of things has passed away'" (21:3,4). This is the rest we hope to enjoy eternally in heaven.

Materials for the tabernacle

⁴Moses said to the whole Israelite community, "This is what the LORD has commanded: ⁵From what you have, take an offering for the LORD. Everyone who is willing is to bring to the LORD an offering of gold, silver and bronze; ⁶blue, purple and scarlet yarn and fine linen; goat hair; ⁷ram skins dyed red and hides of sea cows; acacia wood; ⁸olive oil for the light; spices for the anointing oil and for the fragrant incense; ⁹and onyx stones and other gems to be mounted on the ephod and breastpiece.

¹⁰"All who are skilled among you are to come and make everything the LORD has commanded: ¹¹the tabernacle with its tent and its covering, clasps, frames, crossbars, posts and bases; ¹²the ark with its poles and the atonement cover and the curtain that shields it; ¹³the table with its poles and all its articles and the bread of the Presence; ¹⁴the lampstand that is for light with its accessories, lamps and oil for the light; ¹⁵the altar of incense with its poles, the anointing oil and the fragrant incense; the curtain for the doorway at the entrance to the tabernacle; ¹⁶the altar of burnt offering with its bronze grating, its poles and all its utensils; the bronze basin with its stand; ¹⁷the curtains of the courtyard with its posts and bases, and the curtain for the entrance to the courtyard; ¹⁸the tent pegs for the tabernacle and for the courtyard, and their ropes; ¹⁹the

woven garments worn for ministering in the sanctuary—both the sacred garments for Aaron the priest and the garments for his sons when they serve as priests."

Moses now *invited the entire Israelite community* to bring an offering to the Lord for the building of the tabernacle. They were to take this offering from what they had. *The Lord did not expect the impossible.* The Lord required rich and costly materials. As we have previously pointed out, however, these materials were either available to the Israelites from what they had received from the Egyptians, or they could be acquired in various ways where the Israelites were camped. To be sure, a real effort would be involved in assembling these materials, in some cases a real personal sacrifice. But the Lord did not hesitate to ask for the best when it was to be used for the purpose of letting the people show honor to his name.

We note, moreover, that the items needed for the tabernacle were listed in detail. *The Lord did not keep any information from the people.* He did not cover up his requirements by stating vague generalities. Precious metals, hides of sea cows, gems, and stones—yes, even smaller items such as tent pegs and ropes—were included. Nothing was too costly or too insignificant to be dedicated to the Lord for his service.

Perhaps there were some among the Israelites who were not blessed with gold or precious stones. Yet they could still be a part of this community project. "All who are skilled among you are to come and make everything the LORD has commanded," Moses declared. *They could devote their skills to the Lord by giving of the labor of their hands.* Men could gather and prepare ram skins and hides of sea cows. Women could spin the elaborate kinds of yarn required and make the cloth as described. Craftsmen could fashion the woodwork and the metalwork as specified. There was olive oil and incense to be prepared according to the Lord's exact recipe. Everyone could use his gifts and talents in some way.

In all this we note the one predominant directive: "Everyone who is willing is to bring to the Lord an offering. . . ." *The offerings of material and labor were to be freewill gifts!* No undue pressure was placed upon the people. No legalistic threat was issued. The Lord wanted this outpouring of gifts to come from the hearts of his people. He wanted them to be brought in the spirit of thankfulness for his gifts of grace and to the glory of his holy name.

No better principles of sound stewardship for use in our congregations can be found today than in this chapter of Exodus. The giving of offerings to the Lord is still very much a part of our congregational life. Liberal gifts are needed to support the work of a local congregation at home, as well as to carry out an effective mission outreach at home and abroad. One needs only to look at an annual budget for local congregational needs and for the work of the synod in order to appreciate this. Building programs are very much a part of these needs. A congregation or a synod without some kind of improvement or expansion project is failing to look ahead. And so the call to "bring to the Lord an offering" is ever before us. How are we to approach our people again and again without having to hear the oft-repeated complaint that "all the church wants is our money"?

Chapter 35 begins with and stresses that "this is what the LORD has commanded"; the offering is "for the LORD." The Lord never asks without reason or foundation. This is the Savior-God who is commanding this, the Lord who has revealed himself in all his grace and mercy, the Lord who has made an everlasting covenant with his people, the

Lord who knows that a grateful people will want to show their gratitude to him for his blessings and will need this expression of thanks in order to express their fellowship with him. The Lord doesn't want our gifts because he needs us. We need him, and we need to express this in our life and in our worship. And if the Lord's blessings are important to us, we will want to share them with as many others as possible.

When making appeals for offerings, it is so easy for our sinful natures to lose confidence in this freewill offering method and imagine that we need to interject some kind of legalistic pressure in order for our money drive to be effective. Why not assess people according to their income? Why not demand a certain amount—or else . . . ? We note, however, how the New Testament echoes this spirit of bringing freewill offerings throughout. It is the gospel of Christ that motivates us, as 2 Corinthians 5:14 tells us. It is the grace of our Lord Jesus Christ which gives Christians the spirit of eager willingness to bring gifts that are acceptable to the Lord. A reading of 1 Corinthians 16:14 and 2 Corinthians chapters 8 and 9 is especially helpful in strengthening ourselves in this important biblical principle.

This does not mean that the gathering of offerings is an effortless task. As Moses told the people precisely what was needed, so we should present the needs of the congregation and the synod clearly to the rest of the people in our congregations. There is no reason to apologize for these needs. This is the Lord's work. The Lord's work is our top priority. This means also that the whole congregation should become involved in bringing gifts to the Lord. Moses addressed "the whole Israelite community." He not only encouraged gifts of gold and silver but made arrangements for every kind of skill to be put into the Lord's service. This kind of effort, involving all our people, takes work. It requires organization. But it gives every member of the body of Christ an opportunity to express his love for the Lord.

In remote village areas in Africa, people have very little money. They have other ways, however, of demonstrating their love for the Lord and their devotion to his work. With their own hands, they can build their own churches from materials available to them in the African bush. On days of special thanksgiving to the Lord, they can bring their maize, their ground nuts, their cassava roots to the Lord's altar. They can set aside an area of land for "the Lord's acre," from which the produce is sold at the market as "the Lord's bounty." The Lord does not expect the impossible. Where the spirit of thankfulness is present, the matter of Christian stewardship will be a joy, not the headache some seem to imagine it to be.

The offering

20Then the whole Israelite community withdrew from Moses' presence, 21and everyone who was willing and whose heart moved him came and brought an offering to the LORD for the work on the Tent of Meeting, for all its service, and for the sacred garments. 22All who were willing, men and women alike, came and brought gold jewelry of all kinds: brooches, earrings, rings and ornaments. They all presented their gold as a wave offering to the LORD. 23Everyone who had blue, purple or scarlet yarn or fine linen, or goat hair, ram skins dyed red or hides of sea cows brought them. 24Those presenting an offering of silver or bronze brought it as an offering to the LORD, and everyone who had acacia wood for any part of the work brought it. 25Every skilled woman spun with her hands and brought what she had spun—blue, purple or scarlet yarn or fine linen. 26And all the women who were willing and had the skill spun the goat hair. 27The leaders brought onyx stones and other gems to be mounted on the ephod and breastpiece. 28They also brought spices and olive oil for the light and for the anointing oil and for the fragrant incense. 29All the Israelite men and women

who were willing brought to the LORD freewill offerings for all the work the LORD through Moses had commanded them to do.

These verses describe the response of the Israelites to Moses' appeal for offerings for the tabernacle. The result is reported in chapter 36. Here we are told that the whole community participated. The response was from the heart. Costly materials were freely given. People with skills willingly offered their services. Women spun the elaborately designed materials as specified. Tribal leaders brought precious stones and gems. The freewill nature of the response is repeatedly emphasized in these verses and is summarized in the last verse: "All the Israelite men and women who were willing brought to the LORD freewill offerings for all the work the LORD through Moses had commanded them to do."

It must have been a real joy for Moses to see the people respond this way. Shortly before this, this same nation had been dancing around a golden calf. The Lord in his anger had threatened to cut them off from the blessings of the covenant. Moses had interceded for the people. The Lord had graciously forgiven their sins, and the covenant relationship had been restored. Out of this dark background, the enthusiastic reply must have been especially heartwarming.

There is no greater joy in the Lord's work today than to see a congregation of Christians respond to an appeal for willing service. The apostle Paul too could rejoice when the Macedonian churches gave generously toward an appeal to relieve the poverty-stricken Christians in Jerusalem. Paul gave all glory to God for this willing response. He writes in 2 Corinthians 9:7,8, "Each man should give what he has decided in his heart to give, not reluctantly or under compulsion, for God loves a cheerful giver. And God is able to make all grace abound to you, so that in all things at all times, having all that you need, you will abound in every good work."

May we in such moments of joy also give all glory to God for the victory of the gospel!

Bezalel and Oholiab

30Then Moses said to the Israelites, "See, the LORD has chosen Bezalel son of Uri, the son of Hur, of the tribe of Judah, 31and he has filled him with the Spirit of God, with skill, ability and knowledge in all kinds of crafts—32to make artistic designs for work in gold, silver and bronze, 33to cut and set stones, to work in wood and to engage in all kinds of artistic craftsmanship. 34And he has given both him and Oholiab son of Ahisamach, of the tribe of Dan, the ability to teach others. 35He has filled them with skill to do all kinds of work as craftsmen, designers, embroiderers in blue, purple and scarlet yarn and fine linen, and weavers—all of them master craftsmen and designers.

Moses introduces Bezalel and Oholiab as the master-builders to supervise the work of building the tabernacle with its appointments. Again we note how Moses repeatedly credits "the Spirit of God" for endowing these men and their assistants with special gifts to carry out their designated tasks.

We too should recognize that "every good and perfect gift is from above" (James 1:17) and that it is God who works in us to will and to act according to his good purpose. "All glory be to God on high" also for the practical skills he gives us in our efforts to beautify the house of God where we praise his name.

The first village church in Africa built by the people themselves was on a piece of land donated by Moses Mhlanga, who also donated most of the labor and directed the work. When on dedication day some people wanted to praise Mr. Mhlanga for his efforts, he replied, "The Lord

built this house. We were only playing." In a more sophisti-
cated society with more complicated methods, it is still the
Lord who builds his house.

More than enough!

36 "So Bezalel, Oholiab and every skilled person to whom the
Lord has given skill and ability to know how to carry out all
the work of constructing the sanctuary are to do the work just as
the Lord has commanded."

²Then Moses summoned Bezalel and Oholiab and every skilled
person to whom the Lᴏʀᴅ had given ability and who was willing to
come and do the work. ³They received from Moses all the offerings
the Israelites had brought to carry out the work of constructing the
sanctuary. And the people continued to bring freewill offerings
morning after morning. ⁴So all the skilled craftsmen who were
doing all the work on the sanctuary left their work ⁵and said to
Moses, "The people are bringing more than enough for doing the
work the Lᴏʀᴅ commanded to be done."

⁶Then Moses gave an order and they sent this word throughout
the camp: "No man or woman is to make anything else as an offering for the sanctuary." And so the people were restrained from
bringing more, ⁷because what they already had was more than
enough to do all the work.

The response to Moses' appeal for offerings is overwhelming! The giving far exceeds the need. As the materials
are delivered to Bezalel, Oholiab, and their assistants, the
amount is so great that the people have to be restrained
from further giving!

Is the system of freewill offerings effective? Yes, when
the people are gospel-motivated, when the need is clearly
explained, when the appeal for help is extended to all.
God's Spirit "is able to do immeasurably more than all we
ask or imagine, according to his power that is at work
within us[;] to him be glory in the church and in Christ
Jesus throughout all generations, for ever and ever!
Amen" (Ephesians 3:20,21).

Paul, as mentioned before, experienced the same response from the Macedonian churches. Of them he writes to the Corinthians: "Out of the most severe trial, their overflowing joy and their extreme poverty welled up in rich generosity. For I testify that they gave as much as they were able, and even beyond their ability. Entirely on their own, they urgently pleaded with us for the privilege of sharing in this service to the saints. And they did not do as we expected, but they gave themselves first to the Lord and then to us in keeping with God's will" (2 Corinthians 8:2-5).

There lies the secret of generous giving: "They gave themselves first to the Lord." They did so because they appreciated the grace that God had given to them, as Paul adds, "the grace of our Lord Jesus Christ, that though he was rich, yet for your sakes he became poor, so that you through his poverty might become rich" (verse 9). When Christian people begin to appreciate this grace of God in the gift of his Son, Jesus Christ, they too will give themselves to the Lord. There will be such an outpouring of gifts for the work of the church and the spread of the gospel that the church treasury will be filled to overflowing.

May we therefore in our stewardship programs appeal to our people as Paul did to the Corinthians: "What I want is not your possessions but you" (2 Corinthians 12:14).

Exodus 36:8–38:31 details the construction of the tabernacle. These verses follow almost word for word the record of the instructions that the Lord gave Moses on Mount Sinai in chapters 25, 26, 27, and 30. This section is not useless repetition. It shows how carefully the Israelites adhered to the instructions of the Lord in every detail.

⁸All the skilled men among the workmen made the tabernacle with ten curtains of finely twisted linen and blue, purple and scarlet yarn, with cherubim worked into them by a skilled craftsman.

⁹All the curtains were the same size—twenty-eight cubits long and four cubits wide. ¹⁰They joined five of the curtains together and did the same with the other five. ¹¹Then they made loops of blue material along the edge of the end curtain in one set, and the same was done with the end curtain in the other set. ¹²They also made fifty loops on one curtain and fifty loops on the end curtain of the other set, with the loops opposite each other. ¹³Then they made fifty gold clasps and used them to fasten the two sets of curtains together so that the tabernacle was a unit.

¹⁴They made curtains of goat hair for the tent over the tabernacle—eleven altogether. ¹⁵All eleven curtains were the same size—thirty cubits long and four cubits wide. ¹⁶They joined five of the curtains into one set and the other six into another set. ¹⁷Then they made fifty loops along the edge of the end curtain in one set and also along the edge of the end curtain in the other set. ¹⁸They made fifty bronze clasps to fasten the tent together as a unit. ¹⁹Then they made for the tent a covering of ram skins dyed red, and over that a covering of hides of sea cows.

²⁰They made upright frames of acacia wood for the tabernacle. ²¹Each frame was ten cubits long and a cubit and a half wide, ²²with two projections set parallel to each other. They made all the frames of the tabernacle in this way. ²³They made twenty frames for the south side of the tabernacle ²⁴and made forty silver bases to go under them—two bases for each frame, one under each projection. ²⁵For the other side, the north side of the tabernacle, they made twenty frames ²⁶and forty silver bases—two under each frame. ²⁷They made six frames for the far end, that is, the west end of the tabernacle, ²⁸and two frames were made for the corners of the tabernacle at the far end. ²⁹At these two corners the frames were double from the bottom all the way to the top and fitted into a single ring; both were made alike. ³⁰So there were eight frames and sixteen silver bases—two under each frame.

³¹They also made crossbars of acacia wood: five for the frames on one side of the tabernacle, ³²five for those on the other side, and five for the frames on the west, at the far end of the tabernacle. ³³They made the center crossbar so that it extended from end to end at the middle of the frames. ³⁴They overlaid the frames with gold and made gold rings to hold the crossbars. They also overlaid the crossbars with gold.

The tabernacle

³⁵They made the curtain of blue, purple and scarlet yarn and finely twisted linen, with cherubim worked into it by a skilled craftsman. ³⁶They made four posts of acacia wood for it and overlaid them with gold. They made gold hooks for them and cast their four silver bases. ³⁷For the entrance to the tent they made a curtain of blue, purple and scarlet yarn and finely twisted linen—the work of an embroiderer; ³⁸and they made five posts with hooks for them. They overlaid the tops of the posts and their bands with gold and made their five bases of bronze.

37 Bezalel made the ark of acacia wood—two and a half cubits long, a cubit and a half wide, and a cubit and a half high. ²He overlaid it with pure gold, both inside and out, and made a gold molding around it. ³He cast four gold rings for it and fastened them to its four feet, with two rings on one side and two rings on the other. ⁴Then he made poles of acacia wood and overlaid them with gold. ⁵And he inserted the poles into the rings on the sides of the ark to carry it.

⁶He made the atonement cover of pure gold—two and a half cubits long and a cubit and a half wide. ⁷Then he made two cherubim out of hammered gold at the ends of the cover. ⁸He made one cherub on one end and the second cherub on the other; at the two ends he made them of one piece with the cover. ⁹The cherubim had their wings spread upward, overshadowing the cover with them. The cherubim faced each other, looking toward the cover.

¹⁰They made the table of acacia wood—two cubits long, a cubit wide, and a cubit and a half high. ¹¹Then they overlaid it with pure gold and made a gold molding around it. ¹²They also made around it a rim a handbreadth wide and put a gold molding on the rim. ¹³They cast four gold rings for the table and fastened them to the four corners, where the four legs were. ¹⁴The rings were put close to the rim to hold the poles used in carrying the table. ¹⁵The poles for carrying the table were made of acacia wood and were overlaid with gold. ¹⁶And they made from pure gold the articles for the table—its plates and dishes and bowls and its pitchers for the pouring out of drink offerings.

¹⁷They made the lampstand of pure gold and hammered it out, base and shaft; its flowerlike cups, buds and blossoms were of one piece with it. ¹⁸Six branches extended from the sides of the lampstand—three on one side and three on the other. ¹⁹Three cups shaped like almond flowers with buds and blossoms were on one branch,

three on the next branch and the same for all six branches extending from the lampstand. ²⁰And on the lampstand were four cups shaped like almond flowers with buds and blossoms. ²¹One bud was under the first pair of branches extending from the lampstand, a second bud under the second pair, and a third bud under the third pair—six branches in all. ²²The buds and the branches were all of one piece with the lampstand, hammered out of pure gold.

²³They made its seven lamps, as well as its wick trimmers and trays, of pure gold. ²⁴They made the lampstand and all its accessories from one talent of pure gold.

²⁵They made the altar of incense out of acacia wood. It was square, a cubit long and a cubit wide, and two cubits high—its horns of one piece with it. ²⁶They overlaid the top and all the sides and the horns with pure gold, and made a gold molding around it. ²⁷They made two gold rings below the molding—two on opposite sides—to hold the poles used to carry it. ²⁸They made the poles of acacia wood and overlaid them with gold.

²⁹They also made the sacred anointing oil and the pure, fragrant incense—the work of a perfumer.

38 They built the altar of burnt offering of acacia wood, three cubits high; it was square, five cubits long and five cubits wide. ²They made a horn at each of the four corners, so that the horns and the altar were of one piece, and they overlaid the altar with bronze. ³They made all its utensils of bronze—its pots, shovels, sprinkling bowls, meat forks and firepans. ⁴They made a grating for the altar, a bronze network, to be under its ledge, halfway up the altar. ⁵They cast bronze rings to hold the poles for the four corners of the bronze grating. ⁶They made the poles of acacia wood and overlaid them with bronze. ⁷They inserted the poles into the rings so they would be on the sides of the altar for carrying it. They made it hollow, out of boards.

⁸They made the bronze basin and its bronze stand from the mirrors of the women who served at the entrance to the Tent of Meeting.

⁹Next they made the courtyard. The south side was a hundred cubits long and had curtains of finely twisted linen, ¹⁰with twenty posts and twenty bronze bases, and with silver hooks and bands on the posts. ¹¹The north side was also a hundred cubits long and had twenty posts and twenty bronze bases, with silver hooks and bands on the posts.

¹²The west end was fifty cubits wide and had curtains, with ten posts and ten bases, with silver hooks and bands on the posts. ¹³The east end, toward the sunrise, was also fifty cubits wide. ¹⁴Curtains fifteen cubits long were on one side of the entrance, with three posts and three bases, ¹⁵and curtains fifteen cubits long were on the other side of the entrance to the courtyard, with three posts and three bases. ¹⁶All the curtains around the courtyard were of finely twisted linen. ¹⁷The bases for the posts were bronze. The hooks and bands on the posts were silver, and their tops were overlaid with silver; so all the posts of the courtyard had silver bands.

¹⁸The curtain of the entrance to the courtyard was of blue, purple and scarlet yarn and finely twisted linen—the work of an embroiderer. It was twenty cubits long and, like the curtains of the courtyard, five cubits high, ¹⁹with four posts and four bronze bases. Their hooks and bands were silver, and their tops were overlaid with silver. ²⁰All the tent pegs of the tabernacle and of the surrounding courtyard were bronze.

²¹These are the amounts of the materials used for the tabernacle, the tabernacle of the Testimony, which were recorded at Moses' command by the Levites under the direction of Ithamar son of Aaron, the priest. ²²(Bezalel son of Uri, the son of Hur, of the tribe of Judah, made everything the LORD commanded Moses; ²³with him was Oholiab son of Ahisamach, of the tribe of Dan—a craftsman and designer, and an embroiderer in blue, purple and scarlet yarn and fine linen.) ²⁴The total amount of the gold from the wave offering used for all the work on the sanctuary was 29 talents and 730 shekels, according to the sanctuary shekel.

²⁵The silver obtained from those of the community who were counted in the census was 100 talents and 1,775 shekels, according to the sanctuary shekel—²⁶one beka per person, that is, half a shekel, according to the sanctuary shekel, from everyone who had crossed over to those counted, twenty years old or more, a total of 603,550 men. ²⁷The 100 talents of silver were used to cast the bases for the sanctuary and for the curtain—100 bases from the 100 talents, one talent for each base. ²⁸They used the 1,775 shekels to make the hooks for the posts, to overlay the tops of the posts, and to make their bands.

²⁹The bronze from the wave offering was 70 talents and 2,400 shekels. ³⁰They used it to make the bases for the entrance to the Tent of Meeting, the bronze altar with its bronze grating and all its

utensils, ³¹the bases for the surrounding courtyard and those for its entrance and all the tent pegs for the tabernacle and those for the surrounding courtyard.

A few items in this lengthy section deserve special notice:

Verse 8 of chapter 38 tells us, "They made the bronze basin and its bronze stand from the mirrors of the women who served at the entrance to the Tent of Meeting." Of minor interest in this passage is the fact that women in those days used mirrors as a means of checking on their appearance. They made them out of polished bronze. These they now willingly gave up to serve as material for the bronze basin, which the priests would use to wash themselves. Of greater interest is the fact that women served at the entrance of the tabernacle. Their presence is also mentioned in 1 Samuel 2:22. What service these women performed is not explained. Perhaps they dedicated themselves to a life of prayer and fasting, as we hear about later in the case of Anna at the time of Christ, mentioned in Luke 2:36,37. Perhaps they were women who devoted themselves to a life of virginity in order to serve the Lord with praying and fasting, as some suppose happened in the case of Jephthah's daughter, recorded in Judges 11:39. The Bible does not give us any details on this matter.

Concerning the ark, the item of chief importance in the tabernacle, we are told that Bezalel, the chief architect of the entire project, took its construction under his personal supervision. Verses 1 to 9 of chapter 37 call attention to this fact.

In verses 21 to 31 of chapter 38, we are given the total amounts of gold, silver, and bronze used in the construction of the tabernacle. It is estimated that the weight of the gold was a little over 1 ton; of silver, a little over 3¾ tons; and of bronze, about 2½ tons. With gold worth today some $500 per ounce, the tabernacle's value would be almost impossible to imagine. Even at that time it was considerable. The silver mentioned included only that collected as atonement money. In order to collect this money, all men 20 years old and older were counted. Their number totaled 603,550—the same number given in the report of the census we find in Numbers 1:46.

39 From the blue, purple and scarlet yarn they made woven garments for ministering in the sanctuary. They also made sacred garments for Aaron, as the LORD commanded Moses.

²They made the ephod of gold, and of blue, purple and scarlet yarn, and of finely twisted linen. ³They hammered out thin sheets of gold and cut strands to be worked into the blue, purple and scarlet yarn and fine linen—the work of a skilled craftsman. ⁴They made shoulder pieces for the ephod, which were attached to two of its corners, so it could be fastened. ⁵Its skillfully woven waistband was like it—of one piece with the ephod and made with gold, and with blue, purple and scarlet yarn, and with finely twisted linen, as the LORD commanded Moses.

⁶They mounted the onyx stones in gold filigree settings and engraved them like a seal with the names of the sons of Israel. ⁷Then they fastened them on the shoulder pieces of the ephod as memorial stones for the sons of Israel, as the LORD commanded Moses.

⁸They fashioned the breastpiece—the work of a skilled craftsman. They made it like the ephod: of gold, and of blue, purple and scarlet yarn, and of finely twisted linen. ⁹It was square—a span long and a span wide—and folded double. ¹⁰Then they mounted four rows of precious stones on it. In the first row there was a ruby, a topaz and a beryl; ¹¹in the second row a turquoise, a sapphire and an emerald; ¹²in the third row a jacinth, an agate and an amethyst; ¹³in the fourth row a chrysolite, an onyx and a jasper. They were mounted in gold filigree settings. ¹⁴There were twelve stones, one for each of the names of the sons of Israel, each engraved like a seal with the name of one of the twelve tribes.

¹⁵For the breastpiece they made braided chains of pure gold, like a rope. ¹⁶They made two gold filigree settings and two gold rings, and fastened the rings to two of the corners of the breast-

piece. ¹⁷They fastened the two gold chains to the rings at the corners of the breastpiece, ¹⁸and the other ends of the chains to the two settings, attaching them to the shoulder pieces of the ephod at the front. ¹⁹They made two gold rings and attached them to the other two corners of the breastpiece on the inside edge next to the ephod. ²⁰Then they made two more gold rings and attached them to the bottom of the shoulder pieces on the front of the ephod, close to the seam just above the waistband of the ephod. ²¹They tied the rings of the breastpiece to the rings of the ephod with blue cord, connecting it to the waistband so that the breastpiece would not swing out from the ephod—as the LORD commanded Moses.

²²They made the robe of the ephod entirely of blue cloth—the work of a weaver—²³with an opening in the center of the robe like the opening of a collar, and a band around this opening, so that it would not tear. ²⁴They made pomegranates of blue, purple and scarlet yarn and finely twisted linen around the hem of the robe. ²⁵And they made bells of pure gold and attached them around the hem between the pomegranates. ²⁶The bells and pomegranates alternated around the hem of the robe to be worn for ministering, as the LORD commanded Moses.

²⁷For Aaron and his sons, they made tunics of fine linen—the work of a weaver—²⁸and the turban of fine linen, the linen headbands and the undergarments of finely twisted linen. ²⁹The sash was of finely twisted linen and blue, purple and scarlet yarn—the work of an embroiderer—as the LORD commanded Moses.

³⁰They made the plate, the sacred diadem, out of pure gold and engraved on it, like an inscription on a seal: HOLY TO THE LORD. ³¹Then they fastened a blue cord to it to attach it to the turban, as the LORD commanded Moses.

³²So all the work on the tabernacle, the Tent of Meeting, was completed. The Israelites did everything just as the LORD commanded Moses. ³³Then they brought the tabernacle to Moses: the tent and all its furnishings, its clasps, frames, crossbars, posts and bases; ³⁴the covering of ram skins dyed red, the covering of hides of sea cows and the shielding curtain; ³⁵the ark of the Testimony with its poles and the atonement cover; ³⁶the table with all its articles and the bread of the Presence; ³⁷the pure gold lampstand with its row of lamps and all its accessories, and the oil for the light; ³⁸the gold altar, the anointing oil, the fragrant incense, and the curtain for the entrance to the tent; ³⁹the bronze altar with its bronze grat-

ing, its poles and all its utensils; the basin with its stand; ⁴⁰the curtains of the courtyard with its posts and bases, and the curtain for the entrance to the courtyard; the ropes and tent pegs for the courtyard; all the furnishings for the tabernacle, the Tent of Meeting; ⁴¹and the woven garments worn for ministering in the sanctuary, both the sacred garments for Aaron the priest and the garments for his sons when serving as priests.

⁴²The Israelites had done all the work just as the LORD had commanded Moses. ⁴³Moses inspected the work and saw that they had done it just as the LORD had commanded. So Moses blessed them.

In this chapter the various items of clothing for the priests are again mentioned as they were fashioned according to the Lord's instructions. The phrase "as the LORD commanded Moses" is repeated in this chapter nine times. Everything was made exactly according to specification.

After the work of preparing the material for the tabernacle and the garments for the priests was completed, everything was carefully inspected by Moses. He was satisfied with what he saw and blessed the people for their faithful work.

All things were now ready for the setting up of the tabernacle for its use.

"Set up the tabernacle"

40 Then the LORD said to Moses: ²"Set up the tabernacle, the Tent of Meeting, on the first day of the first month. ³Place the ark of the Testimony in it and shield the ark with the curtain. ⁴Bring in the table and set out what belongs on it. Then bring in the lampstand and set up its lamps. ⁵Place the gold altar of incense in front of the ark of the Testimony and put the curtain at the entrance to the tabernacle.

⁶"Place the altar of burnt offering in front of the entrance to the tabernacle, the Tent of Meeting; ⁷place the basin between the Tent of Meeting and the altar and put water in it. ⁸Set up the courtyard around it and put the curtain at the entrance to the courtyard.

⁹"Take the anointing oil and anoint the tabernacle and everything in it; consecrate it and all its furnishings, and it will be holy.

¹⁰**Then anoint the altar of burnt offering and all its utensils; conse-crate the altar, and it will be most holy. ¹¹Anoint the basin and its stand and consecrate them.**

¹²**"Bring Aaron and his sons to the entrance to the Tent of Meeting and wash them with water. ¹³Then dress Aaron in the sacred garments, anoint him and consecrate him so he may serve me as priest. ¹⁴Bring his sons and dress them in tunics. ¹⁵Anoint them just as you anointed their father, so they may serve me as priests. Their anointing will be to a priesthood that will continue for all generations to come." ¹⁶Moses did everything just as the LORD commanded him.**

"Set up the tabernacle," the Lord said to Moses. The workers had completed their task. All was ready. This command of the Lord was given "on the first day of the first month." In verse 17 of this same chapter, we are told that this happened "on the first day of the first month in the second year."

We remember that the Israelites began their year, according to the Lord's instructions, with the Passover festi-val. According to our calendar year, this took place the month of April. The Israelites arrived at Mount Sinai "in the third month" after leaving Egypt (19:1). We know that Moses twice spent 40 days upon Mount Sinai. Some time elapsed in preparing for the giving of the law, as well as between the first and second stay of Moses upon the mountain because of Israel's worship of the golden calf. From all this we can estimate that it took the Israelites about a half-year to prepare the items for the tabernacle and its contents according to the Lord's instructions.

After the various items were put into place according to the Lord's instructions, they were anointed with oil to conse-crate them, or to set them apart for the Lord's service. Anointing with oil signified that these items were set apart for the use of a God who was holy and for the worship of his holy name.

In verses 12 to 15, we are told that Aaron and his sons were also anointed with oil for the service of the Lord. According to Leviticus chapter 8, this consecrating of the priests must have taken place some time later, after the Lord had given Moses instructions concerning the various sacrifices that the priests were to perform in the tabernacle services.

Once the materials for the tabernacle were prepared, the setting up of the tabernacle itself was not a major task. The Lord had designed it as a portable structure so that it could be set up and dismantled for moving from place to place, as we see in the following verses.

So the tabernacle was set up

¹⁷So the tabernacle was set up on the first day of the first month in the second year. ¹⁸When Moses set up the tabernacle, he put the bases in place, erected the frames, inserted the crossbars and set up the posts. ¹⁹Then he spread the tent over the tabernacle and put the covering over the tent, as the LORD commanded him.

²⁰He took the Testimony and placed it in the ark, attached the poles to the ark and put the atonement cover over it. ²¹Then he brought the ark into the tabernacle and hung the shielding curtain and shielded the ark of the Testimony, as the LORD commanded him.

²²Moses placed the table in the Tent of Meeting on the north side of the tabernacle outside the curtain ²³and set out the bread on it before the LORD, as the LORD commanded him.

²⁴He placed the lampstand in the Tent of Meeting opposite the table on the south side of the tabernacle ²⁵and set up the lamps before the LORD, as the LORD commanded him.

²⁶Moses placed the gold altar in the Tent of Meeting in front of the curtain ²⁷and burned fragrant incense on it, as the LORD commanded him. ²⁸Then he put the curtain at the entrance to the tabernacle.

²⁹He set the altar of burnt offering near the entrance to the tabernacle, the Tent of Meeting, and offered on it burnt offerings and grain offerings, as the LORD commanded him.

³⁰**He placed the basin between the Tent of Meeting and the altar and put water in it for washing, ³¹and Moses and Aaron and his sons used it to wash their hands and feet. ³²They washed whenever they entered the Tent of Meeting or approached the altar, as the LORD commanded Moses.**

³³**Then Moses set up the courtyard around the tabernacle and altar and put up the curtain at the entrance to the courtyard. And so Moses finished the work.**

Here we are told step-by-step how the pieces of the tabernacle were put together and where the various items of the tabernacle were to be placed.

The *ark of the covenant,* with its poles in place, was set behind the curtain in the Most Holy Place.

The *table for the bread of the Presence* was situated on the north side of the Holy Place; the *golden lampstand,* on the south side of the Holy Place. (The entrance of the tabernacle, as we have stated previously, was toward the east.) The *gold altar of incense* also stood in the Holy Place, in front of the curtain separating the Holy Place from the Most Holy Place.

The *altar of burnt offering* was in the courtyard toward the entrance on the east side, with the *basin* (for the priests to wash themselves) between the altar of burnt offering and the entrance to the tabernacle.

All was in readiness for the Lord's approval, which was indicated to the people in a most unusual and effective way, as the closing verses of chapter 40 tell us.

The glory of the Lord

³⁴**Then the cloud covered the Tent of Meeting, and the glory of the LORD filled the tabernacle. ³⁵Moses could not enter the Tent of Meeting because the cloud had settled upon it, and the glory of the LORD filled the tabernacle.**

³⁶**In all the travels of the Israelites, whenever the cloud lifted from above the tabernacle, they would set out; ³⁷but if the cloud**

did not lift, they did not set out—until the day it lifted. ³⁸So the cloud of the LORD** was over the tabernacle by day, and fire was in the cloud by night, in the sight of all the house of Israel during all their travels.**

In the closing verses of this book, we hear about two kinds of cloud. Both have been described before. One kind was the cloud that appeared to the Israelites as they began their departure out of Egypt. It was by day "a pillar of cloud to guide them on the way" and by night "a pillar of fire to give them light, so that they could travel by day or night." By means of this cloud, the Lord guided the Israelites on their journey. Wherever they camped, the cloud was over the place of encampment. The Israelites did not break camp and continue on their journey until the cloud lifted to guide them on their way. This method of God's guidance is again described in even greater detail in Numbers 9:15-23, as Israel departed from this camping place at Mount Sinai. Wherever the tabernacle was set up, the cloud would cover it. At night it looked like fire. This cloud did not cease to guide them until they finally reached the promised land of Canaan.

The other cloud mentioned in these closing verses is distinct from the cloud that rested over the tabernacle. This cloud filled the tabernacle, so that even Moses could not enter this place. This cloud is here called "the glory of the L*ORD*." We have heard this expression used a number of times in this book. We remember how at times it was associated with fire or with a demonstration of the Lord's goodness. It always indicated some special revelation of the Lord's grace and mercy toward his people. Here the glory of the Lord, in the form of a cloud, filled the tabernacle to demonstrate to the Israelites that the Lord had truly accepted this structure as his dwelling place. The Lord later revealed his saving presence to his people in the very same manner at the dedication of the temple in Jerusalem, described in 1 Kings 8:10,11.

How appropriate that the book of Exodus closes with this final visible demonstration of the glory of the Lord. Let us recall some of the previous appearances of the Lord's glory. In the opening chapters of the book, the glory of the Lord appeared to Moses in a burning bush and called him to lead the Israelites to the Land of Promise. At the Red Sea, the Lord told Moses, "I will gain glory for myself through Pharaoh and all his army" (14:4). On that occasion the Lord miraculously rescued his people by giving them safe passage through the sea while the army of Pharaoh was destroyed. In the Desert of Sin, Moses told the people, "In the morning you will see the glory of the LORD" (16:7), and in the morning they saw the glory of the Lord appear in the cloud as he promised them meat (quail) in the evening and bread (manna) in the morning. The glory of the Lord was revealed on Mount Sinai as the Lord made his covenant with his people through the giving of his law. The glory of the Lord settled on Mount Sinai in the form of a cloud when this covenant was confirmed. After Israel sinned by worshiping the golden calf, the Lord revealed himself to Moses and showed Moses his glory by proclaiming his name, the LORD, the compassionate and gracious God, the God who at the same time would not leave the guilty unpunished. The face of Moses reflected the Lord's glory as he came down from the mountain after the Lord's covenant with Israel had once more been confirmed.

Now, after the tabernacle was erected, the glory of the Lord filled the tabernacle to let his people know that here they could find the assurance of the forgiveness of their sins and fellowship with the God of their salvation. Here their offerings could be brought to atone for their sins; here by their offerings they could demonstrate their devotion to him as his kingdom of priests and his holy people. Here they could bring praise and thanksgiving to his name and find fellowship with their gracious God. Here they could bring their prayers to the throne of his grace. Here he dwelt among them as their God, and here they were his people.

In what more effective way could this book have been brought to a close! Jehovah had truly proved to the Israelites that he was their covenant-Lord. He delivered them out of Egypt. He established his covenant with them on Mount Sinai. He gave them the place of the covenant, the tabernacle, as his very own dwelling. His people were now prepared for the journey onwards to the promised land of Canaan. This is salvation history at its finest!

As we conclude our study of the book of Exodus, we are left with this impression of the tabernacle in the wilderness, where the Lord saw fit to fill that sacred place of the covenant with his glory.

On the basis of our New Testament Scriptures, we know that this tabernacle, with all its blessings for God's people in Old Testament times, was "a copy and shadow of what is in heaven" (Hebrews 8:5). By means of it, God demonstrated his presence among his people, strengthening them on their journey to that promised land of Canaan. There he would fulfill his covenant made with Abraham, Isaac, and Jacob, a covenant centered in the promise of a Savior for all mankind. Until that Savior would come, God's people in the Old Testament would be under the law, under the covenant relationship established upon Mount Sinai. They would be like children in need of the discipline of "guardians and trustees," as Galatians 4:1-3 tells us. We have noted that fact especially in all the ceremonial rules and regulations that the Lord gave his people as a part of the Sinaitic covenant.

"But when the time had fully come, God sent his Son," as Paul tells us in verses 4 and 5, "born of a woman, born under law, to redeem those under law, that we might receive the full rights of sons." When Jesus, the Son of God, came into this world, he "tabernacled" among us. He was the eternal Word who became flesh. "In Christ all the fullness of the Deity lives in bodily form," Paul declared in Colossians 2:9.

The true God not only dwelt personally among the people of this earth; he became sinful mankind's substitute. He took the place of all people under the law, fulfilling all its demands perfectly. He suffered and died as a sacrifice for the sins of the world. When Christ died, the curtain of the temple in Jerusalem that separated the Holy Place from the Most Holy Place was "torn in two from top to bottom" (Matthew 27:51). As our Great High Priest, "he went through the greater and more perfect tabernacle that is not man-made, that is to say, not a part of this creation" (Hebrews 9:11). That "greater and more perfect tabernacle" is our heavenly home, which Christ purchased and won for us "by his own blood, having obtained eternal redemption" (verse 12).

And as Israel journeyed to the promised land of Canaan, so we also are on our way to the eternal dwelling of our heavenly Father, the tabernacle of God with men, where we will be his people and he will be our God, where the old order of things has passed away. That is our goal, the end of our journey.

So often on this journey, we are much like the Israelites of old—unappreciative of God's blessings, as Israel was at Marah, or in the Desert of Sin, or at Rephidim. Yet a gracious Lord abundantly provides for our needs, as he provided his ancient Israel with manna in the desert or with water from a rock. So often we are afraid, as Israel was at the Red Sea. Yet with his majestic power, the Lord leads us with his right hand, just as he led Israel safely through the sea before the mighty waters crushed the enemy. So often we are tempted to rebel against God, as Israel did when it worshiped the golden calf. Yet because of Christ's intercession, God gives us time to come to our senses and repent, even as the Lord spared Israel after Moses' intercession and led them to repentance, also graciously renewing his covenant with a stiff-necked people.

Under God's guidance we pray that our way is from grace to glory and that our earthly pilgrimage will lead us safely to the promised land above. We pray that our studies in the book of Exodus have strengthened that hope in us!

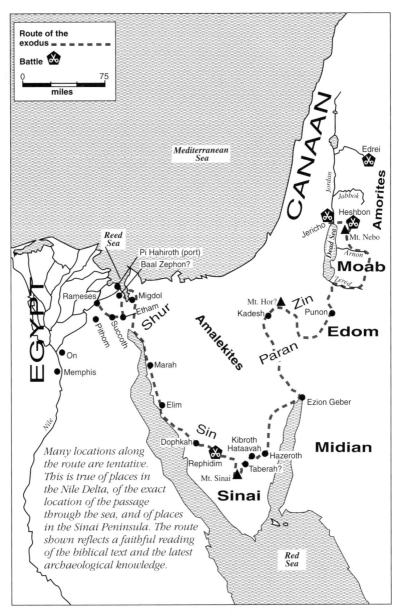

Many locations along the route are tentative. This is true of places in the Nile Delta, of the exact location of the passage through the sea, and of places in the Sinai Peninsula. The route shown reflects a faithful reading of the biblical text and the latest archaeological knowledge.

The exodus